INDIAN CULTURE IN CENTRAL ASIA

EDITORS

DR. RAKESH KUMAR DUBEY

DR. SIROJIDDIN S. NURMATOV

PUSTAK BHARATI
TORONTO CANADA

Editors : Dr. Rakesh Kumar Dubey

Dr. Sirojiddin S. Nurmatov

Book Title : Indian Culture in Central Asia

Published by :
Pustak Bharati (Books-India)
180 Torresdale Ave, Toronto Canada M2R 3E4
email : pustak.bharati.canada@gmail.com
Web : www.pustak-bharati-canada.com

Copyright ©2022

ISBN : 978-1-989416-80-8

ISBN 978-1-989416-80-8

Editorial

After the collapse of the Soviet Union in 1991, the countries of Kazakhstan, Uzbekistan, Turkmenistan, Tajikistan and Kyrgyzstan are jointly known as Central Asian countries. In ancient times, the region situated between India, Iran and China was called Central Asia or Chinese Turkistan. Relations between India and Central Asia have been established since ancient times and due to its proximity to India, the region became known as a 'Close Neighbour.'

Looking at the history, it is known that the Harappan civilization had trade and social relations with Central Asia during the Vedic period and even the pre Vedic times. With the rise and spread of Buddhism in India, China, Korea, Mongolia, Japan as well as the region of entire Central Asia came under the widespread influence of Buddhism. During the period of Emperors Ashoka and Kanishka, Buddhism was spread more vigorously there. The well known 'Silk Route' passed through Central Asia and due to which India not only had trade relations with Central Asia, but also Indian civilization and culture were widely promoted in that region. India's political, economic and cultural relations with Central Asia continued even in the medieval period, for which many literary evidences are available and many archaeological evidences continue to be found.

India had good relations with the Soviet Union that formed after the Bolshevik Revolution in Russia, but India's relations with the Central Asian countries formed after the disintegration of the Soviet Union in 1991 have been better. There are many political agreements between India and Central Asian countries and many organizations are working to strengthen these relations. The current government of India is determined to strengthen its relations with the Central Asian countries and the main focus has been on the issue of connectivity, energy, trade and security.

In the present book an attempt has been made to trace the cultural relations between India and the Central Asian countries and to throw light on the archaeological remains of Indian civilization found in the Central Asian countries and the present signs of India's language, literature, art and culture. The scholars who helped with the articles deserve appreciation and thanks. The views expressed in the articles are the authors' own and the editors do not necessarily agree with them. It is hoped that this book will be useful and helpful in further deepening the relations between India and Central Asia.

Dr. Rakesh Kumar Dubey
Dr. Sirojiddin S. Nurmatov

Contents

1. Buddhism in Central Asia : A Historical Perspective

Dr. Jitendra Pratap Singh

In the second and first millennia B.C, a series of large and powerful states developed on the Southern periphery of central Asia. The xiongnu empire (209 B.C.-93 A.D.) may be seen as example for later Gokturk and Mongol empires. Central Asia, as a distinctive region was first introduced by the German Geographer Alexander Von Humboldt in 1843.

However since its introduction, the borders of central Asia have been subject to multiple definitions and multiple names. Inner Asia Turkestan, Middle Asia, Tran Soxiana, Soviet central Asia and Eastern Turkestan are a few of the names used to identify this region and the political borders attributed to each definition are also different.

The Encyclopedias Britannica defines central Asia as the "Central region of Asia extending from the Caspian Sea in the west to the border of western China in the east. It is bounded on the north by Russia and on the south by Iran Afghanistan and China." The region consists of the former soviet republics of Tazakhstan, Ujbekistan, Tajikistan, Kyrgyzstan and Turkmenistan. [1]

The History of Civilization in central Asia, published by Unesco defines central asia as the region between Iran to Mongolia including Iran, Pakistan, Afghanistan, Kazakhstan, Uzbekistan, Kajikstan, Kyrgyzstan, Turkmenistan, Chinese province of Xinjiang and Magnolia.[2]

The difinition is based on the historical, Cultural, Social economic and other traits which interlinked these countries for centuries.

Language of Central Asia

The study of Buddhism in central Asia is further

complicated by the multiple languages and scripts used a central Asia some of which vanished centuries ago.

The Manu scripts of Central Asia provide evidence of these extinct language and scripts. The language and scripts include Phags-pa, Arabic Avestan, Bactrian, Bramhi, Chinese, Gandhari, Gupta, Judaco-persian, Kharosthi Khota nese, Kitan, kok Turkie Mongolian Nagri, New persian, Pehlevi Sanskrit, Syriac, Turkic and Uighir etc.

The lost languages and scripts stimulated a great interest among academics as well as private collectors, creating a market for objects from central asia, which resulted in the indiscriminate destruction of archaeo logical sites to obtain Manu scripts and objects during the early part of the twentieth century .

Historical Sources of Buddhism in Central Asia

The best source for studying the past is contemporary original documents. However, such documents of great antiquity are indeed rare. Palm leaf manuscripts were used extensively in South Asia, However, due to the hot and humid climate prevailing in this region such manuscripts invariably decayed. The practice of copying the decaying manuscripts on fresh palm leaves continued in Buddhist temples in Sri Lanka and in other South-East Asian countries where the Theravada tradition prevailed. Nevertheless this constant copying inadvertently resulted in minor deviations and changes. The Chinese having invented paper and printing became meticulous record keepers. In China the books were reprinted numerous times and as in the case of palm leaf manuscripts. The reprints sometimes had minor variations.

Sri Lankan and Indian Sources

According to the Sri Lankan historical chronicle the Mahawamsa, Buddhism was first introduced to the Gandhara region during the third century BCE. The ven. Majjhantika was sent to Kamira and Gandhara under the patronage of king Ashoka (reign 273-232 BCE) After The conclusion of the third Buddhist council. The Mahawamsa further records that MaJjhantika Thera performed miracles and saved people from hail and floods caused by the Naga king of Gandhara. Subsequently The Naga king and his followers were converted to Buddhism. The Greek and Aramaic inscription of King Asoka discovered in Kandahar in modern Afghanistan further substantiates.[4]

The fact that Buddhism was introduced to this region during the 3rd C BCE. The Kandahar inscription is not only clearly states.

"After a full ten years, king Pioda sse had the text Dhamma published to men and from this moment he made men merciful and everything prosperous all over the earth"[5]

The Kandahar inscription is not the only one of king Ashoka's which alludes to the dissemination of Buddhism to the Gandhara region in central Asia.

The rock Edict 5 of King Ashoka states- **"In the past there were no Dhamma Mahamatras (?) but such officers were appointed by me thirteen years after my coronation. Now they work among all religions for the establishment of Dhamma, for the promotion of Dhamma, and for the welfare and happiness of all who are devoted to Dhamma."** They work among the Greeks, the Kambojas. The Gandharas, the Rastrikas, the Pitinikas and other peoples on the western borders"[6]

These sources indicate that at least by the 3rd C BCE, it not before, Buddhism was known in the Gandhara region of Central Asia.[7]

Chinese Sources

The introduction of Buddhism to China invariably led to closer contacts with the central Asian kingdoms, especially with regard to obtaining and translating Buddhist texts. Such text from India and Central Asia were translated into Chinese, initially by foreign monks from central Asia. An Shigao from Parthia was one of the earliest and most famous translators of

Buddhist texts into Chinese.

An Shigao arrived in the city of Luoyang in 148 CE and established the most important centre for the translation of Buddhist texts to Chinese.

An X Uan also from the kingdom of Parthia, Zhi LouJia Chan from Scythia (Iran), Kang Me ngxiang and Kang Ju from Sogdian (part of Uzbekistan) were among the foreign monks from Central Asia who were prominent translators of Buddhist texts during the second Century CE.

The Tradition of Central Asian Monks translating Buddhist texts to Chinese continued with FO *Tuteng* from Central Asia becoming prominent around 310 CE and Kumarjiva (344-413 CE) from Qiusi Kingdom were among the key Translators,

These records of prominent Central Asian works provide an important link in the study of Buddhism in Central Asia, especially about Buddhism in modern Iran where archaeological evidence for the existence of Buddhism has thus for not been discovered. Since the time of the western Han Dynasty (206 BCE-8CE); the Chinese imperial court kept meticulous records, not only about the day to day information of the court but also about the various nations they came into contact with. Since the western Han Dynasty, the Chinese Historical Chronicles incorporated a section called "western Region" which provides detailed descriptions of kingdoms beyond the great wall of China. It is in this 'western Region' section that we can find information about Central Asia.' The Emperor WUD i(140-87 BCE) sent a mission to central Asia led by court official Zhang Qian which led to the opening of communication, trade and diplomatic relations between China and the central Asian kingdoms. The Historical chronicle of the Eastern Han Dynasty (8-220 CE), also known as the later Han Dynasty in the chapter on "Western Regions" (xi yu Juan) section 15, states that the Buddhist way of life was practiced in North western India.[9] Buddhism is mentioned in the western Regions. Chapter mainly in the record of India.

However the names of ruler's population trade commodities and other details of the central Asian, Kingdoms are recorded. Other than the historical chronicles of China, the records of the Buddhist monks who travelled to India in search of Buddhist texts also provide a glimpse of Buddhism in central Asia. The Buddhist monk Faxian who travelled to India through central Asia, left a comprehensive record of Buddhism to the region in his A record of Buddhism kingdoms.

Fa xian refers to the kingdom of Shen-shen thus. "After travelling for seventeen days-reached the kingdom of Shen-Shen, a country rugged and hilly, with a thin and Barron soil." The king professed (our) Law.[10] and there might be in the country more than four thousand monks, who were all students of Hinayana. The common people of this and other kingdoms as well as the Shamans, all practice the rules of India, only that latter do so more exactly and the former more loosely.

Kharosthi Document from Central Asia

The Kharosthi Documents with provenance were primarily discovered by Aurel stein at the site of Niya in the **xijiang Province** of China, but many other documents were discovered without provenance due to illicit trade. The Niya manuscripts have been dated to Circa 235-325 CE and the language used in these documents is a North Indian version of Prakrit related to Gandhari.[12] The Niya documents include references to Buddhism and portray the contemporary beliefs of the ordinary people-A Letter from Niya about a dispute between two parties provides the names of two monks. Bamgusena and Pacgoyae. and the death of person" I have heard the bad news that Anasena is dead. As a result of that news, we have experienced the shafts of great sorrow and grief in our hearts. That is something beyond even the powers of a Buddha, or a Pratyekabuddha, or an Arhant or a Universal Monarch. All come to the same end. Care must be exercised how we go virtuous acts performed and purity maintained.[13] Another documents reveals a Buddhist ritual and the virtues brought by practicing it. These documents also prove that Buddhist monks sometimes acted as witnesses and scribes to legal documents.[14] The other Kharosthi manuscripts discovered include a text of the Dhamrmapada written in The Gandhari Language found near Khotan in the **Xinjiang Province** of China and a collecttion of Kharosthi manuscripts in Gandhari believed to have been part of a monastic collection or a library of the Dharmaguptaka school or Buddhism dating to the early first century CE ad consisting of Buddhist poetic compositions of the Dharmmapada Anavatapta gatha, Khadgavisand Gatha, Avadana texts etc.[15] These documents provide contemporary accounts of the lives of Buddhist devotees.

Brahmi Script Documents from Central Asia

Bramhi script was used in central Asia by different communities to record their language. Documents in Sanskrit, Khatanese and Tocharian were mainly written using Brahmi script, Brahm, documents were discovered at the Dun Huang Mogao Grottoes Cave 17, (Gansu Province, China) Kizil Grottoes, Tumshuk, Khadalik, Mazar Tagh, Domoco, Yarkhoto and Endere in the Xingiang Province of China. There is an interesting array of manuscripts in Khotanese, the most fascinating being The "Book of Zambasta," a Buddhist poem written at the request of an official called Zambasta is the longest indigenous literary composition in Khotanese that has survived to the modern era.[16] These text include the Ratnakuta Sutra, Sanghata Sutra and Suvarnabh asottama Sutra.

Among the language using the Brahmi script are the two extinct Indo-European languages known as Tocharian A and Tocharian B. Tocharian A was widely used in the Turfan Area of the Xinjiang province of China and Tocharian B was used in the modern Kuche area and sometimes called **Kuchean**.

Tocharian as with Khotanese, has been extinct for centuries and is only known to us through the text which have been discovered. The Tocharian texts were mostly translations of Buddhist texts but, there were also monastic correspondences and accounts,

Commercial documents, Caravan permits, etc. One of the longest manuscripts in tocharian. A is the Maitreyasamiti-Nataka (a Buddhist text) discovered near Yanqi in the xinjiang province of China in 1974.[17]

Sogdian Documents of Central Asia

Sogdian an extinct Indo-Iranian language was used in the kingdom of Sogdiana, which comprised the modern cities of Samar Kand and Bukhara of Uzbekistan and the cities of Panjakent and Fergana of Tajikistan, Sogdian Buddhist text were mainly discovered at the Dunhuang mogao cave 17 in the Gansu province of China, probably due to the fact that there were Sogdian Colonies in Dun huang as well as in the modern xinjiang province of China.[18]

Sogdian Buddhist texts were also found in Khotan Kuche and Shorchuk in the xinjiang province.

Buddhist texts include Jataka storises such as "Vessantara Jataka" Sutras such as Vajracchedika prajnaparamita Sutra, Mahaparinirvana Sutra, Vimalakirthin irdesa Sutra, Avatas-maka Sutra, Lankavatara Sutra and Tantric and Dharani texts such as Padma Chintamani Sutra, Nilakantha dharani. These Sogdian Buddhist text indicate the role played by the Sogdians in promoting Buddhism in Central Asia as merchants translators and in the role of Sogdian Colonies outside Sogdina.[19]

Archaeological Evidence for Buddhism in Central Asia

Buddhist tradition encourages donations to monasteries as a crucial method of gaining merit (Karma) for the lay followers of the religion. Since the time of Buddha lay patrons use this method to gain merit by constructing temples and funding Buddhist Art and manuscripts to help them in their path to

Nirvana. Thus Buddhist Art reminds suppports and reinforces the eternal truths of the religion and its development and style remain integral to the history of the religion and the regional cultures it encountered.

Buddhist art was used as an integral part of Buddhist instruction as well as bringing merit, which encouraged the patrons to spend lavishly an mountains and art.

Early Buddhist Art (prior to the first century CE) did not include the image of the Buddha, but was represented by anionic symbols such as the wheel of Dharma and a footprint are represented in the early sculpture of Sanchi and Bharut in India and also Sri Lanka. The Buddhist sites located in central asia region. Such as Iran Turkmenistan, Pakistan, Peshawar, Shah-ji-ki-Dheri, Thareli, Sahri Bahlol, Ali Masjid, (Khyber pass) Takht-i-Bahi, Taxila, Jaulian Monastery, Mohra Moradu monastery, Aziz Dheri, Gandhara, Bamiyan, Hadda, Shotorak, xinjiang province, Kashgar, Khotan, Rawak Monastery Kuche Kizil Grottoes Duldul-akur monastery, Subashi monastery. Turfan, Kazakhistan, Kayalyk monastery, Akyrtash monastery, Tamgaly Tas, Kyrgyzstan, Navikat monastery of Chu Valley, Tajikistan, Uzbekistan etc.

Buddhism disappeared from central Asia many centuries ago leaving only one deserted monasteries and temples as reminder of a religion which flourished in the region for over a millennium CE. However, despite Islamic restrictions on Idolarty worship, many of the Buddhist temples have survived as ruins despite the passage of time and vandalism.

Buddhist sites such as the caves at Bamiyan in Afghanistan and Kizil in the Xinjiang province of China were used by the locals for various purposes such as temporary shelters and for storage.

As Islam started to take root in central the patronage of locals tured to Islam and many of the monasteries Lacked the funds to maintain their temples as demonstrated by the lack of new construction in the second Millennium CE despite

Buddhism Surviving in small communities.
The Role of Central Asia in the Dissemination of Buddhism

Historical sources indicate that the dissemination of Buddhism outside India took place in the third century BCE during the reign of Emperor Ashoka (273-232 BCE). With the introduction of Buddhism to Gandhara; Central Asia became a Catalyst in spreading Buddhism to other part of central Asia and East Asia. With the establishment of the Kushan Empire (1st to 3rd Century CE).[20] With its domain including modern Afghanistan Pakistan, Samarkhand, Bukhava of Uzbekistan, Dushrable of Tajikistan and extending to India's Narmada river in the South.[21] Buddhist Philosophy started expanding into other areas of central Asia due to the political stability which made travel and Trade more convenient within the region. Buddhism was one of the religious practiced in the Kushan empire and it came to prominence under the rule of Kanishka-II (2nd century CE)[22] The biggest contri-bution to Buddhism by Kanishka-II was the convening of the Fourth Buddhist council in Kashmir and the compilation of the text of the Maha Sanghika and Sarastivada schools in Sanskrit. The discovery of Sanskrit Buddhist text in central Asia as well as at Dunhuarg Mogao Grottoes Cave17, confirms the use of Sanskrit as the literary language of Buddhism in central Asia as well as in the Transmission of Buddhism to east Asia. Along with Buddhism, Brahmi and Kharosthi scripts were adopted by the central Asian Kingdoms to record their own languages which did not have scripts of their own. The introduction of Buddhism Changed the whole cultural religious and social land scope of central Asia, introducing writing and changing the art and architecture of the area.[23]

The numerous artefacts discovered in central Asia in cludes reliquaries and pots for instance with Buddhist inscription, the ceramics from Termez in Tajikistan with Kharosthi and Brahmi script, dedicatory inscriptions on reliquaries and pottery with a Kharosthi. Buddhist dedicatory inscription from Balkh in Tajikistan etc.[24]

Inscriptions on artifacts especially those on earthenware donated to the Buddhist clergy indicate that Buddhism was part of the daily life of the community and not reserved to the monasteries only During the first Millennium CE, Central Asia played a crucial role in the dissemination of Buddhism. The Tang Dynasty (7th century CE) Buddhist records of China state that a second century BCE. Chinese court official who travelled to central Asia brought back information about Buddhism to China.[25]

The Biography of Prince Ying of the Chu Kingdom mentions a vegetarian feast given to the Buddhist monks and layman in 68CE, which is the earliest contemporary reference to Buddhism and a Buddhist Community in China.[26]

Regardless of how or when Buddhism was introduced to China, Buddhism in China was largely influenced by central Asia, especially as it was the central Asian Buddhist monks who translated the Buddhist canon to Chinese and also introduced many Buddhist text to China.

Along with Buddhist philosophy Buddhist art and architecture were also developed in central Asia, influenced by the Buddhist art of India statues and paintings of Buddha, Bodhisattva and the Arahants, stupas and other religious monument and objects, infiltrated Central Asia and Changed the central Asian cultural and social landscape forever. Even though Buddhism disappeared from Central Asia many centuries ago the remaining art and architecture are a direct testimony to the prominence of Buddhism in Central Asia.

Conclusion

Buddhism in Central Asia has a long and complex history. Theravada, Mahayana and Vajrayana Buddhist schools were all prevalent in various parts of Central Asia during various periods of its history. Buddhism was the most important religion in Central Asia during the first Millennium CE and started to decline in modern Iran and Uzbekistan as early as the Third century CE due to persecution by Zoroastrianism. In order areas Buddhism flourished as the major religion until the conquest of Arabs of Central Asia and introduction of Islam which led to some destruction of Buddha statues as ideal worship was not encouraged in Islam. Despite Islamic religious restrictions very little evidence of wanton destruction of Buddhist monasteries by the Arabian armies has been found through excavations unlike at Dalverzin-Tepe and in Iran where there is evidence of Zoroastrianists destrianism . In order area Buddhism flourished as the major religion until the conquest of Arabs of Central Asia and introduction of Islam which led to some destruction of Buddha Statues as idal worship was not encouraged in Islam. Despite Islamic religious restrictions very little evidence of wanton destruction of Buddhist monasteries by the Arabian armies has been found through excitations unlike at Dalverzin-Tepe and in Iran where there is evidence of Zoroastrianists destroying living Buddhist monasteries. During the conquest of Genghis Khan in Central Asia, many of the Buddhist monasteries was destroyed due to the destruction of the cities by the army of Gengeis Khan.

Central Asia also played an important role in the dissemination of Buddhism in china and other East Asian Countries. The Buddhist art of Central Asia was important in the development of art of China and the Buddhist clergy of Central Asia were important as translators of Buddhist text in China. Buddhist texts in different language used in central Asia convey the fact that Buddhism was disseminated in local languages.

Buddhism is not a living religion in Central Asia anymore even though there are few Buddhists still remaining in central Asia such as the Han Chinese who migrated to the xinjiang province of China during the Qing Dynasty (1644-1911 CE), the koreans who settled in Uzbekistan and Oirat-DJungar in

Kazakhstan. The ethnictics of Central Asia who embraced Buddhism during the first Millennium CE are no longer Buddhists, and even some of the languages, Cultures and even people have been absorbed by different languages and cultures. This is evident from their disappearance of Tocharian A and B, Khotanese, Bactrian and Sogdian from central Asia. These multiple language and cultures were the true corner stone of Buddhism in Central Asia which has left a rich inheritance of Buddhism, Buddhist art and architecture in the landscape where Buddhism is no longer in existence as a living religion.

References

1. http://www.britannica.com
2. History of civilization of central Asia, Vol. I, UNESCO Publishing, 1992 pp. 19-27 and p.p. 476-480
3. Refer to http://idp.bl.uk/website for details of the Dunhuang Cave 17 artifactsartefacts including the language and scripts discovered.
4. The Mahavamsa or The great Chronicle of Ceylon, translated into English by Wilhelm Geiger, Buddhist Culture centre Dehiwala, 2007, pp-82-87
5. Malalasekera, GP, Encyclopedia of Buddhism, Vol. II, Government of Ceylon, 1966, P-184
6. Dhammika, ven. S, The Edicts of King Ashoka, Kandy, 1993, P.3-4
7. http://www.dailymail.com.uk/news/article-1329650/company-digging-Afghanistan-unearths-2-600-year old-Buddhist-monastery.html
8. Chen, Kenneth, Buddhism in China.A Historical Survey, Princeton University press New Jersey, 1964

9. Hill, John E (Tr.). The western Regions according to the Hou Hansh : the xiyuu Juan ("Chapter on the western Regions from Hou Han Shu) 2003
10. our law referers to Buddhism in this context.
11. Legge, James, A record of Buddhistic kingdoms : Being an account by the Chinese Monk Fa-Hien of his travels in India and Ceylon (AD399-414) in Search of Buddha Book of Dicipline, Lok Virsa, Islamabad pp-12-14
12. Burrow, T, A Translation of Kharoshthi Documents from Chinese Turkestan, Royal Asiatic Society London, 1940
13. Burrow, T. A Translation of the Kharosthi Document from Chinese Turkestan, Royal Asiatic Society London. 1940 p.p.-82-83
14. It is written by the scribe and Monk Samghamitra. "It is authoritative in very district" Lin, Meicun, "A new Kharosthi wooden Tablet from China,"Bulletin of the school of oriental and African studies Vol-53, Issue 2, University of London, 1990, P-285
15. Solomon, Richard, Ancient Buddhist scrolls from Gandhara : The British Library, Kharosthi Fragments, University of Washington Press, Seattle, 1999
16. EMMerick, RE, (ed. and Tr.), Book of Zambasta : A Khotanese poem on Buddhism," London oriental Series, vol. 21, Oxford University Press 1968.
17. Ji, xianlin, werner Winter & Georges-jean Pinault, "Fragments of the Tocharian A Maitrya Samiti Nataka, of the xinjiang Museum, China, Trends in Linguistics : Studies and Monographs : 113, Mounton De Gruyter, Berlin 1998
18. Walter, Mariko, Namba, "Sogdians & Buddhism," Sino-Platonic Papers," No-174 (Nov-2006), Philadelphia, 2006, P-22
19. Ibid – p.p-39-42
20. Puri, B.N., "The Kushans," History of Civilizations of Central Asia-The Development of Sedentary and Nomadic

Civilizations: 700 BC to AD 250 (Vol-II), UNESCO Publishing, 1994 p.p-247-263
21. Reference map. 4 in the History of Civilization of Central Asia –The Development of Sedentary and Nomadic Civilizations : 700 BC to AD 250, UNESCO Publishing, 1994
22. As the dated of all the emperors of Kushan are disputed I have provided the century according to the data of History of Civilization of Central Asia- The Development of Sedentary and Nomadic Civilizations : 700 BC to AD 250, Vol II UNESCO Publishing 1996.
23. History of Civilizations of Central Asia-The Crossroads of Civilizations : AD250 to 750, Vol-III, UNESCO Publishing 1996.
24. Vo robyova-Desyatovskaya "Buddhism," History of Civilizations of Central Asia-The cross roads of civilization; AD 250 to 750, Vol. III, UNESCO Publishing 1996, pp-431-448
25. Chen, Kenneth, Buddhism in China-A Historical Survey, Princeton University press, New Jersy, 1964, p.p-29-32
26. Ibid-p.p-34-35

Books

1. Aalto, Penlti, On the role of Central Asia in the Spread of Indian Culture influence. In Chandra, Lokesh (eds.) India's contribution to world thought and culture Chennai, Vivekananda Kendra Prakashan : 1970
2. Agnihotri, Prabhu Dayal, Patanjali Kalin Bharat Delhi : Eastern Books-2007
3. Gopal, Dr. Surendra, India and Central Asia : Cultural, Economic, and political links, Delhi : Shipra Pub. 2001
4. Kumar, B.B. India and Central Asia : Links and Interactions India and Central Asia. In Roy, JN Kumar, BB(eds.) classical to contemporary periods, Delhi, Astha Bharti Pub. 2007

5. Lubaraskya, A, Indian Settelers in Central Asia, Vivekanand Kendra Patrika. 1973. feb, 2(1)
6. Singh, J.P. Ramayan Kalin Bharat, Shivalik Prakashan, New Delhi 2014

Asst. Professor (History)
New Standard College of Higher Education,
Salethu, Raebareli (U.P.)
Mob. No. : 9452231064

2. Ancient Trade Relations between India and Central Asia and their Influence

Dr. Kaustav Chakrabarti

Abstract

India and Central Asia have enjoyed a long and lasting relationship since ancient times. The Indian sub-continent along with Afghanistan, was contiguous to its neighbouring cultural zones such as Central and West Asia, and has enjoyed geographical affinity, cultural proximity and the fruits of economic exchange. Trade and commerce freely flourished in this socio-cultural zone. This paper tries to give an insight into the various aspects of Trade and Commerce that flourished from the pre-historic times down to the late ancient period.

Key words : Trade, India, Central Asia, Kushan, Arabs, Jews

The Antecedents

Indian Civilization is of hoary antiquity, antedating even the invasion of Aryans from the snowbound North-Western passes of the Himalayas. With the discovery of Mohanjodaro and Harappa in 1922 by two Indian archaeologists, namely Messrs. Rakhaldas Banerjee and Dayaram Sahani, the concept of the 'ancient' in Indian history was pushed still further and is currently estimated to be at least five thousand years old.

Harappan Trade and its Central and West Asian Linkages

The Harappan Civilization covering present day India, Pakistan and even parts of Afghanistan developed along independent lines, and was founded on the bedrock of trade and commerce with its West and Central Asian counterparts. The Sumerian merchants who frequented this region brought back large quantities of bronze and copper artefacts, which are testified by good quantities of Sumerian seals, probably used as currency. Again the discovery of a piece of fabric in Sumer bore the imprint of a Harappan seal. Akkadian sources refer to Harappan merchants paying visits to places like "Dilmun", "Magan" and "Meluhha". Of these places, Meluhha has been identified with Mohanjodaro. "Dilmun" and "Magan" were probably in the Persian Gulf. One striking similarity between the cities of Mesopotamia and Sumer alongside their Harappan counterparts was the large number of irrigation canals. Both Harappa and Mesopotamia were agrarian societies, with the surpluses being extracted for the upkeep of their respective "priest" kings and bureaucracy. As no weapon of violence has been found at Harappa, it's a matter of conjecture that probably religion acted as a "pacifier" of a potentially restive populace, though in the Mesopotamian case, the state was strong enough to deal with any rebellion.

At Harappa, Lothal was an important port. It was discovered by the Archaeologist, Professor S.R. Rao in the early fifties of the last century. The stone anchor found at Lothal probably points to it being a deep water port. Lothal, presently in the Indian state of Gujarat, acted as a port for long distance trade between Harappa and West Asia. The main items of export from India were ivory products, cotton cloth[1], gems and jewellery, peacock feathers and so on. Lapiz Lazuli was imported from Afghanistan. It was probably a status symbol for the ruling houses at Harappa, and also a valuable medium of exchange. One cultural commonality between Harappa and Mesopotamian civilization was the veneration of the bull and bull motifs in sculpture and painting.

The Aryan Ingress into the Indian Sub-Continent and its cultural and commercial ramifications

Linguistic groups from the Central Asian Steppes, commonly known as Aryans, made inroads in to the Indian Sub-Continent during BCE 1500. They were a group of

---

[1] The Greek for Cotton is "Sindon", probably from Sind or the Indus

nomadic pastoralists, little given to agriculture and sedentary lifestyle. They used horses and iron weapons and moved with their entire livestock and families. This nomadic group of horsemen probably moved in two directions, namely India and Persia. The latter eventually came to be known as Iran or *Aranyam* after their conquerors. The word "Arya" in the Indo-Iranian language means, literally of noble birth. The **Behistun Inscription** of the Persian Emperor Darius I describes him as *Arya Putra* (Son of an Arya), *Arya Citra* etc. For the next seven hundred years or so, several such Indo-European speaking groups migrated across the length and the breadth of Eurasia. The Indo-Aryans spoke Sanskrit as their mother tongue which is akin to Latin and Greek.

The *Vedas* or the sacred books of the Aryans are among the oldest known living scriptures in the world. The *Rig Veda* was translated into English by Professor Friedrich Max Muller. It comprises 1028 hymns invoking various deities and soliciting their support. Apart from rituals, one gets an idea of the geographical areas and the flora and fauna from Vedic Literature. The geographical area referred to in the Rig Veda includes that drained by the western tributaries of the Indus such as *Gomati* (modern Gomal), the *Krumu* (modern Kurram), the *Kubha* (modern Kabul) and the *Suvastu* (modern Swat), and the eastern limit being formed by the Ganges and the Yamuna. The Rig Veda mentions certain metals, such as *Ayash*, supposedly Iron.

Sedenterization of the tribes and the formation of Janapadas

By the sixth century BCE, the Aryan tribes gradually settled down among the indigenous people and formed distinct *janapadas* or settlements. There had been twenty nine such janapadas during the lifetime of Lord Buddha BCE (543-483). Of these, sixteen were prominent, either as Kingdoms or as Tribal Republics. The latter were known as Sodasa Maha Janapada. They could be classified as follows:

1. Kasi
2. Kosala
3. Anga
4. Magadha
5. Vajji
6. Malla
7. Chedi
8. Vatsa
9. Kuru
10. Pancala
11. Matsya
12. Surasena
13. Asmaka
14. Avanti
15. Gandhara
16. Kamboja

Kasi (modern day Benares or Varanasi) constituted the eastern most limit of Aryan migration and settlement, and was a monarchy, while Kamboja was in the North Western Frontier Region adjoining Pakistan and Afghanistan. It was a Republic. Kamboja's close proximity to Central Asia and Iran made it susceptible to influences from the Persians, Greeks and the Scythians. Taxila or Takhshashila was a university town and a centre of Buddhist culture. It drew students from all over India and also from Central Asia.

Trade and Commercial activities during the days of the Janapadas

The formation of the Janapadas or human habitations in what had been wilderness in the past gave considerable boost to trade and commerce. The powerful kingdom of Magadha provided security to the traders or *sreshthis*. The emergence of the Maurya Dynasty under the tutelage of Chandragupta Maurya BCE (322-298) gave a powerful impetus to long distance trade.

Important Trade Routes

The *Arthashastra* of Kautilya or Chanakya, the Prime Minister and advisor to Chandragupta, is an important source of information regarding contemporary socio-economic conditions. This book refers to two types of trade routes, namely the *Uttarapatha* or the Northern Trade Route and the *Dakshinapatha* or the Southern Trade Route. The *Uttarapatha* went all the way up from the imperial capital at Pataliputra to as far as Valhika or Bactria or modern Balkh in Afghanistan. The eastern terminus of the great northern trade route was Tamralipta or modern Tamluk in the present day state of West Bengal. The Mahabharata in its *Shantiparva* refers to the *Uttarapatha* and its link to the countries of the Yavanas.[2]

Pushkalavati or modern Charsadda in the North West Frontier Province was an important meeting place for traders in horses from Central Asia and Kamboja. As the Indian climate was not suitable for horse breeding, so Persian, Arabian and Central Asian Turkmen horses were in much demand for their health, strength and beauty. Marco Polo, the Venetian Traveller to India during the Early Medieval Period of Indian history, had witnessed and referred to a similar trade in Arab horses along the Malabar Coast.

The Mauryan period in Indian history also coincided with the emergence and development of Buddhism that reached its peak under Ashoka the Great BCE (267-232). The Emperor made Buddhism into a state religion and propounded his famous philosophy of *Dhamma*, which was an ethical code of conduct entailing social and individual responsibility. The Rock Edicts of Ashoka found as far as Mansera and Shabazgarhi in the Hazara district of Afghanistan give an

---

[2] The Sanskrit *Yavana* originates from the Greek Polis of Ionia, Ion and Yavana being phonetically one and the same. Incidentally, the Hebrew Yavneet is phonetically close and similar to the Sanskrit and Greek terms.

estimate of the extent of his empire, and India's commercial and cultural outreach to lands beyond the Indus. This brings us to the famous Silk Route which was the commercial lifeline of Eurasia.

The Silk Route

The Silk Route running from China to the Eastern Mediterranean was the most lucrative of all trade routes in antiquity. India being at the cross roads of the eastern and western civilisations gained much from this commercial artery. It derives its name from the lucrative trade in Silk between China and the Roman Empire. The old Silk Route touched Sikkim in the eastern most part of the Indian sub-continent to Kargil in the Western Himalayas in the westernmost part, thereby linking the trade of China and Tibet to that of Trans-Oxiana and the Roman Empire. India served as conduit in the East-West trade, with Central Asia being an important transit. The importance of trade through the Silk Route was enhanced further with the influx of the Sakas and the Kushans into the Indian Sub-Continent.

The Saka-Kushanas and their Imperial-Commercial Outreach

The decline of the Maurya Empire after the assassination of its last ruler Brihadrata in BCE 183 led to a series of foreign invasions in the form of the Indo-Greeks, the Parthians, the Sakas, and the Kushanas.

The Yeu-Chi or the Tocharians who were also known as Kushans were one of the five nomadic tribes of this branch from the steppes of north Central Asia bordering China. Driven westwards by the Huns, they first occupied Bactria and gradually moved to the Kabul valley and seized Gandhara after crossing the Hindukush. Finally, they established their suzerainty in the lower Indus region and the greater part of the

Gangetic Basin. In the process of their conquest of the Indus-Gangetic region, the Kushans displaced both the Sakas and the Parthians.

Kushana rule in India was inaugurated by the House of Kadphises. The House of Kadphises was succeeded by the House of Kanishka. Under Kanishka, the Kushan Empire stretched from the Oxus to the Ganga, from Khorasan in Central Asia to Varanasi in Uttar Pradesh. Kanishka was the greatest of all the Kushana rulers. His capital was at Pursuhapur or modern Pesahwar. This is attested by Kalhana's *Rajatangini*.[3]

Commercial Linkages with Central Asia and their Influence

As with thriving empires everywhere, trade and commerce constituted an important source of revenue. The Central Asian roots of the Kushanas served them extremely well in this regard.

Kanishk's (sic) control extended not only over the fertile valley of Fargana, but over the whole of the silk route from the eastern borders of Sinkiang to the Iranian border.[4] Samarkand and other cities of Soghdia were also under his domination.[5] Realising the importance of trade, the Kushans paid special attention to developing trade routes.[6]

The Kushana presence in India is corroborated by the discovery of large numbers of gold coins. It's obvious that merchandise along the silk route had to be paid for in gold.

---

[3] Rahul Sankritayana, *History of Central Asia Bronze Age-Chenghiz Khan*, New Age Publishers Private ltd., Kolkata, 2007, pp.108-109

[4] Rahul Sankritayana, *History of Central Asia*, op.cit, p.108

[5] Ibid

[6] Ibid, p.109

India received much gold from the Altai Mountains in Central Asia. The very word Altai means 'golden mountain', and the whole of Asia was supplied with gold from Altai.[7]

Kanishka was a patron of Buddhism, and he convened the Fourth Buddhist Council at Kundalvan in Kashmir. It was here that Buddhism split into Mahayana and Hinayana sects under the supervision of Asvaghosa and Vasumitra.

It was through the patronage of the Kushanas and the traders along the Silk Route that Buddhism spread to Central Asia, and influenced the civilisations in the Eurasian region.

Indian Contacts with the Mediterranean and West Asia
India's Jewish Contacts

Ancient Hebrews had some kind of commercial contacts with India. The first mention of Jews in connection with India occurs in the Bible itself. In the Book of Esther which probably dates from the second century B.C., mention is made of the decrees of the Persian monarch Xerxes (Ahasueras in the Bible) relating to Jews scattered throughout the 127 provinces of his empire stretching 'from *Hodu* (India) to *Kush* (Ethiopia)" (Esther 1:1). The richness of this land was known to King Solomon (Shlomo in Hebrew). Solomon made a throne out of ivory and the sandalwood (procured from India) was used for ornamenting the musical instruments of the Temple, as also the palings of the bridge, which led from the Palace to the Temple.[8] Even a few Hebrew words are believed by some scholars, notably Max Muller, to be of Indian origin.[9] The Hebrew word for Sandalwood is *"Almug"*, the Sanskrit of

---

[7] Paraphrased, p.37

[8] *The Jews And India-II*, B.V.Jacob in *Shema*, Calcutta, September 1949, V.4, No.4, p.10

[9] A.L Basham, *The Wonder That Was India*, Rupa, New Delhi, 1993, p.232

it being *"Valgum"*; the Hebrew for ape is *"Koph"*, the Sanskrit *"Kapi"*. In Hebrew, peacock is *"Tukiim"*, in Tamil "Tokei". The word *"Eleph"* for ivory is derived from the Sanskrit word *"Ibha"*.[10] Arabian traders took Rice to Europe from Dravidian ports, the word rice being an abbreviation of the Spanish *"Arrez"* derived from the Arabic *"Aruz"* and simultaneously the Hebrew *"Orez"*, which in turn are simply adapted from the Tamil *"Arisi"*.[11] All this can be said to indicate the development of maritime relations between India and the Middle East at an early date.

Polity and Economy in the late Ancient Period in India

The decline of the Gupta Empire in the wake of the Hun invasion led to the rise of petty principalities across the subcontinent. The seventh to the twelfth centuries in Indian history was a period of transition. The old imperial unity was gone and regionalism was the new feature. However, the Maukharis of Kanauj and the Pushyabhutis of Thaneswar were able to forge a new empire under the leadership of Harshavardhan circa CE (606-647). Harshavardhan's reign saw the renewal of cultural efflorescence and literary activity. The Chinese traveller and Buddhist scholar Hiuen Tsang visited India and was a guest of the emperor for fourteen years. In course of his travels across Central Asia, the former went through territories ruled by Turkish chiefs who were Buddhists by religion. As a symbol of their faith in Buddhism, the Turks erected a huge Buddhist monastery near the Sogh River.[12] The Turkish and the Mongol word for Vihar was Bukhar, hence the name Bokhara.[13] He also studied at the

---

[10] *The Jews And India-II*, B.V.Jacob in *Shema*, Calcutta, September 1949, V.4, No.4, p.10

[11] Ibid

[12] Rahul Sankritayana, *History of Central Asia*, op.cit, p.71

[13] Ibid, p.71

Buddhist seminary of Nalanda which attracted students from China, Japan, Korea, Tibet and Central Asia. The Scholar Kumarjiva's mother was a Central Asian Princess from Kucha.

From the sixth century CE onwards, there was a general decline in trade and the decay of urban centres. Trade with the Western Roman Empire had decayed due to the Hun invasions and silk trade with Persia and the eastern Mediterranean practically stopped by the mid sixth century. The general decline in commercial prosperity is corroborated by the absence of gold coins that had characterised the Silk Route trading era.

The Arabs and their monopoly of Indian Trade

The mid sixth century CE witnessed the virtual monopolisation of the India Trade by the Arabs. The Nabateans, had already carried on a lucrative trade in perfumes, spices and silk with the Far East.

The advent of Islam and its spread across half the world by the mid seventh century CE since the death of the Prophet Muhammad (PBUH) was a phenomenon of great significance for humanity. Islam was a religion of the Scripture and Urbanisation. The Prophet (PBUH) himself had been a merchant under the tutelage of his future wife and mentor Khadija. Islam's spread was therefore fortuitous in bringing the fruits of brotherhood and prosperity to humanity at large.

Arabs traders had settled along India's Malabar Coast for a long time in antiquity and intermarried with the local women. They took advantage of the favourable monsoon wind to sail between India and West Asia bringing forth the merchandise of both lands in ample quantities. Arab travellers and traders like Suleiman, Al-Idrisi and Al-Masudi on their visits to Al-Hind (India) spoke of the general prosperity of the country. They praise the Rashtrakuta kings for their sympathetic and complete regard for the Arabs.[14] Ports on the Eastern and the Western Coasts of India provided great opportunities to Arab traders to bring their products and likewise export them to distant lands. The Arab writers refer to many ports in this area Qayrah (Kaveripattanam), Manifattan or Malifattan (Nagapattanam), Abatu (Adirampattanam), Tanda (Todi), Daqtan (Devipattanam) and Fatni (Kilakarai).[15] Arab traders externalised India's West Asian links with far-reaching cultural and economic significance.

Conclusion

Trade and Commerce between India and Central and West Asia not only sustained the Indian Sub-Continent but also led to political and cultural bonds of friendship and cooperation. Traders and Missionaries frequented the Silk Route and carried new good and ideas to distant lands. The discovery of numerous Buddhist stupas, statues, and frescoes in the Central Asian heartland is indicative of this strong cultural intercourse.

Bibliography
Books
1. Basham, A.L. *The Wonder That Was India*, Rupa, New Delhi, 1993
2. Gopal, Lallanji, *The Economic Life of Northern India*, C.A.D. 700-
1200, Motilal Banarasidass, New Delhi, 2013
3. Nainar S.M.H. *Arab Geographers' knowledge of South India*,

---

[14] Lallanji Gopal, *The Economic Life of Northern India*, C.A.D. 700- 1200, Motilal Banarasidass, New Delhi, 2013, p.145

[15] Cited from S.M.H. Nainar , *Arab Geographers' knowledge South India*, Madras, 1942, Index s.v. in Lallanji Gopal, The Economic Life of Northern India, op.cit, p.147

Madras, 1942
4. Sankritayana, Rahula, *History of Central Asia Bronze Age-Chenghiz Khan*, New Age Publishers Private ltd., Kolkata, 2007

Journal(s)
Shema (The Hebrew University of Jerusalem, Israel)

**Asst. Professor of History,
City College,
Kolkata-700009,
West Bengal, India**

3. Ancient Trade Relations and Pattern of Trade between India and Western and Central Asia

Dr. B. K. Tyagi

Relations of India with the Western and the Central Asia have been culturally, economically, religiously, and politically very strong since times immemorial. Asia as a whole, as well as each of its constituent sub-regions, are extraordinarily diverse regarding geography, climate, economy, social and cultural traditions as well as social composition and culture.

The cultural roots between India and West Asia point towards some of the stark similarities between them because no other country in the Asian continent have had as long and sustained historical engagement with the West Asia as that of India and that underlines the significance of present day relevance of their mutual relations which make their historic meeting unique and unparallel.

It is very difficult in differentiating one region from another. After all, over the centuries, peoples, goods, languages and customs have crisscrossed the continent mainly as the result of conquest and commerce. Through the ages, there have been several periods of heightened contact and various types of interactions between India and West Asia.

India's links with the West Asia by land as well as sea routes goes back to very ancient times. The Arabs admired with keen interest many other aspects of Indian culture and civilization as well. They translated several Indian works spread over a wide variety of subjects but did not remain satisfied with only the translations and went on to work out original compositions based on or derived from the treatises they translated. The other fields of Indian knowledge they studied included works on snake poison, veterinary art, and books on logic, philosophy, ethics, politics, and science of war. In this process, their vocabulary was also enriched considerably.

About the economic relations between them, one can find several accounts from mid-ninth century by the Arab and other travellers such as Sulaiman the merchant, Al-Masudi, Ibn-Hnqual, Al Idrisi, etc., which testify the existence of a flourishing commercial exchange between the both. Evidence for a very active interaction in the cultural spheres including marital relations, however, goes back to the eighth century and earlier. The Great Indian Emperor Chandragupta Maurya had been married to Helena the daughter of Seleucus, a resident of Syria and was the commander of Alexander the Great. Customs and traditions: Even the advent of Muslims and Islam into India was through this region which has today evolved as the Hindu-Muslim or Ganga-Jamuni tehzib or a culture of mixed etiquettes and courtesy paving the way for the emergence of Sufism and other liberal-humanist Muslim sects in India and such liberal sects like Wahabi in West Asia.

Central Asia is known as the heartland of the Asian continent. Since China, India and Iran are situated around Central Asia they have been profoundly influenced by Central Asia and vice-versa. There are several conceptions of Central Asia. According to the Chinese conception, "Central Asia comprises the entire area beyond the great wall or the Western frontiers."1 According to Indian conception, "Central Asia comprises the entire area beyond the Himalaya and Hindukush in the north."2 According to Iranian conception, "Central Asia comprises the entire area between the Pamir and the Ural mountains."3 For a long time Central Asia was popularly known as Turkistan - Eastern and Western. Eastern Turkistan came under the influence of China and Western Turkistan was under the supremacy and colonial subjugation of Tsarist Russia.

The American scholars have used the term 'Inner Asia'

instead of 'Central Asia' for the entire region. After the establishment of U.S.S.R. Central Asia was defined as Soviet Central Asia, which consisted of Turkmenistan, Tajikistan, Uzbekistan, Kyrgyzstan and Kazakhstan. Central Asia's geographical and strategic locations as well as its rich mineral and hydro-carbon resources have always lured great powers on many occasions.

Although the term 'Central Asia' is in general use, it has never been clearly defined region. In 19th century, it was taken by Britain as stretching from the Caspian Sea in the West to the Kansu province of China in the East, and from Western Siberia in the North to the Himalayan Approaches to British India in the South. This region covered the Khanates of Khiva, Bukhara, and Khokand. In the maps after formation of U.S.S.R. this area is shown as occupied by the Kazakh, Turkmen, Uzbek, Kyrgyz, and Tazik Soviet Socialist Republics; the Sinkiang-Uygur Autonomous Region of China and by the independent states of Afghanistan. And now after the dissolution of U.S.S.R. in 1991, it confined to the republics of Turkmenistan, Tajikistan, Uzbekistan, Kyrgyzstan and Kazakhstan.

In the 2nd century B.C. when the Saka tribes emigrated from Bactria to North India via Pamir, they carried with them elements and traditions of Central Asian Culture.4 Some arms and articles excavated in Taxila are believed to be of Central Asian origin. However, ancient relations between India and Central Asia reached its zenith during the Kushana period.

During the early centuries of Christian era, with the Central Asian traditions, Saka-Parthian and Kushana elements were developed in the North-Western, Western and the Central regions of India. Saka-Parthian and Kushana culture flourished appreciably with the Central Asian traditions. It was not only in social and artistic activities but also in economic mobilization of this region and other political parts come under the rule was mixed with the cultural elements. Kushana sculptures and inscriptions5 clearly show the influence of Central Asian traditions on Indian culture especially in Gangetic region. The Kushana pattern represented on Kushana coins, testifies to the spread of Zoroastrianism and its coexistence with the Indian religion of Buddhism and Shaivism.6 Similarly the excavations at Adzhina Tepe in South Tazikistan have revealed Buddhist monastry with paintings and sculptures clearly depicting the Indian cultural influence.

During the Kushana period, people came to India from Central Asia and embraced Buddhism and even held official posts of administration. A Kushana inscription from Taxila mentions the building of a Buddhist Chaitya (monastry) by a Bactrian. Kushana sculptures show the influence of Central Asian traditions. The helmet worn by the statues of kings is typically in Indo-Sythian specimen.7 Such type of head dress was unusual in India at that time but it was popular in Central Asia very much. The Gandhara School of art, purely Buddhist in character, was influenced by the Graeco-Roman tradition which developed the Central Asian art and tradition as well. The Buddha and Bodhisattvas are fashioned in accordance with the canon as interpreted by the Gandhara School.8 In addition, there was interaction in literary traditions too. The Bactrians translated Buddhist texts from Sanskrit and even interpreted their own.9 Sanskrit inscriptions in Brahmi and Kharosthi at Kara Tepe, proves that Indian monks and scholars not only preaches Buddhism in Central Asia but also brought with them Indian culture and traditions.

The earliest archaeological evidence available attests to circulation of gold coins during this period which is recognized to the Central Asian impact. The Kushana period witnessed large scale circulation of gold coins. The numismatic evidence clearly reveals the development of internal and foreign trade between Central Asia and India.

These cultural ties influenced the socio-economic system

in India. Varna system came to an end with the generation of new castes by the intermixture of the Varnas and foreigners. Besides it, there was ruling aristocracy on the land due to the feudal tendencies in spite of the developing phase of money,10 but it was confined to the cities only.

With the establishment of intensive trade relations between the Far-East and the West and beyond up to the eastern provinces of the Roman Empire, via the overland trade route known as the 'Silk Road', the economy of Central Asia linked up with India. The Central Asian traders did not confine their trading activities to the East and West only. They conducted trade with their Indian counterparts via the routes that branched off towards the main Silk Route towards India. As such the development of this overland trade gave an impetus to the process of urbanization as numerous towns skirting the trade routes developed into main trading centres dealing with internal as well as international trade.11

In the 3rd century A.D. Bactria was regarded as a great centre of Indian civilization and the river Oxus was spoken of as a river of Buddhists and Bramans because thousands of Brahmans and Buddhist monks had settled in these regions.12 The other important centres of Buddhist learning in this region were Kotan, Yarkand, and Kuchi etc. Huien Tsang, while passing through Central Asia also indicates these relations.

During the Gupta period from 4th century to 6th century A.D., the international trade of India had developed with the West especially with Rome. The important Northern land route used by the traders was from Taxila via Kapisa, Bactria, Hekatompylos and Ecbatana onwards to India which was considered as the sole supplier of precious stones.13

Fahien and Hiuen Tsang visited India in the 5th and 7th century A.D. respectively, through a great North-Western route that ran via Central Asia and Bactria through the passes of the Sulaiman range to India. Besides it, there was a less frequented route as well in the North-East from Tonkin through Kamarupa (Assam) across Pundravarhana (North Bengal) to Magadha (Bihar).14

The quantum of trade was very insignificance from Orenburgh by the land route to Khiva, Bukhara, and India because of long distances and difficulties in transporting goods and because of the waterless steppes through out the journey and severe danger from robbers and the nomad Kirghizs of the small hords and Kara Kalpak.15

Regarding the convenient route for journey, and other information of trade between Russia and India a report was made by Lieutenant General Count V.A.Zubov,16 that for their trade with India through the Caspian Sea, the most advantageous base was Astrabad. The place was healthy and the port was very good. The journey through the province of Khorasan and Kandhar up to the borders of India by the most convenient path, running through mountains which separated India from Persia came to 1,000 Versts. In spite of great heights and other difficulties, there existed a very convenient road to Kabul, situated in the centre of the fine province of Jabulistan in Afghistan. Since Kabul Island was on the bank of the river Begat and Amu Darya was not far from the area, the above route was very ancient and convenient and it was through that route that goods were received from India.

Silk Road, also called Silk Route, ancient trade route, linking China with the West, that carried goods and ideas between the two great civilizations of Rome and China. Silk went westward, and wools, gold, and silver went east. China also received Nestorian Christianity and Buddhism (from India) via the Silk Road.

With the gradual loss of Roman territory in Asia and the rise of Arabian power in the Levant, the Silk Road became increasingly unsafe and untraveled. In the 13th and 14th centuries the route was revived under the Mongols, and at that time the Venetian Marco Polo used it to travel to Cathay (China). It is now widely thought that the route was one of the main ways that plague bacteria responsible for the Black Death pandemic in Europe in the mid-14th century moved westward from Asia.

Originating at Xi'an (Sian), the 4,000-mile (6,400-km) road, actually a caravan tract, followed the Great Wall of China to the northwest, bypassed the Takla Makan Desert, climbed the Pamirs (mountains), crossed Afghanistan, and went on to the Levant; from there the merchandise was shipped across the Mediterranean Sea. Few persons travelled the entire route, and goods were handled in a staggered progression by middlemen.

The trade between India and Central Asia during the period carried on by means of kafilas, and in some few cases by independent parties of traders. Mongomerie17 made it clear that the great routes used for this trade were:-

The first route was from Sukur, via the Bolan Pass into Afghanistan; second via Dehra Ismail Khan, and the Derbund Pall, into Afghanistan; third from Peshawar via the Khyber Pass, to Afghanistan (or Kabul); fourth from Amritsar via Kashmir and Ladakh, to Yarkand and Eastern Turkistan generally; fifth from Amritsar, Jullandhar, or Ludhiana via Nurpur, Mandi and Kullu from there by Ladakh to Yarkand and Eastern Turkistan; sixth varies from other routes from the plains across the Himalayas to Ladakh; seventh route between India and eastern Turkistan avoiding Ladakh and the territories of Maharaja Jammu altogether; eighth route between India and Lassa.

India was trading with western Turkistan generally under more unfavourable circumstances than Russia, for Khiva, Bukhara, Herat, Samarkand, Kohan and Balk can communicate more easily with the Caspian sea than with Peshawar and indeed were generally closer to the Caspian than they were to Peshawar.18 The Russians had a capital communication with the Caspian by means of the Volga and the navigation of the Caspian was entirely in their hands.

The routes between India and Eastern Turkistan or Little Bukhara were less known. It consisted of those from the Punjab and the North-West provinces. Only three among the several were available for traffic, the first via Kashmir and Leh, the second via Mandi, Kullu and Leh, and the third via Shivela, Garo and Rudok.

The natural channels of trade between Afghanistan, Persia, Western Turkistan and India were the passes of the Sulaimani range and those leading to Peshawar.19 First, among these, was the Mulla Pass near Gandava, in the Khelati Hills level which was completely safe, and one that could be travelled in all seasons. Second was the Bolan Pass, leading through Shikarpur to Sukur on the Indus, through which the trade of Afghanistan passed from Kandhar into Sindh, a distance of 400 miles. This road was generally levelled and the trade through it was at Rs.50,000 per annum.20 Third was the Ghulwaire or Guleri Pass, opposite Dehra Ismail Khan. This, though somewhat unsafe, was the chief trade route between Afghanistan and the Punjab, which was estimated at an amount of £291,000 per annum, and was in the hands of hereditary clans of merchants called provindahas.21 The fourth was, Tatara and Abkhava Passes leading from Kabul to Peshawar; these were practicable all the year and the trade was on the increase, approximately valued £2,77,150 per annum. Through these passes was the route from Bukhara which was 820 miles way or from 40 to 45 days journey by the Hajigak Pass of the Bamian range, the route was usually preferred and some what by the passes of the Hindukush.22

The natural and the most direct channel of trade for the countries of Eastern Turkistan, including Kashgar, Yarkand and Khotan, would be through the territories of the Maharaja of Jammu and Kashmir via Leh and Shrinagar to Amritsar. In distance in all, it was 1,100 miles, if the route to Leh through the valleys of the Shayak River and the Karakoram Pass was taken, and 983 miles through the very difficult route over the

Sasor Kitian Passes. But owing to the insecurity of the road between Yarkand and Leh and heavy import duty upon goods passing through Kashmir territory, the trade for the most part passed into India via Bukhara and Kabul.23 A considerable portion of trade was brought by a more circuitous and difficult road through Kulu and Mandi, simply to avoid the exaction of the Kashmir custom-house.24 The trade between Eastern Turkistan and India by the Leh route was estimated at £ 23, 504.25

There are four corridors which link India with ancient Silk Roads.

The road through high Tibetan plateau and down to the Ganges – to Sravasti.

The Road through valleys and mountains of western Nepal to the fertile valleys of the Ganges.

The Silk Roads through the Karakoram via Srinagar, Leh and Sangju Pass covering Western Himalaya.

The road down the Ganges – Delhi to Chandraketugarh in West Bengal.

Geopolitically West Asia occupies an important position in international relations due to its geographical location and proximity to continents and countries – South Asia, China, Central Asia, Europe, and Africa. The region is strategically significant due to its enormous energy resources, trade route links to different parts of the world and the fact that it is a place of origin for the Abrahamic religions. It is the world largest oil-producing region accounting for 34% of world production, 45% of crude oil exports and 48% of oil proven reserves. All powers seek a stake in the affairs of the region due to the abundance of natural resources. It is also a region plagued with instability largely due to the involvement of external forces, and sometimes due to internal conflicts.

Central Asian trade via Caspian

The trade from Astrakhan via Caspian Sea during the period could be divided into two main branches-goods sent to the west and south west coast of the sea from Persia, and trade on the eastern coast with the nomad Turkemans with Khiva and Bukhara. Indian goods went to Caspian Sea via Shigaz and Isfahan only when there was complete quiet in Persia. They went via Kandhar and Astrabad through Balkh, and Bukhara and when caravans could come back in peace and security through the territory of Afghans, who lived on the northern borders of India. The entire trade carried on the Caspian Sea remained in the hands of Asians but due to their interests in personal profits it was declining. The quantum of trade underwent regular fluctuation and it never had a stone foundation. There were proposals26 for construction of a strong and secure trading base at the gulf of Astrabad which was the most convenient centre with all proper facilities and routes from other cities. Second thing that had to develop was the establishment of a trading company with experienced experts. The proposal in this respect was establish and maintain good relations with Afghanistan and other frontier provinces of northern Indian land.

The regional dynamics of the region is rapidly changing. Regional heavyweights like Saudi Arabia, Iran, and Turkey are contending each other's views and divided on the basis of their deep vested interests. At the same time, international players and multi-lateral organizations are also involved in proxy conflicts in the region.

India's commercial and cultural relations with the region have ancient roots. People to people contacts were established between the two great civilizations in those early days when the merchants of the Kulli culture in Southern Baluchistan and the early Sumer dynasties were in existence. Later the period between the rise of Islam in the 7th century A.D. to about the 10th century A.D. may be termed as the golden age of trade relations between India and the Arab world. Our relations are still growing stronger based on common brotherhood, mutual friendship, trade, and commerce.

An important factor influencing India's foreign policy is her socio-cultural affinity of Indian Muslims owing to – Macca and Madina located in this region. Every year more than a lakh Indian Muslims go for Hajj, providing a binding force between two regions. For the past four decades trade, energy and human resource have been the principal drivers of India's economic relations with the Gulf Cooperation Council (G.C.C.). India has been heavily dependent on energy supplies from the region, while Indian expatriates have constituted a substantial share of the regional labor market. Remittances from the region were last estimated to be fifty percent of the total of 80 million USD coming to India.

Though relationship between India and the region has been mutually advantageous, it remains far less diversified and productive than it could be. In the era of globalization and liberalization, the Indian economy has been consistently growing, as have been its requirements for energy. It is important to know that over four-fifths of India's oil and gas requirements are met from external sources. Oil and gas security is important for the country's energy security. India was the third-largest consumer of oil and fourth-largest LNG (Liquefied Natural Gas) importer in 2017. To meet its requirements, India has been heavily dependent on West. Saudi Arabia, Iraq, Kuwait are the chief countries that fulfill the major demands of India's energy. Hence, the strategic importance of West Asia for India has been of utmost importance.

India's soft power is clearly visible in terms of culture, language, skills, Bollywood, food, yoga, its democratic character, neutrality, and non-interference, international law and multilateral diplomacy to name a few. Similarly, the diaspora too adopts various means to influence the government of the homeland and host countries. During the recent time, the reliance on soft power diplomacy as a foreign policy tool has been incorporated by Prime Minister Mr.

Narendra Modi.

The presence of Indian diaspora has also become an important element of spreading soft power prerogatives. They are looked upon as an unofficial ambassador to foreign policy and an important bridging link between two regions. One cannot deny the fact that Indian diaspora in the Gulf has been neglected. However, the role played by the Gulf diaspora is profound in India's development. It is only recently that India accorded importance to the Gulf region as is clearly evident in the diplomatic visits paid by Indian PM to the countries of the West Asia in general and to the Gulf States in particular. His visits to Saudi Arabia, UAE, Qatar, Iran, and Israel have yielded results, like UAE allocating land for the construction of a temple. The Qatar-Saudi blockade, and the ongoing U.S. sanctions over Iranian Nuclear deal are the two contentious issues, which India is watching closely. The change instance of India's foreign policy has been due to the large influx of labour from India to the economies of the GGC, which account for nearly 9 million contributing significantly for both the economies of India and the Gulf.

It is pertinent for India to adapt West Asian policy in a way that the national interest could be promoted in terms of trade, energy security, the export of human resource and security of its labour and remittances. This policy needs to focus on being mutually beneficial, candid and acceptable to many countries of West Asia. Notably, our diaspora policy has become a major source of soft power diplomacy by the Indian government. Our energy security in West Asia is well protected.

Notes

1. Ram Rahul, Modern Central Asia, New Delhi, 1979, p.1
2. Ibid.
3. Ibid.
4. G.M.Bongard-Levin, op.cit.p.99.
5. G.R.Sharma, Kushana Studies, 1968, p.43.
6. Ibid.
7. J.Rosenfield, The Dynastic Arts of the Kushana, Berkeley, 1967, pp.14 -16.
8. B.A.Litvinsky, Outline History of Buddhism in Central Asia, Moscow, 1958, pp.18-19.
9. B.Gaforov, Kushan Civilization and Culture, Moscow, 1968, pp.14 15.
10. .R.S.Sharma, Light on Early Indian Society and Economy,1966, p.78.and G.R.Sharma, Central Asia from 6th century B.C. to 6th century A.D. cited in Amalandu Guha's Central Asia.
11. Alexander Belenitsky, Central Asia, London, 1969, p.97.
12. S.C. Raychoudhary, Social, Cultural and Economic History of India, Delhi, 1983, P.125.
13. P.N.Chopra, B.N. Puri, and M.N.Das, A Social, Cultural, and Economic History of India, Delhi , 1974 pp.132-133.
14. Ibid P.136.
15. Ibid.
16. Lieut. Gen. Count V.A. Zubov, A General Revision of Trade with Asia, 1802, No. 218 p.249-250.
17. Memorandum on Central Asia and its trade with Hindustan, Davies official Reports on Trade with Central Asia.
18. Ibid.10.
19. For. Dept. (Pol.A) May, 1864, 9-12, pp.2-3, minutes by the Hon'ble the Liet. Governor, Punjab.
20. Ibid.
21. Ibid. p.3.
22. Ibid.

23. Ibid.
24. Ibid.
25. Ibid.
26. Surendra Gopal, India and Central Asia: Cultural, Economic and Political Links, Shipra Publications, New Delhi, 2001. p.246.

Select Bibliography
1. Dialogue, A quarterly journal of Astha Bharati, Delhi, Volume 2 No. 3, January-March, 2001, Volume 3, No. 4, April - June, 2002, Volume 6, No. 2, October - December, 2004, and Volume 8, No. 4, April-June 2007, (Consulted on Internet.)
2. Gopal, Surendra. India and Central Asia: Cultural, Economic and Political Links, Shipra Publications, New Delhi, 2001.
3. Guha, Amalendu. (Ed.) Central Asia: Movements of Peoples and Ideas from Times Prehistoric to Modern, Delhi, 1970.
4. Joshi, Nirmala. (Ed.) *Central Asia, The Great Game Replayed,* New Century Pub. Delhi, 2003.
5. Perspectives on Central Asia Vol.II, No.1, April, 1997, Published by the Eisenhower Institute's Center for Political and Strategic Studies. (Consulted on Internet)
6. Rahul, Ram. *Struggle for Central Asia,* New Delhi, 1982.

**Professor and Head,
Department of History,
Govt J. N. S. PG College,
Shujalpur (M.P.) India**

4. A Pathway of Cross-Cultural Influence between Central and South Asia –Buddhism to Baburids

Dr. Dildora Khodjaeva

While studying some areas, their history cannot be neglected, if it is especially related to understanding relations between countries. Without the knowledge of history, we cannot understand the present-day problems, whether they are of national or international level, accurately and objectively. History is considered as the 'queen' or 'mother' of the social sciences, because, it is the basis of philosophy, politics, economics, culture, art and religion. Considering the significant role of history, the paper delves into historical interactions between Uzbekistan and India and highlights cultural impacts between the two regions.

As a vital part of the Eurasian continent–Central and South Asian regions had a strong impact on the development of the world civilization. The regional interactions and cooperation in various spheres extensively shaped cultural and political junctures. It is necessary to indicate that while reviewing historical sources, since ancient times Central Asian region broadly known as Bactria, Turan (Persians called, the land of Turks), Transoxiana (Romans called, 'the land Beyond the Oxus'–Amudarya river) Mawaraunnahr (Arabs called, 'the land Beyond the River') and Turkestan (land of Turks), which mostly represents a territory of modern Uzbekistan. As for historical India, it is generally regarded as an integral part of the whole geopolitical area defined widely as South Asia proper. Therefore, the paper treats Indo-Uzbekistan relations as an interaction between South and Central Asia in the broadest sense.

While scrutinising the historical relations between Central

and South Asia, we have indeed to consider not in terms of decades or centuries but millennia. Whereas between 2000 and 1500 BC, a significant migration of Aryans (Central Asians) brought into Indus Valley the Indo-European languages along with cultural practices such as sacrificial rituals, all of which formed the basis of early Vedic culture. A recent fascinating discovery on 'Genomic Formation of South and Central Asia' (Narasimhan, 2018) provided greater verification to the theory of the Aryan migration.

Moreover, ancient epic narratives – India's two gems – Ramayana and Mahabharata, which are considered as a kaleidoscope of facts consist of important historical phenomena of the Indian sub-continent. As described in the battle of Kurukshetra in Mahabharata texts and mostly interpreted by 20th century scholars, several Central Asian warriors were invited by Kauravas and Pandavas both and participated in the Great War. Central Asian clans including Saka, Kamboja, Tukhara, Pahlva and Huns have been referred to as good birth of Kshatriya in the Mahabharata. The Udyoga Parva (Mahabharata, chapter 7) mentions the fact that the Sakas fought on the side of Kauravas.

Archelogy in the 20th century facilitated clarity and brought to light in many theories of world civilisation history. Thus, a number of archaeologic pieces of evidence provide the existence of cultural binds between the people of Turan/Transoxiana and Indus Valley in the ancient and medieval epochs. The spreading of Buddhism is a clear corroboration, where the archaeological excavations obtained remarkable findings, in Karatepa, Fayaztepa and Dalvarzintepa (Rtveladze 2015; Kumar, 2007) in old Termez (near to Afghanistan). Accordingly, along with Buddhism a large number of inscription in Sanskrit and Prakrit were discovered in old Termez, which date from the 1st century AD. As a matter of fact, that Buddhism moved along the Great Silk Route through Kashmir, Afghanistan, Central Asia and

China, which strongly established in East Asian countries of Korea and Japan.

Geostrategic location of Central Asia, particularly, Uzbekistan in the centre of Eurasian continent presented the region to function as the 'Heartland' in the transcontinental system of the Great Silk Route.

In the history of the Great Silk Route, there are three periods of intense trans-communication:

1. Between China and Central Asia, extending to Rome (206 BCE. – 220 CE.);
2. Between China and Central Asia, Byzantium, the Arab Empires, the Persian Empire, and India (618 – 907 CE.);
3. Between China, Central Asia, Persia, India, and Europe (13th – 14th centuries) (R. Kurin, 2002).

After the conquest of Western Asia in the 3rd BCE. by Alexander the Great, the Mediterranean became linked to the Indus Valley and the Fergana Valley in Central Asia, which opened the route across the Tarim Basin and the Gansu Corridor to China. In this context, Central Asians are considered as earliest agents in progressing the function of the Silk Route exchange and the land of Central Asia was a bridge between cultural activities. With the name of initiating the development commercial gain between the regions, the Silk Road facilitated the transmission of knowledge and syncretisation of different cultural elements through merchants, travellers, pilgrims and missionaries. Language, art, literature customs and religions influenced each other. On the other hand, science, craft and technologies gradually improved along crisscrossed Routes.

It was during the 8th century when Islam was introduced into Central Asia by Arabs, which brought a great cultural transformation of indigenous traditions and developed science and letter in the region. In this regard, Indian Subcontinent witnessed Islamic influence in 7th century in the Malabar region, which was introduced by the Arab traders. However, Central Asian invader Mahmud Ghaznavi (971-1030) facilitated the widening of Islam in the northern part of India. Since cities like Bukhara, Tehran, Isfahan, Gujrat, Punjab and whole Afghanistan was under Ghaznavid Empire, as a great patron of science, literature and admirer of fame, Mahmud tried to bring all eminent scholars to his royal court. Because, as believed during that time, the presence of poets and scholars at the royal court contributed to the prestige and reputation of the King. With the same manner, Central Asia's great minds including scientific scholars Abu Rayhan Al Beruni (973-1050) and poet Abul-Qasim Ferdowsi Tusi (940-1020) accompanied Mahmud of Ghazni. He even attempted to persuade Avicenna to travel with him but was not successful.

Since Beruni escorted Gaznavi on his travels and military campaigns to India, it opened boundless horizons before the genius for learning every aspect of the mysterious land. Although, while Beruni was in Khwarazm (1000 CE), he already had some knowledge about India. His Āsār ul- Bāqiya (the Chronology of Ancient Nation), refers to the Indus Valley and Indian astronomical theories. Beruni spent years in the company of Brahmana priests and scholars, learning Sanskrit, and studying religious and philosophical texts. Al-Beruni's fluency in multiple languages (Arabic, Persian, Latin, Turkic, Hebrew, Greek, Sanskrit Hindi and Syric) enabled him to successfully translate from various texts as well as to compare one religion or culture to another.

During his sojourn in India (1017-1030 AD), Beruni worked productively and based on his knowledge from and of India, he produced prominent books in 12 subjects: Astrology, Mathematics, Astronomy, Geography, Chronology, Anthropology, Geodesy, Mineralogy, Pharmalogy, Religion, Yoga and Ayurveda.

As Beruni explored the region with a rich cultural context, his lucid and objectively depicted encyclopedic book 'Kitab-ul

Hind' or 'Tarikh Al-Hind' (History of India) written in Arabic is a great contribution to the world history and science. The work is considered as one of the first Muslim studies of the Hindu religion as well. The book is divided into 80 chapters and enlightens various subjects on philosophy, astronomy, alchemy, iconography, religion, festivals, social life, customs, measures, metrology and law. While writing Al-Hind, Beruni along with his personal observations, referred to Sanskrit sources, like the Gita, Puranas, Upanishads, Patanjali and Vedas, etc. According to the sources, as a scholar and roving world citizen, Beruni had an extraordinary ability to conduct and engage in harmonies dialogue with different cultures. Therefore, Gaznavids, Mahmud and his successor Masoud, found the presence of Beruni in their court very useful. Since Al-Beruni firmly believed that, instead of fighting wars and trying to destroy each other, great cultures should try to learn from each other. Al-Beruni's adequate knowledge brought notable mutual understanding between Muslim and other cultural worlds.

It was during the Empire of Delhi Sultanate (1206-1526) when Turko-Islamic culture stretched over a large part of the Subcontinent and its influence got off the ground shaping Indian architecture, literature, language, art, belief, outfit and cuisine. As a result, the first Islamic architecture of India, the Quwwat-ul-Islam mosque was built between 1193 to 1197. Along with the mosque, to call for prayer, construction of Qutub Minar – a tower started in 1193 by Qutubiddin Aybak, however, it was completed with further addition by his successor Iltutmush in 1230 and later by Feroz Shah Tughlaq in 1368. Today, Qutub Minar is considered as the highest brick minaret in the world.

Since the Sultans of Delhi realised the geographic and seasonal changes of India, they tried to create comfort during hot seasons to make weather cool with the help of (monsoon rain) water reservoirs, which can be considered as an initial ancient integrated ecosystem at Hauz-e-Khas (from Persian means, 'special lake'). Another accomplishment of the Delhi Sultanate was a madrasa, established by Tughlaq in 1352 and was considered as one of the leading Islamic Institutions of that time. Thus, with urbanization, Delhi Sultanate flourished as other leading commercial and cultural centres of the world like Baghdad, Cairo and Istanbul. As Tarikh-i-Feroz Shahi by Ziauddin Barani (2015) confirms: 'the royal capital of Delhi had emerged as a great city and had become a source of envy for Baghdad and a cause of jealousy for Egypt, equal to Constantinople and comparable to Bait al-Maqdis (Jerusalem)...in every branch of learning'.

The intensive interaction between Central and South Asian people facilitated Sufi networks at the Subcontinent. As the Goodwill Ambassadors, Sufis integrally carried social harmony among the societies. Consequently, the influential Sufi saints, like Khwaja Mu'inuddin Chisti (1142-1236), Baba Fariduddin Ganj-i- Shakar (1179-1266), Syed Muhammad Nizamuddin Auliya (1238-1325), Nasiruddin Chirag- e-Dehlavi (1274-1356) won the hearts of the people of India. Today, there are several Sufi shrines of Chistiya and Qadiriya dargahs serving thousands of worshipers throughout India.

Since the 13th-14th centuries are considered as a zenith of Sufism, when the mystic poet-musician Amir Khusrau became a patron-saint for musicians. He had introduced genre Qawwali (devotional Sufi songs) among Muslims of the Subcontinent. In this context, it is relevant to mention that Hazrat Amir Khusrau Dehlavi (1253-1325) is indeed a precise example of Indo-Turkic amalgamation. From his father's lineage, he belonged to Kesh (known as Shahr-e-sabz in Uzbekistan) of Turkic origin and his mother was from the Rajput community. His father, Amir Saifuddin Mahmud, fleeing the ravages of Chingiz Khan, migrated from Uzbekistan and found refuge in India during the reign of

Eltutmish. Accordingly, Khusrau gained true knowledge of Turkic, Indian, Iranian, Arabic and Greek cultures and philosophy. Perhaps, based on his rich experience, Khusrau contributed to the creation of a new linguistic medium – known as Hindavi, as well as compiled a Hindi-Persian dictionary. Moreover, it is not only the merging of languages, he combined musical customs as well. In this context, there are many surveys done on Khusrau's role in the development of Hindustani music and its classical instruments. According to scholars (F. Azizova, 1999; D. Karomat, 2015), Khusrau contributed to the systematic process of synergising between Indian and Central Asian musical art styles, as a result, he invented and developed the Ragas.

It is noteworthy to mention that spreading Muslim cultural traditions influenced Hindi poetry, which is felt in the writings of Naat and Bhakti verses, whose system of imagery bears affinity to that of Sufi poetry. Thus, Sufism and Bhakti stood on common grounds of ideology and practice. Moreover, Indo-Muslim synthesis had played a considerable influence upon the development of medieval Punjabi literature (A. Shamatov, 2011), which later affected emerging Sikhism in South Asia.

As history bears witness, through the regular diverse exchanges on Silk Route, the formation of the interstate cultural association was flourished among the Central and South Asia. Especially, it reached its zenith during the Empire of Baburids – the longest dynasty of India (1526-1857), which is popular as Mughal dynasty. The Baburids expanded their kingdom throughout the Indian territory such as Delhi, Lahore, Agra and Fatehpur Sikri coinciding with the Mawaraunnahr's glorious metropolises of Samarqand, Bukhara, Khorasan, and Balkh (Foltz, 1998).

The dynasty of Babur in the Indian subcontinent: Humayun, Akbar, Jahangir, Shah Jahan, Aurangzeb, Farrukhsiyar, Muhammad Shah and Bahadur Shah presented a lot of treasures to the land – India. In this context, the paper emphasises the important contribution of Baburids to India's architecture, landscape, science, technology, literature, art, culture and so forth.

Turkic ruling class, especially, Temurid/Baburid dynasty, with the taste of town life, had always tried to develop a luxurious atmosphere by building palaces and creating gardens along with lakes. While studying the history of Temurid gardens, it is recognised that they mostly created a 'cultural zone' for socio-cultural activities, marriage ceremonies, festivities as well as other entertainments like sports, and even for composing poetry. Although, as Abul Fazl remarks in Aina-i Akbari that 'formerly peoples planted their gardens without any order, but since Babur's arrival (1526) in India, more methodological arrangement of garden was made'. Thus, Babur introduced into South Asia a concept of Chaharbagh (fourfold), a symmetrical innovative garden. Precisely, a walled-in garden, subdivided into four quarters by raised walkways and canals, which was pervasive throughout this ancestral homeland Ferghana and his kingdom of Kabul.

As Babur settled down in Agra, he founded Bagh-e Hasht-Behesht (Garden of Eight Heaven) on the east bank of the Yamuna river at Agra, which Babur mentioned in his memoirs (Baburnama) the moments of during Ramadan (A. Beveridge, 2006) Moreover, Babur founded Mehtab Bagh (Moonlight garden) in Agra, where over a century after Taj Mahal was built and made a perfect reflection of the Taj in the moonlight.

It is a well-known fact that Babur was always nostalgic of his homeland fruits and products. Therefore, fruits, vegetables, trees, seeds and flowers had been imported from Central Asia. Under the supervision of skilled Turanian horticulturists, the imported seeds and trees of Central Asia were planted and cultivated on Indian soil.

As an important aspect of Baburid's period was immigration of Turks, Persians, Afghans and Arabs, who settled down in the subcontinent, leading to the formation of composite culture and synthesis of civilization. Once Akbar took the throne, the impulse of creativity of the imperial constructions reflected on the architecture in the region. The construction of his father Humayun's tomb is considered as a perfect approach of a composition of the garden and architectural elements of its own time. As the first major Baburid monument, Humayun mausoleum (built during 1565-1572 AD) drew inspiration from the Temurid architecture and a meticulously symmetrical plan combined with red sandstone and white marble, which made an architectural metaphor for the Indianisation of the Turko-Islamic style. Some fifty years later, Humayun's mausoleum influenced the architecture of the Taj Mahal.

During Jalaluddin Akbar's period (1556-1605) the traditional Turko-Islamic architecture was enriched with some synthesis of Hindu/Jain/Buddhist styles. Architectural syncretism emerged at Akbar's new great capital city Fathepur Sikri, where construction patterns reflected his philosophy represented in his period's political and religious unity. Moreover, the Buland Darwaza (Gate of Magnificent) at Akbar's Fatehpur Sikri was modeled on the entry gate at Ak Saray palace at Shahr-e Sabz (A.H. Dani, 1993).

The zenith of Baburid royal classical architecture campaign in India shined with the foundation of world-renowned Taj Mahal, which was commissioned by Shah Jahan (1628- 1658) in memory of his favourite wife Arjumand Banu. There are many legends and controversies surrounding about the construction, which started in 1632 AD and was completed in 1648 AD. Historical records list several personalities responsible for the foundation of this greatest example of Indo-Islamic architecture. According to Nizomutdinov (1966), the Taj's architect was an Ottoman, Muhammad Isa Effendi, and the chief draftsman, Muhammad Sharif, was from Samarqand, the head sculptor, Ata Muhammad, was from

Bukhara. As a global project of its own period more than 20,000 workers along with skilled artisans from India, Central Asia, Persia, Ottoman and Syria took part to construct the finest treasure of India. Taj Mahal's ornamental materials had been brought from all around Eurasia: nephrite, jade and crystal from Central Asia, turquoise from Tibet, lapis lazuli from Badakhshan and Afghanistan, chrysotile from Egypt and, main marble and red sandstone from India, also forty- three type of precious, semiprecious stones: topaz, onyxes, coral, mother pearl, garnets and sapphires were used from all around India (F. Ching, 2014).

One more achievement of Shah Jahan was the foundation of his imperial capital Shahjahanabad (1628-1658 AD) spread out over a large area along the banks of river Yamuna in the south-eastern parts of Delhi. Shahjahanabad was an example of a sovereign city model, where the magnificent Lal Qila (Red Fort) and Jama Masjid were located in the central part of the city. Since Shahjahanabad was a walled city with gates – Dilli, Lahori, Kashmiri, Kabuli, Ajmeri, Turkman, Khizri, Lal, Badarroo and Faresh Khana Darwazas – connected to the town. The Gate (Darwaza-Darvoza) concept, similarly can be observed in old Tashkent city system, like Samarqand, Ko'kcha, Chig'atoy, Kamolon, Sag'bon, Labzak Darvozas and so forth. Moreover, adding Turkic suffix 'Abad' (prosperous) after some name, also was related to Central Asian custom, which was used for an urbanised region. Accordingly, the structure of Mohalla, also had been adopted from Central Asia and developed in Shahjahanabad. With developing of the city, royal Hammam Turkish bath concept, which was basically introduced by Babur in the Subcontinent, became accessible to the common public as well. The urban-cultural achievements under the Baburid period were the result of civilizational synthesis of elements from India, Central Asia and Persia, where Islamic culture was dominant.

The Baburid period in India became a melting pot of religions, languages, art and cultures. There was no single domain untouched or neglected in this epoch, the greatest growth was witnessed especially in literature, fine art, music, poetry, and dance, where great patronage was provided by Baburid rulers for fostering the Empire. The Baburids brilliant cultural contribution to the Subcontinent, which is something that cannot be described in a paragraph or two. The remarkable culture which Baburids fostered in India owed a considerable debt to Central Asian legacy (Foltz, 1998).

The court language of the Baburid Empire was considered to be Persian, however, simultaneously Turkic was used as conversational language as well, between the civilian community from Central Asia. Perhaps, there was a group of native Indian and Central Asian soldiers who were combined under one army. Subsequently, a new vernacular language was generated in militaries by their interactions with each other. The military camp was called O'rda in Turkic, from which the word Urdu originated. According to Farooqi (2008), the name 'Urdu' seems to have begun its life as zaban-e urdu-e mualla-e Shahjahanabad (the language of the exalted city/court of Shahjahanabad, that is, Delhi). Over time that long name shrank simply to Urdu. The name Urdu was first used by the poet Ghulam Hamadani Mushafi, which is considered the golden period of Urdu poetry, the 18th – 19th centuries.

Indeed, it is not immediately that Urdu came up as a language, historically a strong base had been made through many centuries if we consider the initial step from the Aryan immigration and intense interaction with Central Asian region, later interexchange with Arabs, then invention by Muslim conquerors, such as of Turkic origins and Afghans. Between all of these stages, there was a great contribution by Khusrau to Hindavi/Rekha. And the prime time for this language was when the Baburid dynasty created a favourable condition for the flourishing of Urdu. Therefore, Urdu is enriched with the combination of many Arabic, Persian and Turkic words. In fact, Uzbek language is also an amalgamation of the same mentioned languages.

Indian Culture In Central Asia

Since Central Asia is considered a polyglot society, as well Indians, significant strides were made for the development of the translation sphere. Under the patronage of wise Baburid Emperors, as a powerful medium for transmission of ideas towards making civilised society at the subcontinent, literary translations came up, through which various believers could enlighten the opinions.

It was Akbar, literally as the Great ruler had courageous enough to cross the religious borders and resolve the complex issues between society. With synthesising the best elements of various religions Akbar conceived absolute peace and harmony at his mighty and magnificent Empire. It should be acknowledged, that implementation of the concept 'Din-e Ilahi' (Divine Faith) influenced the social and cultural integration of his time, which was the highest understanding by humankind. It was Akbar, who had first acknowledged for unification the country, it is not always necessary to use the hard power, the instruments of cultural powers are the best devices for implementation. His policy effected even on the country's economic growth as well, which is mentioned in many sources related into the economic history of India, that during 16th century the GDP of India was the highest in the world economy of that period.

It was during Akbar's reign, the first Translation Bureau department was established in India, where various works on science, religion, history and epics had been translated in Sanskrit, Persian, Arabic, Turkic and other Indian languages. The efforts of Hindus and Muslims created a social unity, that acquired popularity on humanistic ground. One of the significant points was the introduction of printing technology in India by European missionary-printers. By transporting and establishing the printing press at the Baburid court, it fostered the contribution of science and education.

As the great patrons of literature, many historical works and biographies composed during the Baburids period, hereby some famous and significant are, Baburnama (by Babur), Humayunnama (by Gulbadan Begum), Akbarnama, Ain-i Akbari, Navaratnas (by Abul Fazl), Muntakhab-ul Tawarikh (by Abdul Qadr Badauni), Tabaqati Akbari (Nizamuddin Ahmad), Tazkirat-ul Waqiat, Tarikh-i Humayunshahi (by Jauhar Aftabchi), Ramcharitmanas (Tulsidas), Sursagar (Surdas), Padmavat (Malik Jayasi), Padshahnama (Abdul Hamid Lahori) and so forth.

As the most influential rulers of Indian history, Baburid imperial court gave a new impetus to the development of artistic fabrics. This period was characterised with the emergence of various types of fabrics, new technology and expansion of the range of colours.

Baburids had a strong influence on exquisite craftsmanship, artistry and textile technique in India. To encourage sophisticated silk, Akbar established silk weaving centres- Karkhanas at Fatehpur Sikri, Lahore, Ahmedabad, and Kashmir (I. Habib, 1997). Moreover, the imperial court supported the production of cotton and patronised textile techniques, subsequently, a hybrid of silk and cotton, known as 'mashru' was innovated (R. Crill, 2015). Later, the most exquisite cotton fabric, delicate and elegant in production– known as 'malmal', was generated. Among other techniques, during Akbar and Jahangir's reign, 'zardozi' (a fabric worked with gold threads), embroidery improved more generally. This traditional motif belongs to one of the ancient crafts of Uzbekistan and most widespread pattern in Bukhara. Since two regions were in contact through Silk Route and other personal sources, they perhaps, influenced each other by borrowing various motifs, while at the same time preserving their individual traditions and uniqueness.

Originally from Central Asia, the dynasty's rulers skilfully sought to fuse the two traditions in an attempt to harmonise cultural relations. Although, Turkic culture had been already presented to the Subcontinent from the Gaznavids period,

Baburid rulers achieved that cultural synthesis. Perhaps, it was during Akbar's time that culmination took a definite aesthetic aspect of its own. Through the court historiographer Abul Fazl's work there is some adequate information on imperial court etiquette, food habits and man outfits etc., during Babur to Akbar's time. After surveying the history and observing the Central Asians clothing, it is clear that present-day garments, such as kurta, salwar, pyjama were the evolution of Baburid fashion.

Concerning women's attire, there are a lack of adequate sources, until the arrival of Mehrunissa (Nur Jahan) to the imperial court in 1611. As an empress (wife of Jahangir), with sheer intelligence and strong character, she gained immense power in all matters of administration in the kingdom. Nur Jahan was the first lady in the entire Empire to be portrayed in the hunter's attire that was evidently worn by men. She has been credited with the introduction of many innovations and techniques. Particularly, Nur Jahan's contribution in the field of textile, fashion and couture culture include, Chikonkari embroidery (needlework on cotton) and badla (silver threaded brocade), and kinari (silver threaded lace), Nurmahali (a complete set of garments designed for bridegrooms), farsh-i chandani (sandalwood carpets). It was the rose perfume (itr) discovered-courtesy of Nur Jahan's mother Asmat Begum, which later was named as 'Itr-i Jahangiri'. Perhaps, it inspired Nur Jahan to invent an initial form of conditioner in her own time, whereas all the clothes were scented with rose water. Her love for flowers was reflected through the motifs in the dresses and costumes of the period (R. Das, 2013). It would be fair enough if we state, the imperial court's successful innovations are still influential and their elegant attires, accessories are in vogue even in the modern era.

Through amazing social networking, far and wide caravan routes from Central Asia to India and Egypt to Libya, the stuffed triangle-shaped snack garnered immense popularity among travelers. This popular Central Asian snack 'somsa', known as sanbusak, sanbusaq, sambosa (Middle East), sanbosag (Iran) samosa (India) survived over the centuries and carries across the globe. Compared to Central Asian Samsa, Indian samosa have a difference in stuffing and baking techniques, except that the triangle shape remains. The same way, Central Asian cuisine, which was brought by Baburids, an amalgamation of two regions experience and taste. As a researcher and being from Central Asia and knowing the taste and technology of cuisine of the native land and India, basically there are quite a few differences found between Central Asian and Indian 'Mughlai cuisine'.

From Babur onwards, in consequence, each Emperor made his contribution to enrich the menu for today's 'Mughlai' cuisine and raised cooking to an art form. As observed, since Humayun spent much of his life in Iran and on the other hand influence of his Iranian wife Hamida, most Persian foods were introduced to the Baburid imperial court menu by them. With the influence of Persian cuisine and the combination of a lot of flavors and nuances new traditional Kashmiri cuisine was shaped, for example, food varieties such as Pasanda, Kofta, Rogani Josh, Haleem, Goshtaba, Zafarani Kokur, and so forth. Liberal Emperor, Akbar, and his successors evolved traditional cooking styles, a fused taste of cultures. As a result, Uzbeki palov converted into Biryani. While scrutinizing the history of biryani, sources are linking it to the Persian etymology birian (grill, roast), but as an observer finds, it is derived from Uzbek/Turkish language bir yon/yan (one side, separate), as the cooking technology proves it. Biryani is mostly prepared layered with the meat at the bottom of the cooking pot, a layer of rice is placed over it and other ingredients one put over it layer by layer. If we consider the cooking technology, the meaning biryani, logically and etymologically exactly the same with Uzbeki 'bir yan' - rice one side and other ingredients are another side. In addition, Uzbeki nan (non), kabab (kabob), korma (qovurma), khichra (kichiri) halwa (holva) became popular and Indianised as well.

Much more can be mentioned – the humanistic Baburid legacy developed and generated the highest cultural identity for the people of the Indian subcontinent. This can be observed in the architecture, gardens, science, literature, fine arts, music, attire, cuisine, beliefs and so forth. Even in modern-day, after nearly three centuries, the influence of cultural amalgamation plays a significant factor in the region, which was presented by Baburids.

Overall, history is not about feeling good about oneself but rather understanding and analysing the past. Thus, understanding a historical interconnection between Central and South Asia, we observe a creative process of assimilation that worked mutually, which contributed to enrich each other in many spheres of cultural activities.

References :
Azizova, Farogat (1999). Shashmaqom and Raga, Academy of Science of Tajikistan, Dushanbe.
Barani, Ziauddin (2015). Tarikh-i Firoz Shahi, translated from Persian into English by Ishtiyaq Ahmad Zilli, New Delhi: Primus Books.
Berridge, G., Keens-Soper, M. and Otte, T.G. (2001). Diplomatic Theory from Machiavelli to Kissinger, Palgrave, UK.
Ching, Francis (2014). Architecture: Form, Space and Order, New Jersey: John Wiley and Sons.
Crill, Rosemary (ed.), (2015). The Fabric of India, London: Victoria and Albert Museum.
Dani, Ahmad Hasan (1993). New Light on Central Asia, Lahore: Sang-e-Meel Publications.
Das, Rajripa (2013). Mughlai Libaas: The Transmigration of Central Asian Fashion to the Indian Subcontinent in the 16th and 17th Century, Dissertation-MLitt Art History, University of Glasgow.
Farooqi, Mehr Afshan (2008). 'Language of Whose Camp?',

Outlook, 21 February. Available at: https://www.outlookindia.com/ website/ story/language-of-whose-camp/236758.

Foltz, Richard (1998). Mughal India and Central Asia, New York: Oxford University Press.

Habib, Irfan (ed.), (1997). Akbar and His India, Delhi: Oxford University Press.

Karomat, Dilorom (2015). 'From the Sultanate to the Mughals: Literary Sources as a Mirror of Musical Relations between India and Central Asia', in Anita Sengupta and Mirzokhid Rakhimov (eds.), Insights and Commentaries South and Central Asia, KW Publishers PVT Ltd, New Delhi.

Kumar, B B. (2007). 'India and Central Asia: Links and Interactions India and Central Asia', in Roy, J.N. Kumar, B.B (eds.), Classical to Contemporary Periods, Delhi: Astha Bharti Pub.

Kurin, Richard (2002). 'The Silk Road: Connecting People and Cultures', in Caria M. Borden (ed.), The Silk Road: Connecting Cultures, Creating Trust, pp. 23-27. Washington DC: The Smithsonian Institution.

Narasimhan V.M., Patterson N.J., Moorjani P. et al. (2018). 'The Genomic Formation South and Central Asia', BioRxiv, 31 March. DOI: http://dx.doi.org/10.1101/292581.

Nizomiddinov, I. (1966). XVI-XVII asrlarda O'rta Osiyo va Hindiston munosabatlari (The Relations Between Central Asia and India during XVI-XVII centuries), Fan, Tashkent.

Rtveladze, Edvard V. (2015). 'The Great Indian Road: India-Central Asia-Transcaucasia', in Anita Sengupta and Mirzokhid Rakhimov (eds.), Insights and Commentaries South and Central Asia, KW Publishers PVT Ltd, New Delhi.

Associate Professor,
Tashkent State University of Economics,
Uzbekistan

5. History of The Development of Indology in Uzbekistan

Prof. Mukhibova Ulfatkhon

Historically, interest in India and its study in Central Asia is rooted in the distant past. Indology as a science has existed in Uzbekistan for 75 years. The same age as independent India, the Department of Indian Philology was founded in 1947. During its existence, the Indian branch has trained more than 1,500 specialists. Not only envoys from other CIS countries studied here, but also scholars from other countries such as Poland, Germany, Bulgaria, Mongolia, Cuba and Vietnam trained by qualified lectors.

In this regard, programs for the exchange of specialists were successfully implemented, according to which, over the past period, well-known Indian scientists, professors such as J. Sarkar, Kamar Rais, Bholanath Tiwari, H.A. Farukh, K.U. Hashimi, Muhammad Amin lectured at the Department of Indian Philology. And in recent years, due to improved ties with Indian universities, professors from J. Nehru University Devendra Chaubey, Khoja Ikramuddin, Anwar Alam and Akhlaki Akhan were invited to teach.

Hindi is studied as a foreign language at the Lal Bahadur Shastri School No. 24, in front of which a bust of M. Gandhi was installed in 1974, as well as at the academic Lyceum at the Tashkent State University of Oriental Studies. Hindi as a foreign language is also taught at the University of World Languages.

The main center of Indology is the Tashkent State University of Oriental Studies, which originates in the Central Asian University, later becomes part of the Tashkent State University since 1947. The Department of Indian Philology, established at the Oriental Faculty in the same year, still

59

remains the main and major center of Indology not only in Uzbekistan, but also in Central Asia.

The history of Indology is very rich both in terms of training highly qualified personnel for the country and so in terms of a comprehensive study of India..

Speaking about the personnel issue, it should be especially noted that many Indologist graduates of the Oriental Faculty, as completely developed personnel, held responsible positions in the highest state bodies of Uzbekistan, contributing to the development of international relations with foreign countries, both during the existence of the USSR and after the formation of the independent Republic of Uzbekistan. It is worth mentioning the names of the most active, well-known graduates, Indologist Orientalists, who represented the interests of our country on the world stage as diplomats.

Mr. Fatih Teshabaev[1] is an outstanding Indologist, Candidate of Philosophical Sciences, defended his PhD thesis on the ancient Indian philosophy in Moscow. He spoke Hindi, Urdu, Punjabi, Arabic, Persian, English, German and French. His career began as Chairman of the Friendship Society of Uzbekistan. But his main focus was the diplomatic mission, which started in 1969, when he held the position of chief economist at the USSR Embassy in India. After F.Teshabayev has worked in various positions in the Presidential Apparatus of Uzbekistan. In 1991, he was appointed Deputy Minister of Foreign Affairs of independent Uzbekistan. In 1993, he was appointed Ambassador Extraordinary and Plenipotentiary of Uzbekistan to the United States, then Uzbekistan's represent-tative to the UN. Since 1997, he has been the Ambassador Extraordinary of Uzbekistan to Great Britain and Northern Ireland. He became an honorary member of the Academy of Science and Culture of the State of California, was awarded

---

[1] O'zbekiston sharqshunoslari bibliografiyasi.(Bibliography of Orientalists of Uzbekistan, in uzbek) Toshkent, 2011. –P.320.

the Governor of the State of Tennisi "Goodwill Ambassador". After graduation, he was a member of the scientific group of the grant "Philosophy of the Peoples of the East" at the Institute of Oriental Studies, where the result of his scientific activity was the book "Philosophy of Ancient India".

Mr. Omon Khatamov[2] is an Indologist, Candidate of Historical Sciences, defended his Ph.D. thesis in Moscow. A prominent public figure, worked as Deputy Minister of Foreign Affairs of the Republic of Uzbekistan, made a certain contribution to the development of Indian-Uzbek relations at the diplomatic level in the first decade of the period of independence of Uzbekistan.

Mr. Surat Mirkasymov is an outstanding Indologist and diplomat. For many years he worked as the Ambassador of Uzbekistan to India. For many years he worked (1967-1991) in the Friendship Society for Cultural Relations of Uzbekistan and in recent years he became the Deputy Chairman of the Friendship Societies. Held the position of the assistant (1969-1974) for Cultural Relations of the USSR Embassy in India, then became Vice-Consul at the USSR Consulate in Calcutta. After that he worked as the First Secretary of the Embassy (1982-1985). At the next stage, he continued his diplomatic work by becoming director of the USSR Cultural Center in Delhi. Since 1991, S. Mirkasymov held the position of Deputy Chairman of the National Association for Cultural Relations of Uzbekistan. Since 1993, he was sent as a representative on a diplomatic mission to the Republic of India and then for many years he continued his career as the Ambassador of Uzbekistan to India. Currently, Currently, S. Mirkasymov is giving a course of lectures on international diplomacy at the University of Oriental Studies.

---

[2] O'zbekiston sharqshunoslari bibliografiyasi.(Bibliography of Orientalists of Uzbekistan, in uzbek) Toshkent, 2011. –P.353.

Mr. Tashmirza Khalmirzaev[3], a prominent Indologist, candidate of philological sciences, defended his PhD thesis in Moscow. For a long time, he worked as the dean of the Oriental Faculty of the Tashkent State University, then as the head of the Department of Indian Philology. After he switched to diplomatic work and served in the consular department of the Embassy of Uzbekistan in Karachi, after that he was appointed the first secretary at the Embassy of Uzbekistan to Pakistan. He created the first Urdu-Uzbek dictionary (2003), then the Urdu-Russian dictionary (2013), which were published in the capital of Pakistan, Islamabad.

Mrs. Rano Gulyamova[4] defended her Ph.D. thesis in Moscow in 1976. Thesis was based on the works of Vishnu Prabhakar. For many years, she was the head of the Department of Indian Philology.At present, the daughter of Ms. Gulyamova, Mrs. Gulera Shermatova, teaches the Hindi language and literature at the University of Oriental Studies, continues the work of her mother and writes a doctoral work on the memoirs of Vishnu Prabhakar.

[3] O'zbekiston sharqshunoslari bibliografiyasi.(Bibliography of Orientalists of Uzbekistan, in uzbek) Toshkent, 2011. –P.355..

[4] O'zbekiston sharqshunoslari. (Orientalists of Uzbekistan, in uzbek). Toshkent, 1996. –P.484.

Mr. Muzrobiddin Tashmukhamedov[5]- Indologist, Candidate of Historical Sciences, defended his Ph.D. thesis in Moscow, worked for many years at the USSR Embassy to India. In 2003 he was invited as a professor to Columbus University, Ohio, USA, in 2005 he became a member of the International Association for Central Eurasian Studies in the USA.

Mr. Mukhtar Shapsanov[6]- Indologist, Candidate of Historical Sciences, defended his Ph.D. thesis in Moscow. For many years he worked as an interpreter for the GKES at the USSR Embassy to India. He built a school for children in his native city of Karshi.

One can recall many other Indologists who have contributed to the development of various branches of independent Uzbekistan.

Science and study are parallel branches of any specialty. Indology also includes both scientific and educational activities. Educational activity is a school, a lyceum and a higher educational institution, where the foundation for science is laid. Indologists of our Republic have been simultaneously developing both educational and scientific work.

In the field of science, Indology is notable for the fact that India is studied comprehensively, namely, scientific research is devoted to the study of the peculiarities of language and literature, history and philosophy, economics and politics of this region. To date, numerous linguistic and literary research works cover the period from the Middle Ages to the present.

Of particular note is the scientific activity of an

---

[5] Oʻzbekiston sharqshunoslari bibliografiyasi. Bibliography of Orientalists of Uzbekistan, in uzbek) Toshkent, 2011. –P.326..

[6] ʻzbekiston sharqshunoslari. (Orientalists of Uzbekistan, in uzbek). Toshkent, 1996. –P.430.

outstanding Indologist-linguist, an expert in many Indian languages, both northern and southern, Doctor of Philology, Professor **Azad Shamatov**[7]. His name as the leading Indologist of Uzbekistan is known not only in India, but also in many Indological centers of both Asia and Europe. He specialized primarily as a linguist-dialectologist. He was the only specialist who knew well all both Western and Eastern dialects of Hindi. In addition, he studied such South Indian languages as Tamil, Telugu, Marathi, Kannada and Odia. He is the author of many monographic studies and scientific articles. He has repeatedly participated in International Conferences on Indology in London (1999), Montreal (2000), Moscow (2004, 2014), as well as in India, Pakistan, Ukraine, Georgia, Estonia, Poland, Hungary, Mauritius, Germany, Italy, France and many other Asian and European countries. He has won research grants from the USA (Fulbright), Germany (DAAD) and India (Anand Coomaraswamy) and has developed several studies in linguistics. For many years he worked as the head of the Department of Indian Philology at the Tashkent State Institute of Oriental Studies. In 2014, the Government of India awarded A. Shamatov the Dr. George Grierson Award for his services to the development of Indology in Uzbekistan and beyond.

Mrs. Tamara Khodjaeva[8], Associate Professor, one of the leading indologists of Uzbekistan, Candidate of Philological Sciences, has made a huge contribution to the study of modern Indian literature, as well as the history of cultural and literary ties between Uzbekistan and India. She is the author of about ten monographic studies, more than ten

---

[7] O'zbekiston sharqshunoslari bibliografiyasi. Bibliography of Orientalists of Uzbekistan, in uzbek) Toshkent, 2011. –P.385..

[8] O'zbekiston sharqshunoslari bibliografiyasi.(Bibliography of Orientalists of Uzbekistan, in uzbek) Toshkent, 2011. –P.370.

textbooks on the Hindi language and literature. She is the only specialist in Punjabi literature in Uzbekistan. Her research papers have been published in Uzbek, Russian, Hindi, English and Punjabi.

Translation work brings nations together and creates opportunities to get to know each other better. India has become famous on a global scale due to its ancient philosophy, rich centuries-old history, and its multifaceted art. The ancient epics of India *the Ramayana and the Mahabharata* are the heart of the Indian people, this is the whole inner world of the peoples of the Indian subcontinent. They reflect all national and universal values, all customs and rituals, the entire history of the subcontinent and the worldview of the peoples of India. Knowing *the Ramayana or the Mahabharata* means knowing India, understanding their interests and aspirations. In India, they do not get tired of creating serials based on these two epics.

One of the qualified Indologists of the department is Mrs.Shirin Jalilova, who defended her Ph.D. thesis on the topic *"Terms of kinship and properties in the Hindi language"* in Moscow. She is the only specialist who deals with ethnography, she is interested in the religious and philosophical views of the peoples of India and the ancient Indian customs and the lexical composition of Hindi. Wrote the monograph *Culture of Ancient India.*

Mr. Amirulla Fayzullaev, the well-known Indologist-translator devoted his whole life to translation. He translated many stories, novels of famous Indian writers such as Yashpal, Premchand, Krishan Chandar, Tagore and many others into Uzbek and introduced Indian literature to the Uzbek people. However, his translation into Uzbek of the series *Mahabharata and Ramayana* has become a huge contribution to the approach of the peoples of India to Uzbekistan. Both series were shown several times on Uzbek television. Specially organized television programs with the participation of Indologists were assigned to responses to letters from viewers who showed great interest in the epic *Mahabharata*. In 2019, the translator Amirulla Fayziev was awarded the Dr. George Grierson Award by the Government of India for his services to the development of Indology in Uzbekistan. Amirulla Fayziev devoted his whole life to translation work, being the editor of the journal "Literature of the Peoples of the World" and published his translations of the works of Indian writers.

As you know, the Middle Ages is a period of Muslim and Indian culture merge on the territory of India, where the rule of the Baburids in northern India played a big role. Thanks to this period, the encyclopedic memoir *Baburnama* of the emperor Babur appeared. Many scholars of the West and East are engaged in the study of this work. Uzbekistan also has a school for the study of *Baburnama*, in the dissemination of which a doctor of Philology, indologist **Mr.Ansariddin Ibragimov**[9] played a significant role. His PhD and doctoral dissertations are devoted to the study of *Baburnama* which is considered to be a special contribution to the development of Indology in Uzbekistan. His daughter, continuing the work of her father, defended her doctoral thesis on translations of *Baburnama* into Urdu.

The literature of medieval India, called Bhakti literature, is one of the richest and most varied legacies of this ancient country. It was during this period that the Baburid Empire dominated, which contributed to the development of not only literature, but also all branches of the socio-cultural sphere of India. **Ms. Ulfathon Mukhibova,**[10] the student of Professor A.Shamatov, Doctor of Philology, Professor, is engaged in studying this literary heritage. On the basis of the scientific

---

[9] O'zbekiston sharqshunoslari. (Orientalists of Uzbekistan, in uzbek). Toshkent, 1996. –P.124.

[10] O'zbekiston sharqshunoslari bibliografiyasi. (Bibliography of Orientalists of Uzbekistan, in uzbek) Toshkent, 2011. –P.231.

grant *Literature of the Baburid era*, she thoroughly studied the literature of the Baburid era not only in Hindi, but also in Urdu, Persian and Turkic languages. As a result of research with a group of scientists she published six monographic studies on the literary heritage of the Baburid era in four languages. During a long stay in India, she improved her qualifications in language and literature at such Indian universities as J. Nehru University, Agra University, Sahitya Academy, Kendriya Hindi Sansthan. Participated in many international conferences in India, Russia, USA, Georgia, Kazakhstan, Mauritius, Holland, South Korea, Iran and other countries showing achievements of Uzbek Indology abroad. She published more than 100 articles on the ancient, medieval and modern literature of the peoples of India.

One of the features of India is multilingualism, which from time immemorial continues to be a peculiar side of this state. Dakhini is one of the languages of medieval India. **Mrs. Muhayo Abdurakhmanova**[11], Candidate of Philological Sciences, Associate Professor specializes in the Urdu language and Dakhini, its medieval form. She has traveled many times to India and other countries of Asia and Europe for her research work. In collaboration with Indian scientists, she has published 2 monographs: in the Urdu language in 2019 together with Professor of the J. Nehru University Khoja Ikramuddin, and also in 2020 with the participation of Professor of the Delhi University Chandra Shekhar *Selected Ghazals of Ghalib*.

Mr. Sirajiddin Nurmatov[12], one of the youngest Indologists, a student of Professor A. Shamatov, is engaged in

---

[11] O'zbekiston sharqshunoslari bibliografiyasi.(Bibliography of Orienta-lists of Uzbekistan, in uzbek) Toshkent, 2011. –P.17.

[12] O'zbekiston sharqshunoslari bibliografiyasi.(Bibliography of Orienta-lists of Uzbekistan, in uzbek) Toshkent, 2011. –P.255.

linguistic research on the Hindi language. In his Ph.D. dissertation, he conducted a comparative study of the Hindi and Sinhalese languages using the example of a numeral. Currently, he continues his research in his doctoral dissertation "Formation and development of the system of numerals in the Indo-Aryan languages", revealing features of Hindi, Sanskrit, Pali and Apabharansha. He made presentations at International conferences held in India and Russia. Published more than 50 articles on linguistics.

One of the first specialists in the history of India is considered to be Doctor of Historical Sciences, Professor **Timur Giyasov,** who devoted his whole life to teaching students studying the history of the countries of the East, in particular India.

The research of ancient and modern philosophy of India was carried out by such Indologists as F.Teshabaev, S.Yuldashev and B.Abidov, who have published hundreds of articles on the philosophy of India, dedicated to prominent philosophers of India as Ramaswamy, Vivekananda, Ramanuja, Ramananda, Iqbal, Tagore and others. Of particular note is the huge contribution of our University of Oriental Studies to the study of the philosophy of the East thanks to the head of the Department of Philosophy, Professor Matbua Akhmedova. As a result of the involvement of the above-mentioned Indologists-philosophers for the implementation of the scientific grant "Philosophy of the Peoples of the East", a monograph "History of Philosophy of India: from antiquity to modernity" was published.

The University always cooperates favorably with embassies in the process of studying a particular issue. In particular, in connection with the centenary of receiving the Nobel Prize by the world-famous poet, philosopher, public figure, musician, educator of India and Bangladesh Rabindranath Tagore, in 2013, the department jointly with the Embassy of India and Bangladesh organized a scientific seminar with the participation of all Indologists of Uzbekistan, as a result of which a collection in three languages dedicated to this event was published. In August 2019, events were held to mark the 150th Anniversary of the birth of the great son of India M. Gandhi, in December of the same year, the Mahatma Gandhi Indology Center, together with the Embassy of India in Uzbekistan and the Lal Bahadur Shastri for Indian Culture held a seminar dedicated to the birthday of the famous poet Mirza Ghalib.

At present, much is being done at the Tashkent State University of Oriental Studies in the field of practical and scientific study of the Hindi language, the literatures of the peoples of India, history, philosophy, economics and foreign policy of India. Over the past period, the teachers of the department have published more than 50 monographs, 65 textbooks, 15 translations of works by Indian writers and poets, 11 different dictionaries.

In 1994, the Department of Indian Philology was renamed the "Department of Languages of South Asia" in order to expand the number of languages taught at the department, among which Bengali, Indonesian, Malay and Vietnamese should be mentioned.

The department has prepared more than 50 candidates and doctors of sciences in linguistics, literary criticism, history and philosophy of India. These specialists are still successfully working in various institutions of Uzbekistan.

In 2006, at the Department of South Asian Languages, on the initiative of Mr. Skand Tayal, the Ambassador of the Republic of India to Uzbekistan, Mahatma Gandhi Indology Center was founded to improve Indological science in Uzbekistan. The Center hosts scientific conferences, seminars, various events in cooperation with the Embassy of India to Uzbekistan and Lal Bahadur Shastri Center of Indian Culture in Tashkent. In particular, with the support of Ambassador Mr. Skand Thayal, International Conferences on Indology actual issues were held in November 2006: *Conference of*

Indologists, as well as in March 2008: *Central Asia - India Dialogue. Building a Partnership on the Foundation of Rich Cultural and Historical Heritage.* The materials of the Conferences have been published as a collection of research papers.

To date, about 1,000 students have been studying the Hindi language at higher educational institutions, schools and academic lyceums in Uzbekistan.

In Uzbekistan, translations of works by Indian writers have been carried out. In particular, in 1961, Tagore's works five-volume edition dedicated to the 100th Anniversary of his birth was published. Uzbek Indologists translated the novels of Premchand, Krishan Chandar, Yashpal, the great epics of India *the Ramayana* and *the Mahabharata*, the tales of *Panchatantra, Hitopadesha,* the novel of the Tamil writer Chinnappa Bharati, the presentation of which was in India in the presence of the writer himself. In 2010, Mahatma Gandhi's book *My Life* was translated by Amirulla Fayzullaev into Uzbek, then it was republished in 2019.

In order to improve cultural and scientific ties between the universities of India and Uzbekistan, in the 2018-2019 academic year, at the invitation of the university administration such professors of J. Nehru University as Anwar Alam, Devendra Chaubey, Khoja Ikramuddin and Akhlaki Ahan conducted lectures and practical classes on linguistics and literature of Hindi and Urdu for one month.

The cultural and scientific ties between Uzbekistan and India began to develop especially rapidly after the arrival of Delhi University Professor **Chandra Shekhar**, who was appointed Director of the Lal Bahadur Shastri Center of Indian Culture. With his assistance, for the first time in the history of Indology, thirteen Hindi teachers of universities, lyceum of oriental languages and Hindi school named after Lal Bahadur Shastri in Tashkent trained under a teachers' special program at Kendriya Hindi Sansthan in Agra and received certificates. Also, with the support of the Embassy of India in Uzbekistan, in 2020, a major monography *Literature of India* was published by assoc. prof. T. Khodjaeva and prof. U. Mukhibova, Indologist lecturers of the university.

The universities of Uzbekistan widely celebrated the Gandhi's 150th birth anniversary. In particular, on August 28, 2019, a seminar *Public Diplomacy in the Philosophical Teachings of Mahatma Gandhi* was held in Tashkent. The event was organized by the SCO Public Diplomacy Center in Uzbekistan, the Embassy of India to Tashkent and the Tashkent State University of Oriental Studies (TSUOS). The event was attended by representatives of the diplomatic corps in Tashkent, the Committee on Interethnic Relations and Friendly Relations with Foreign Countries under the Cabinet of Ministers of the Republic of Uzbekistan, as well as scientists-indologists. Mr. Anil Kumar Shastri, the Chairman of Lal Bahadur Shastri Management Institute, the Trustee of Lal Bahadur Shastri National Memorial Trust as well as Dr. Shobhana Radhakrishna, the Chief Specialist of the Gandhi Forum on Ethical Corporate Governance, participated in the seminar.

Many Indologists have been awarded various awards from India and other foreign countries for their merits in the development of Indology in Uzbekistan. In particular, in 1988, the diplomat F. Teshabaev was awarded Jawaharlal Nehru Award, and a special award "Goodwill Ambassador" by the Tennessee Governor, the USA, as well as he was considered for honorary membership of California Academy of Sciences, the USA. Professor A. Shamatov (2014) and famous translator Amirulla Fayzullaev (2020) were awarded the Dr. George Grierson Award. Professor U. Mukhibova (2007) and Ph.D. S. Nurmatov (2017) were honored the award "For merit in the development and dissemination of the Hindi language" by the Indian Consulate of Cultural Relations (ICCR)".

In recent years, Uzbekistan has been rapidly reforming higher education system in order to improve the quality of trained specialists in all areas. In particular, in 2020, a Double Degree Memorandum was signed between the Tashkent State

University of Oriental Studies and Gujarat University for a master's degree (linguistics, Hindi) after the official trip of the President of Uzbekistan Shavkat Mirziyoyev to Gujarat. In July 2022, five TSUOS senior students successfully graduated Gujarat University and became the first holders of a double master's degree.

Currently, many graduates of the Department work in the Ministry of Foreign Affairs of Uzbekistan, in the Embassies of Uzbekistan, the Institute for Strategic and Interregional Studies, diplomatic missions of Uzbekistan in foreign countries, Uzbekistan Airways, the Institute of Oriental Studies of the Academy of Sciences of the Republic of Uzbekistan and other organizations, continuing to contribute to the development of bilateral cooperation with India.[i]

Bibliography

1. Aulova R., Rahmatov B, Sodiqova M. Hindiy tili darsligi. (Hindi language textbook) Toshkent, 2008.
2. Библиография востоковедов Узбекистана. (Bibliography of Orientalists of Uzbekistan, in rassian) Tashkent, 2005.
3. Muhibova U.U. Hind adabiyoti (qadim va o'rta asrlar). (Indian Literature (Antiquity and Middle Ages)) Toshkent, 2008.
4. O'zbekiston sharqshunoslari. (Orientalists of Uzbekistan, in uzbek). Toshkent, 1996.
5. O'zbekiston sharqshunoslari bibliografiyasi.(Bibliography of Orientalists of Uzbekistan, in uzbek) Toshkent, 2011.
6. Rahmatov B., Sodiqova M, Nurmatov S, Sulaymonova M. Hindiy tili darsligi. (Hindi language textbook) Toshkent, 2008.

**Head of South Asian Languages Department,
Director of Mahatma Gandi Indology Center of Tashkand
State University of Oriental Stadies,
Uzbekistan**

6. The Linguistic and Cultural Relations of Central and South Asian Countries

Dr. Sirojiddin S. Nurmatov

A Linguistic Area is well known as a term, representing a specific type of Areal and Historical Community of Languages that emerges up in a course of convergent development of the both cognate and non-cognate types of speech over definite space.

Proceeding from this point there is an idea proposed on regarding emergence and evolution of a such type of formation through the 11th to the 19th centuries within a common geographical space including so called Ajam i.e. Non-Arab Muslim states of Asia as a whole. As we suppose on as a nucleus of the Area apparently served the territories of Mawarau-n nahr (Transoxiana) and Khurasan as well as the northern, central and most portions of southern India and at last East Turkestan too. The approach put forth above in fact lays down a ground to suggest a concept on Central and South Asia as a Medieval Linguistic Area as a whole.

Summing up a different renowned views concerning various problems of Areal Studies with special reference to the one of Linguistic Area one should state that since as a basis of the phenomenon there were traditional Languages in Contact relationships taking place in Diachrony as a result of intensive Interlingual Contacts is due to be considered as a Socio-Cultural and Historical one evolving on within a certain space and epoch as well[1].

At first this relates to the Area proposed above because the given phenomenon occurred there as preconditioned and

---

[1] Please refer to C. Masica, M.B. Emencan, F.B.I., Keiper, N.B. Gurov and G.A. Zograph etc.

motivated by such Socio-Cultural setting as expansion of Islamic Culture where Arabic and Persian (Tajik) served as basic means of intercourse while Turki and Hindustani respectively functioned as regional mediator-languages in Central and South Asia. Actually as a main starting point of the one should be recognized an era of Islam's penetration of these regions as a brand new type of religion commencing as early as through the eighth to the ninth centuries.

First of all it should stated that though the Islam came and expanded over South Asia much later than to Central Asia, the new Religion's ideological foundations, had already undergone some significant changes by the thirteenth to the fourteenth centuries, after substantial adjustment to alien ethnic and social environment.

For instance, let's take advantage of the famous Arab Traveler, Ibn Battutah's account of the marriage happened to one Muslim noble, with a sister of the Sultan of Delhi, which provides a revealing picture of the great extent to which the Muslims had adopted the Hindu marriage ceremonies even in those early days[2]. Such kind of novations, according to the specialists seems to have become a result of Sufi activities for the most ardent propagators of that had adopted a number of basic principles belonging to Hindu Philosophy School of Vedanta and Yoga. Simultaneously, along with Sufism, there Bhakti (Devotional)movement of Hindu origin, was catching on. Both movements usually had been founded on some postulates of Vedanta, like appeal to everybody to comply with feeling of love to all surroundings and to dedicate oneself to boundless self-renouncement.

To the opinion of prominent Russian Philologist I.P.Minaev, «A lot of Devotional Movements in Medieval India had one rational grain which might be observed in their

---

[2] The Delhi Sultanate, the fifth volume of the History and Culture of the Indian People. -Bombay, 1960.-P.611.

often but not unsuccessful efforts to find a link between Islamic Monotheism and Hindu Polytheism and to make reconciled the both extremities as well as to unite the Muslims in their belief[3]» .

Approximately, the same picture showing a growing trends to-Socio-Cultural synthesis in Islamic Central Asia, one should refer to such authorized Historian as B.A. Litvinsky, who states that «A Genesis and Contents of numerous phenomena, pertaining to Medieval Islamic Spiritual and Material Culture, should be sought in Buddhism[4]», to which one ought to add also Zoroastrian, Manichean and Shamanite components, of the Pre-Islamic Culture of this region as well.

So then it may be stressed on that over both regions under review there were definite cultural, religious, social, ideological and everyday personal interactions, between Local people and New-Comer Muslims, which though occurred far from being synchronically but resulted in gradual absorption of alien elements by local environment. Hence ultimately there a favorable conditions had been established for Linguistic Interference too.

So firstly the one have been formed and spread over, both regions, because of an evolution of Islamic Culture, Enlightment and Literature, mainly through the means of Arabic and Persian (or Central Asian Tajik). On the wake of coexistence and competition in the same sphere of communication, the latter's gradually came to be differentiated functionally. So that, Arabic came to serve as a Medium of Religious Confessional intercourse, while Persian defined itself

---

[3] Minaev I.P. The Old India. The notes on AfanasyNikitins, Travelcgte, Saffit-Petersberg. 1881. -P.31 (in Russian).

[4] See Buddhism and Central Asian Civilization, in the collection « The Indian Culture and Buddhism». - Moscow, 1972. -P. 163 (in Russian).

as an entirely recognized means of Literary and especially Poetic activities.

A continuous specialization of Persian to perform this function during the eleventh to the eighteenth centuries in Its own turn led to its formation as effectively acting mediator-language, favoring a wide Borrowing of Arabo-Persian or Muslim Lexicon and Phraseology alike along with Syntax patterns and Word-Building Affixes and Models. Besides a direct historical development of The New Persian (I.e. Persian and Tajik languages) and to some extent intermediary Influence of the Arabic (through the last one) played a sufficient role in the formation process of some written literary forms of speech in Indian Subcontinent.

In addition to as it well known in order to identify - the Linguistic Interference Process and Its outcomes for the Languages in Contact there is a concept becoming the most crucial which relates to proportional dependence of the Interference nature and intensity on genealogical and typological factors as well.

For instance, concerning South Asia with particular emphasis on Its Indo-Aryan zones one could notice a specific correlation of Arabic, Iranian and Indo-Aryan speeches where the former exhibits a typical representative of Afroasian Family, while the latter's being a member's of Indo-Iranian group of the greater Indo-European Family in fact are connected mutually by genetic relations.

In this connection it is Important to point out that during the Interaction between Arabic and Indian Languages., as a mediator, served usually these of Iranian one, because the Borrowing and Adaptation of Arabic Lexicon, initially was done within a frame work of Iranian system, in particular of New Persian, through the VIIth to the XVIIIth centuries. Only after that Arabic Lexicon, which has already become basically an integral part of Iranian Languages Lexical Systems, started to be handed over, to the Indian ones. Therefore, a penetration of Arabic words into Indo-Aryan speeches, went on already in that sound cover, and in that grammatical form as well which these had acquired in Iranian Languages i.e. these had been accepted and realized by New Indo-Aryan Languages either in Persianized or in Tajikized shapes.

Secondly within a whole range of Languages in Contact Theory Problems, there Impeccable significance belongs to Bilingualism problem proper, which extends particularly to these cases when the Languages are interacted in immediate geographical contiguity lasting a long period of time and producing often both a deep Linguistic Interference and Mixing-up.

As far as it concerns, with a majority of cases, there non-contiguous type of Bilingualism, takes place, which of course provides an existence of definite socially or professionally connected groups, speaking both languages in contact. The same situation does affect South Asia, as a whole. Apart from a specific social group, of Newly Converted Muslims, which arouse there including bilingual persons, there was a lot of individuals with special speech behavior, depended on Interference level, who in certain situation, used to be regarded as original standard by monolingual ones. Such factors gained a great importance in those cases where the speech behavior of these people would enjoy special social prestige. In particular, it relates to speech of either Muslim clergy or Sufi saints and teachers alike having a wide access to common people masses as well as to writers and poets as masters of literary cultivated speech whose compositions being mostly translated from another languages, mainly from Persian and Arabic having transferred along with these a lot of words in course of substitutions.

Thirdly, with regard to Interlingual Relations, as a substantial source, to benefit enriching and developing a Lexico-Phraseological Resources of the speech one should keep in mind, that in such cases, there not only occurs considerable renovation of Lexical Strata Correlation, but starts on an establishment of new type of relations, between and alien units on Phonological, Morphological, Word-Building and Semantical levels of speech hierarchy, which brings about a Systemic Transformational all. In our case the profound and immense process has involved almost entiremillennium affecting majority of systemic levels of speech as well.

The idea also does find its own approval from literary point of view. It should be indicated., as change-over from unilateral impact of Persian literature to the process of mutual enrichment, as well as the Bilingualism in Poetry. This kind of approach demands a following circumstances to be kept in view.

Unlike the Central Asia, where a Muslim literature in fact, predominated without any rivalry having no substantial aesthetical antipodes, it was South Asia which witnessed an existence of mighty and original Ancient Indian Literary Traditions, highly advanced and developed, which could oppose the former. These had at own disposal a strict bounding canons, thoroughly sophisticated Poetics Theory as well as a system of versification many styles and genres being sufficiently perfect accurately elaborated, a rich system of characters and inexhaustible treasury of images going back to unique Epics Masterpieces like«Mahabharata» and «Ramayana» as well as to the great Tale Epics up brought by old Folklore sources.

Therefore, on the wake of relatively not so long atmosphere of alienness and antagonism between these two lines there a new type of relations evolved on during several centuries being supported and patronized both by ruling dynasties and some single persons especially in the field of translation of the most brilliant works into Persian, Turkish and other languages. So that the Medieval Europe soon also became aware of these traditions. Forthcoming links grew on steadily in the form of synthetic trends to rapprochement between two cultures and literatures which gave on appearance of mixed up and intermediate styles in literature and living speech.

As a sequel of these trends one can indicate the Early Hindustani as intercommunal and interprovincial idiom functioning in South Asia as a whole. A primary stage of this language was supposed to be connected with introduction of current vernaculars relating to the first half of the second millennium A.D. in literary usage. The language actually seemed to accomplish a specific mission of supradialectal koine having been influenced strongly by Muslim Cultural and literary traditions and embodied a nucleus of basic northern vernacular Khari Boli (Kauravi) along with neighboring dialects and sub dialects as well as its southern forms existing in alien linguistic environment. It is also a important fact that a lot of these varieties of colloquial speech has acquired a written literary existence under immediate impact of Bhakti and Sufism movements, too.

In this context there is another serious factor to be taken into account like origin and florescence of local Persian Literature in South Asia favoring greatly a stable Persian-Indian Bilingualism as well as Multingualism both of which become extended up to remote southern parts of the Subcontinent. As far as the zones of the most dense concentration of these are concerned this phenomenon gave an impetus to consolidation of those literary forms of speech which were written in Arabic script alike Kashmiri, Panjabi, Dakkhini, Balochi, Brahui, Lendi, Sirayki, Multanietc[5].

Now let us consider several the most important stages of

---

[5] It should be indicated, that within a framework of Persian Literature in India there a specific style evolved on which was called «Sabk-i Hindi» i.e. «Indian style» by Iranologists.

formation the Turki as a regional mediator-language within Linguistic area proposed above.

As it is proverbial a term «Turki» means conditionally united group of regional Turkic Languages of the 18 -19 centuries includingthe Central Asian one, Eastern-Oghuz one, the Trans-Volga region form and the North Caucasus one, acentral position among these is supposed to belong to the Central Asian one, which in fact has got its own unique ethnicity history. In short it runs as following. A ground for common national Turki had been prepared through the 6thto the tenth centuries as a result of mixing-up and assimilation involved old Iranian tribes Saks and Massageth with Yue-Chji and Hunns as well as with another Turkic tribes, like Kangly, Qarluqs, Chigils, Khalajs and partly Uighurs who in total composed a very nucleus of Turkic Ethnic Community.

There were a significant events in the History when Turki used in the Runic and the Sogdiana scripts had been proclaimed as official language of Turkic Kaganate in the sixth to the seventh centuries, the kingdom which arouse in a course of formation a union among the various tribes and nationalities of Altai,Semirechye and Central Asia, covering a whole territory of Mawarau-n nahr and Central Asia. The kingdom managed to exist up to Arabic invasion i.e. up to Advent of Islam in the eighth century.

In this connection it is very important to point out that exactly in this period the Nomadic Old Turkic tribes gradually started to settle down mainly in the Farghana valley and at the vicinity of Shash i.e. modem Tashkent. Starting from the eighth century there prevailing positions in Farghana had been occupied by Qarlmjs and Chigils. As far as Shash is concerned there were Oghuzs who dominated over it. By this period practically there a process of mixing-up of Old Soghdian and Turkic tribes already has finished. According to prominent scholar of the eleventh century Mahmud Qashghari just at that period there was a curious Language Situation formed on which consisted of alternation of Turkic-Soghdian Bilingualism with pure Turkic speech while typical Sogdian idiolects usage has disappeared entirely.

On the forthcoming stage one should regard as a substantial fact the emergence of big town typed settlements in Central Asia where the three varieties of Script were used like Khoresmian, Sogdian and Runic, The latter is apparently goes back to Orkhon-Yenisei Inscriptions considered to be the oldest specimens of Turkic Script at all.

Throughout this period there was going on a formation of written literature in Turki with a specific role played by Karakhanid-Uighur (the tenth to the twelfth centuries) and Golden Horde (the thirteenth to fourteenth centuries) literary traditions. As a peak of this process one usually consider the ChaghataiTurki speech under which anearned written style of that had been formed on the basis of local Turkic Qarluq-Qipchaqdialects through the 15th to the 16th centuries in Mawarau-n nahr (Transoxiana) of Timurid period.

To the eminent Turkologists mind as the most particular feature of the one there was its rapid enrichment with different dialectical elements supported by regional variatious as well as by growing contacts with Qarluq, Oghuz and Qipchaq languages. That's why it has attained eventually a supradialectal form of speech that on the "hand contained a lot of Arabic and Persian Loans and on the another one was based on Arabic script which did not ever put any limits on Vocalic Representation. Thanking to that the Chagatai Literary Tradition itself gained prominence over a vast territories stretching on from Mediterranean right up to Mongolia and the western borders of India as well.

Describing a language situation in Central Asia of that period the specialists use to stress upon the fact that such a phenomena like expansion of various forms of Turkic-Iranian (Tajik) Bilingualism in Samarqand, Bukhara and the neighboring to Iran Turkmen lands along with cultivation of Arabic as a medium of Religion and Science as well as a teaching of Arabic and Persian in local schools altogether has profoundly stimulated enrichment and nourishment of Central Asian Turki with Muslim Loan-Words and Phraseology.

Alike Hindustani in South Asia on the Central Asian Turki there had been created a long literary tradition where besides Religious and Mystical compositions became very famous a Historico-Narrative genres as well as various books dedicated to secular topics, not to speak about official documents and historical statements preserved on too.

Therefore, just alike Hindustani which influenced many South Asian Languages, according to the opinion of prominent Turkologists the Chaghatai and Central Asian Turki played an important role in stimulating different stages during development of the both of the Eastern Oghuz Turki and the Trans-Volga riverbank regional Turki as welll.

Along with that in the next period as soon as. Tajik and Persian were getting on with attaining an official and cultural language functions under politically manifold states in Mawaran-u nahr the more durable and stable became a, process of Bilingualism and Mutual Convergence of Tajik-Persian and Turkic Languages Systems.

While contemplating a comparison of the both regions from the point of language situation in order to construct the Linguistic Area suggested on it should be generalized as following. Having replaced an unilateral impact of Persian (Tajik) literature on local languages and literatures the process of mutual enrichment and bilingualism led actually, to intimacy and rapprochement of coexisting literary traditions thereby making a common ideological and thematical basis strengthened on, as well as common system of characters and even common means of images, and poetics techniques. All these phenomena, came to pass, in the conditions of similar socio-economical setting which was founded as early as, in the 3rd 7thcenturies, under Zoroastrian Sassanid Dynasty and became prevailing over Central Asia, Iran, Afghanistan and most part of India ruled by Timurids Moghuls[6].

Herewith, a forthcoming period in the History of Central and SouthAsia could be delineated, as an epoch, of ceaseless and active Language and Literary Collisions and Clashes along with an epoch of coexistence of increasing Interference, as a whole.

Meanwhile one can note that as far as main differences through the epoch are concerned these in fact depend on following cases.

Firstly a lot of significance should be given to the socio-cultural situation which caused considerable changes in the relations between rivaling two social groups of indigenous and newcomers origin in both regions.

Secondly, one should take into account a distinctive features of recipient environment in general defined by many factors like an-evolution of written literary language, a stylistic regroupings within its structure, a development of literary speech standard and its correlation with spoken one as well as with colloquial vernaculars.

Thirdly, as individual personal contribution to the History of the language should be appreciated a Language Policy of rulers and writers which often used to take the shape of alternation between two main motion forces either Language Purism or a Tendency to Democratize a Language Development.

So now approaching to the problem under discussion from particular linguistic point of view let's remember and bear in

---

[6] Koroglu H. Uzbek Literature - "Short Encyclopedia of Literature". Vol. 7. –Moscow, 1972. –P. 731 (in Russian).

mind that a concept of «Linguistic Area» as well as a general concept of Areal Linguistics are equally based on principal fundamentals of Languages in Contact Theory as a whole. Reviewing a different opinions on this, account one can notice that the most well-grounded one among these seems to be the one of N.Gurov and G.A.Zograph. In particular they share the point, that for Areal Studies there substantially important is a tenets on possibility of Indirect Interference apart from the Direct one. It composed of such cases where an influence of certain language does stimulate a development of some processes and regularities to be already potentially outlined in the another one.

While referring to these two concepts one should get sight of that a Direct Interference is usually understood as «a Linguistical Transfer the Rules from one of the Languages in Contact and mainly from Mother tongue to intermediate system between two languages under comparison»[7].

Unlike the Direct one which brings about some grammatical or stylistical errors the Indirect one is followed by definite peculiarities. So for instance a Direct Syntactical Interference can go ahead leading to Divergence from stylistic standard proper. Ultimately it succeeds in simplification of the rales, providing a transfer from deep structure to surface one and reverse. In such cases usually is that in the Situation of Subordinate Bilingualism there is probably a tendency to refuse a variation prevailed when expressing the same syntactical relations. Meanwhile a Compound Construction would be substituted by a Simple one i.e. by Subordinate Personal Clause unlike that of Infinitive one.

Let's compare following examples. Infinitive one in French . - je l' intends chanter une chanson russe - «I hear him singing

---

[7] Rozentsveig V.Y. Languages in Contact. Concerning Linguistic problems of this theory. -Leningrad, 1972. - P.25 (in Russian).

(literally- to sing) Russian song» and Personal one - j 'entendsqu'ilchanteune chanson russe - «I hear how he sings Russian song».

The same kind of picture is typical for Persian-Hindustani and Persian (Tajik)- Turki Syntactical Interference in Modem Uzbek which conditionally might be regarded as a most developed successor of Medieval Turki in Central Asia. In fact there are two different constructions. First one bases upon unfolded Direct Object with substantiated Participle as a Centre of the Construction where a Subject of the Object is expressed by a special Possessive Affix - Men Karimning ketganini bilaman «I know Karim having gone». The second one represents a Complex Sentence with Subordinate Conjunction *«ki»* which means a wide range of syntactical relations. The Conjunction is usually written in one with Predicate and followed by comma - Men bildimki, siz kelgan edingiz «I knew that you have already come».

Now let's compare those instances with semantically corresponding Constructions in Modern Literary Hindi, which is considered to be direct inheritor of medieval Hindustani.

First the Infinitive one is examined on below: Use tumhaare cale jaane kaa pataa calaa «He came to know about your departure» i.e. about you have departed. Literally «He was reached by news about you have left».

Now let's discuss the Personal one:

Use pataa calaa ki tum cale gaye «He came to know that you have left».

In this connection it should be underlined that in the languages under comparison i.e. in Hindi and Uzbek the second construction based on Complex Sentence with Subordinative Conjunction *«ki»* obviously has been formed under impact of corresponding construction of Persian (Tajik) origin. By the way in the both Hindi and Uzbek this pattern is regarded as more bookish written one than the former which looks rather peculiar to Colloquial Speech proper.

Another important evidence showing an the Indirect

Interference in the languages under comparison there some features representing division of the Nouns into Animate and Inanimate subclasses which in Hindi contaminates with In flexional Category of «Defmiteness» closely linked with the previously mentioned one. Meanwhile in Uzbek such case relates to division into Person and Non-person subclasses as well' as into these of Definite and Indefinite.

As for Hindi alike the most New Indo-Aryan Languages the Definite Object takes the form of the Dative (or the Oblique with the Dative postposition) while the Indefinite Object takes the form of the Direct. For instance: *mai ne kitab kharid li*. «I purchased a book» and mai ne us kitab ko kharid liya «I purchased the book».

The same case one has in Uzbek - Men kitob sotib oldim «I purchased a book» and Men bu kitobni kecha sotib oldim «Yesterday I purchased the book».

As it is seen from the examples given above there in the both languages is perceived typologically a common way designed to represent a deep structure meaning by surface structures either by the Direct form or by the form of the Dative. The difference between the' latter's is conceived only in the forms of the Dative which in Hindi provides the postposition *«ko»*, while in Uzbek it is expressed by the Affix *«ni»* added to the form of the Object.

Apart from these cases the most particular peculiarities to be more specific for the Regional Mediator-Languages after having compared and analyzed many genetically non-cognate and systemically various types of languages spread over the Area one could expose a main typological parameters of the given Linguistic Union or «Sprache Bund» which are apparently more or less typical for various forms of the speech.

1. On Lexica- Semantical level proceeding from general orientalist point of view one can see that side by side with New Indo-Aryan in the orbit of complicated and deep Adaptation and Assimilation Process of Muslim Loans

proved to have been attracted also certain languages of Central Asia (Transoxiana) and Afghanistan being closely to India and having reached various levels of literary development. There are languages of Iranian and Turkic origin. Some traces of such linguistic interaction occur clearly in principal commonness not only of the Cultural or Upper i.e. International Strata in the Vocabulary of both these languages and Indian ones, but even of everyday Lexical Strata too.

2. As a result of that phenomena nowadays the Muslim Lexicon is considered to be a definite typological feature of the most Afroasian, Iranian, Indian and Turkic languages of Asia and to some extent of Europe as well.

3. On Syntactical Level there is a number of common phenomena including similar types of Simple Sentence right up to some types of Compound one too.

4. On Word-Building Level one can notice an usage of productive Prefixal and Suffixal types of formants asending to Iranian and Arabic origins.

5. On Phraseological one among indigenous patterns there is a lot of extremely productive structures with Nominal and Verbal Semantics including Pronominal Compound Verbal Units tracing back to Iranian Prototypes.

6. On Phonetic Level we have observed a substantial strengthening of Phonological status pertaining to such consonants as uvular «q», «qh» and fricative «f» and «z» realized in various positions within the units of the Muslim Lexicon.

The present investigation takes into consideration also the results of the Comparative-Oppositional Analysis of Muslim words after Trubetskoy's method accomplished on the data of the 15th century Turku and several written works in Early Hindustani in wide chronological frame of the epoch of the 15th -17th centuries. According to these the features listed above could be treated as a typical evidence of the Areal' Links

between the languages under comparison.
Moreover, these proved to be retained in Modem Uzbek, Tajik, Dari, Pushtu, Urdu, Panjabi, Kashmiri, Hindi, Sindhi etc.

References :
1. Minaev I.P. The Old India. The notes on Afanasy Nikitins, Travelcgte, Saffit-Petersberg. 1881. (in Russian).
2. Koroglu H. Uzbek Literature - "Short Encyclopedia of Literature". Vol. 7. –Moscow, 1972. (in Russian).
3. Rozentsveig V.Y. Languages in Contact. Concerning Linguistic problems of this theory. -Leningrad, 1972. (in Russian).
4. Zograf G.A. South Asian's Languages. –Moscow, 1990. (in Russian)
5. Shamatov A.N. Dialectical and Archaic Features of Hindustani Morphology in 15th Century.-Tashkent, 1966. (in Russian)
6. Shamatov A.N. Various types and ways of Loan-Words Assimilation in Early Hindustani with special reference to Dakkhini of 14th and 15th centuries. -Moscow, 1982. (in Russian)
7. Varmaa D. Hindii bhaaShaa kaa vikaas. -Delhi, 1962.
8. Bahrii H. BhaaShaa kaa vikaas. -Dilli,1992.
9. The Delhi Sultanate, the fifth volume of the History and Culture of the Indian People. -Bombay, 1960.
10.Buddhism and Central Asian Civilization, in the collection «The Indian Culture and Buddhism». -Moscow, 1972. (in Russian).

**Associate Professor,
South and South-East Asian Languages Department,
Tashkent State University of Oriental Studies,
Uzbekistan**

7. Indian Culture in the works of Abu Rayhan Biruni

Umida Kuranbaeva Sultannazarovna

As every nations' living place, climate, names of months and days are different, the same notion can be mentioned in its pious events and holly days.

They celebrate it in a manner that was derived from their ancestors, like using their expected cosmetics, wearing national old-fashioned clothes and enjoying every minute of that event.

As time inherently passes, it's an absolutely natural notion that changes in such events can't be avoided, due to the differentiating climate and weather.

Central Asian, Asia and Middle East Nations from the very old times have always lived in a close neighborhood, so that can be caused that too many similarities in their cultures and religious events. Till the present time, the works by Abu Rayhan Biruni about history, ethnographies, chronologies, toponymies, calendars, holidays and religious events of the nations mentioned above, takes one of the main places in research works.

The full name of the scientist is Abu Rayhan Muhammad bin Ahmad Biruni (973-1048). According to many Muslim sources of the 10th – 13th centuries (Yakut al-Hamavi etc.) he was born in Khwarezm, in his capital city Kath of the Khwarezmshah era - Afreghids. According to Nawal Balawi, a Pakistani scientist, Biruni's works were more than 1801.

---

[1] Ghurrat al-Zijat or Karana tilaka. Institute of sindhology university of sind. Sind, -Pakistan. 1973. – P. 68; Boilot D. J. L' Oeuvre d'al – Beruni, essai bibliographique. Caire, 1955. – P. 290-311.

Unfortunately, only 33 of these works have come to us2. The well-known orientalist, academician I.Yu.Krachkovsky gives a high appraisal to Biruniy's legacy and says, "It is easier said than not to enumerate the areas of science he is engaged in"3. Biruni is a great scientist-astronomer, geographer, mineralogy, ethnography, history and poet of the medieval East. He is one of the scholars who differentiate people according to their nationality, convictions and positions.

Before starting to write one of his most famous works, which have come down to our days, - "Kitab fi tahqiq ma li-l-Hind min maqula maqbula fi al- 'aql aw mardhula" ("The book containing an explanation of the teachings belonging to the Indians, acceptable by or rejected" by "India" 10304.) Biruni thoroughly and thoroughly studied the science, culture and lifestyle of the Indian people.

The first data related to Indians are cited in such works as "al-Athar al-baqiya min al-qurun al-khaliya", ("The Chronologi of Ancient Nations" or "Chronology")5, "Kitab at-tafhim li'avail Sina'at at al-tanjim" ("Introduction to

---

2 Abu Rayhan Beruni. Pamyatniki minuvshih pokoleniy / Perevod M. Sale. Dop. isp. podgotovka k pechati, vvodniy tekst A. Ahmedova. T. I. Tashkent: Fan. 2015. – S. 35-36.
3 Krachkovskiy I. Yu. (1957). Izbrannie sochineniya. T. IV.Moskva-Leningrad, 1957. –S. 247.
4 Abu Rayhan Beruni. Tanlangan asarlar. T. II. Tashkent: Fan, 1965.–B. 7; Matvievskaya G.P., Rozenfeld B.A. Matema-tiki i astronomi musulmanskogo srednevekovya i ix trudi (VIII - XVII vv.). T.2. Moskva: 1983. – S. 266.
5 Abu Rayhan Beruni. Qadimgi xalqlardan qolgan yodgorliklar. Tanlangan asarlar. T. I. Tashkent: O' zbekiston, 2020. – B. 23; Matvievskaya G.P., Rozenfeld B.A. Matematiki i astronomi musulmanskogo sredneveko-vya i ix trudi (VIII - XVII vv.). T.2. Moskva: Nauka, 1983. – S. 265.

Astrology" or "Astronomy")6 and "Al-Kanun al-Mas'udi" (" Masudic Canon" 1037)7. When studying the history of Indians Biruni, collected information about these people before the trip to India, which are reflected in his previous "India" writings.

There were too many scientists before Abu Rayhan Biruni, who were interested in traditions of Hindoos, who were living in the territory of India and other countries. Aiming to restate above mentioned point, I can exemplify Muhammad ibn Muso Kharezmee (year of death 847), after receiving expected level in a science, was interested in Hindoos' math and geography8.

It can be pointed out that the Indians' math, astronomy, botanics, history and culture were gradually introduced in almost every research work by Abu Rayhan Biruni.

So, what works can be found the information about the culture and religious holidays in?

The chronology of different peoples, the names of months, holidays, traditions, religion, culture, genealogies of kings, prophets and false prophets are described in the work "Al-Asar al-Baqiya min al-Qurun al-Khaliya", written in 1000-1003. In addition, in this work we can find information about

---

[6] Abu Rayhan Beruni. Tafhim. Tanlangan asarlar. T. IV. Toshkent: Fan, 2006. – B. 6; Matvievskaya G.P., Rozenfeld B.A. Matematiki i astronomi musulmanskogo sredneveko-vya i ix trudi (VIII - XVII vv.). T.2. Moskva: Nauka, 1983. – S. 272.

[7] Abu Rayhan Beruni. Tanlangan asarlar. T. V. Toshkent: Fan, 1973. – B. 7; Matvievskaya G.P., Rozenfeld B.A. Matema-tiki i astronomi musulmanskogo srednevekovya i ix trudi (VIII - XVII vv.). T.2. Moskva: Nauka, 1983. – S. 266.

[8] Muhammad Ibn Muso Xorazmiy. Tanlangan asarlar. Matematika, Astronomiya, Geografiya. –Toshkent: Fan, 1983. – B. 173.

Indians living in India and other countries.Furthermore, we can come across with information about the Indians living in India and other countries in this works. The way of celebration of hindoos' holidays is described like this: "The second equinox, which suits the Sindhids' lifestyle, plays main role for hindoo's as the holiday "Mehrjan" for Persians. They present valuable gifts to each other and gathering together in their holy places. After a while they go out for a walk and gathering for meetings, submissing to the world and obeying him"9. Particularly, there were listed names of twelve months on page 105 of this work. To the above mentioned S.F.Starr in his work named "Forgotten enlightment: Golden Age from Arabian conquest of Central Asia to Amir Temur's period" pointed out his thoughts, while he mentioned that there's too little information about hinds" in a work "Architectural derivation from ancient nations" comprehending with "India". This event in the work of Biruni called "Chronology", as the reason why India and other countries were not added , depicted his idea by saying that: I don't come across any person who knows exact data about it , so I gave up that I could not specify clearly10.

The work " Kitab at-tavhim li avoil sinat at-tanjim" ("Tafhim") was_written in 1029-year, is an encyclopedical work that includes 8 chapters: Law, arithmetic, astronomy, geography, astrology, asturlab, ahkami nujum; it is written as the answers to 530 questions. We can come across with valuable information about India and its people. We can find the information that is related to the topic in the chapter "Chronology". In a table below, names of the Indian months

---

9 Abu Rayhon Berun. Tanlangan asarlar. T. I. Toshkent: Fan, 1968. – B. 303.

10 S. F. Starr. Unutilgan ma'rifat: Markaziy Osiyoning arab istilosidan to Amir Temur davrigacha bo'lgan oltin asri.- Toshkent: O'zbekiston, 2018. – B. 385.

and weeks are given. This table helps us to know exact celebration date of holidays, according to exact months and days.

The names of week days in Indians11

Adityavara	Somavara	Mangalavara	Budhavara	Brihaspativara	Shukravara	Shanayshcharavara
Day of Sun	Day of Moon	Day of Mirrix (Mars)	Day of Utorid (Merkuriy)	Day of Mushtariy (Jupiter)	Day of Zuhra (Venera)	Day of Zuhal (Saturn)
Sunday	Monday	Tuesday	Wednesday	Thursday	Friday	Saturday

The work of Abu Rayhan Biruni written in 1030-year, among of other his scientific heritage which is handed down over the years, is consedred as a rare work "Tahqiq mo li-l Hind min ma'qula maqbula fi-l-aql av marzula" or "The book of Indian accurating of trustworthy and unreliable education" is called "India" in scientific literature. This work of Biruni is highly-assessed by Eastern and Western scholars.

Eventhough Biruni had not visited India, he was interested in India, since all of the scholars who lived in Middle centuries was interested in this place's science, culture and history. Before completing the work "India", Biruni learnt about the Indian people that lived in Central Asia, in his works "Osor al-bokiya", "Tafhim" he gave some information about this nation and provided with a full data in "India" work. Indeed, Biruni's "India" is different from other contemporary works and other ones which were written in next years, with factual information and deep scientific analysis. The written sources which were collected by Biruni, is the result of oral survey on Indian religion, philosophy, astronomy, geography, literature, grammar data and poetry. Biruni got acquainted with poem "Mahabharata" and other literatures. He learnt

---

[11] Abu Rayhon Beruni. Tanlangan asarlar. T. VI. Toshkent-Urganch-Khiva: Ishonch, 2006. – B. 117.

Indian culture, lifestyle, traditions, rules and orders of ceremonies in the process of meeting. This collection created foundation of new historically-scientific and memorial book "India"12. Biruni figured out that Indian science developed as well as old Greek subjects.the main task of "India" is to determine the best advances of Indian ideology in different spheres and to observe their sources. This great works demanded that Biruni had to prepare firmly and learn new language in a limited and short time. Biruni admitted that he liked Sanskrit and Indian language classes and emphasized:" I am alone in my period". However it was tough to learn new languages in his 50's. Eventually, he learnt languages adequately to add a lot of transcripted Sanskrit terms in his work13.

An old Indian culture attracted Biruni. Knowing about entirely new sphere for Biruni meant to understand his period's social matters. So, hard work was required, such as inherently reading works of Indian philosophers and scholars which were written in Sanskrit language. He learnt sources in detail such as "Mahabharata", "Bhadgavadgita", "Sankhya" of Kapilan, " Yogasutra" work of Patanjali" and others in Sanskrit language. In his only "India" work he mentioned about almost 180 Indian works, particularly there were works dedicated to Astronomy. He translated the work "Almajistiy" by Ptolemiy, "Basis foundation" by Evklid and his work about usturlab into Sanskrit language. By translating from Indian works "Karana tilaka", "Arkand", "Khandakhadyaka" into Arabic language, he introduced scientific acheivments of the Indians to the Muslims, and vice versa.

---

12 Bulgakov P. G. Jizn i trudi Beruni. Tashkent: Fan, 1972. – B. 206.
13 S.F. Starr. Unutilgan ma'rifat: Markaziy Osiyoning arb istilosidan to Amir Temur davrigacha bo'lgan oltin asri.- Toshkent: O'zbekiston, 2018. – B. 478.

Biruni acquired previous works about India written in Arabic. He admitted more profound ones among them. While writing about India he tried to be a good story teller, not a criticizer14. Biruni's scientific views was reflected on his concepts about Indian literature. He was not satisfied by giving information about various poetry genres in Indian and Sanskrit languages, but he dedicated 13-chapter of "India" for reflections of Indian grammar and books about poems. After having described "chandani" similar to aruz poetry measure, peculiarities of Indian grammar, he pointed out that their books included shkolas. He said that he had difficulties while translating "Uklidus" and "Almajistiy" into Indian language as well as in the process of writing down about Usturlab skill. But he said that he was interested in spreading knowledge and to make aware of others about it. Thus, he mentioned that he meet troubles in translating scientific works into poetry form, but according to his view it was easy way to learn it by heart. In this way, he created stable typology based on poetry measure, he showed in a schematic way by colleting all data. Biruni mostly pointed out about Indian traditions and religious belief.

There were moethnographic date in his than in other searchers' works. While describing Indian weather, flora and fauna, he had learnt perfectly previous scholars and philosophers' works which were not handed in up to now. Except the works that were written in Sanskrit by Indian writers based on the legendary-epic, religiously–philosophical meaning, he used oral information. According to his information, he had Indian friends who collected factual

---

14 Abu Rayhon Beruni. Tanlangan asarlar. T. II. Toshkent: Fan, 1965. – B. 183.

S. F. Starr. Unutilgan ma'rifat: Markaziy Osiyoning arab istilosidan to Amir Temur davrigacha bo'lgan oltin asri.- Toshkent: O'zbekiston, 2018. – B. 118.

materials about India and its people, traditions, their old religions and culture. Most of them were highly-qualified people. Although such kind of Indian informants gave fully real information because he compared and checked their data to ensure himself, If he felt doubts about some vital information, he warned readers to be careful15.

V.V. Bartold emphasized in one of his articles: "There is no answer to the question how XI century scholar was so aware of scientific methods and had broadened horizon?"16 In reality Biruni could not explore India entirely, he had only been to cities below and got acquainted with the culture of these places during the exploration process. "I have found that Lavhur (Lohur) fosters situated in 30o and 10`. The distance from there to Kashmir's center is 56 mile. It includes hills and half of them are fields and as well as this, he gave information about locations of Gazna, Lamgon, Kobul, Purshovar, Kande – amir accomadation, Vayhand, Danpur, Jaylam, Nandna, fosters (the distance between Nandna, fosters and Multon is 200 mile) Sialkot, Mandakkakur, Multon. Biruni said he had not been to any other places except them17, so we can conclude that he had been to Northern-Western parts of India, to be more precise, in some places of Panjob, from Peshovar to Sialkot, in the South to Multan and been to western borders of Kashmir. According to his notice, he defined data about eastern and southern areas by reading works in Sanskrit and observations.

There is a special style of Biruni in his work, he addressed to not only one but also several directions simultaneously not to make readers get bored. If we talk about different subjects

---

15 Biruni va ijtimoiy fanlar. Toshkent: Fan, 1973. – B. 96-97.
16 Bartold V.V. Raboti po istorii islama i arabskogo xalifata.T.VI. Maskva: Nauka, 1966. – B. 263.
17 Abu Rayhon Beruni. Tanlangan asarlar. T. II. Toshkent: Fan,1965. – B. 244.

in some places of book, then discuss them that is not related to our topic, we don't intend to prolong the topic, but in order to keep readers get interested. Because looking the same things always bring impatience and anxiety. If a learner think about different subjects, he seems himself in various gardens, without managing to know about particular one, another one starts and a person thinks every new has its own pleasure, and gets interested in looking through them18.

Biruni gave information about chess in chapter 48. He emphasized that chess (Shatranj) appeared in India initially, changes were added by Greeks. The greatness of Biruni's idea is based on his deep reflection and pureness. Biruni emphasized: "This book ("India") is not a discussion and argument book so I don't give the proof of enemies, and don't reject who are not unfair. It is only narrative book. I am writing all words as real ones, I add Greek words to reflect their correlation with Indians"19. Biruni pointed out that comparing Indian and Greek religions is more profound, so he talked about Zevs, Heracles, Afina and other Greek deitis. As a result, while learning process by comparing, he added more than 25 narrations from Greek works, for instance Indians also did not write down in the skins like Old Greeks, as the proof he gave the words of Sokrat: "I don't move the knowledge from alive peoples' heart to died sheep's skin"20.

If it goes to about Indian holidays, so as to know exact celebration days of holiday and famous days in Biruni's works, we will analyze names of months based on the table in "Osor al-bokiya", "India", "Tafhim", in every book, the names

---

18 Abu Rayhon Berun. Tanlangan asarlar. T. I. Toshkent: Fan,1968. – B. 96.
19 Abu Rayhon Beruni. Tanlangan asarlar.T. II. Toshkent: Fan,1965. – B. 28.
20 Abu Rayhon Beruni. Tanlangan asarlar. T. II. Toshkent: Fan, 1965. – B. 138.

98

of months are similar because they are from one root.

Expressions of the names of Indian months in Biruni works

Names of months			In "India' work 2- division and calling of moths				
"Monuments from ancient nations" (1968 y.)[1]	"Monuments from ancient nations" (2015 y)[2]	"Tafhim"	"India"	Current names	Light half owner of each month	Dark half owner of each month
J-i-t-r	Jaytra	Jaytra	Chaytra	Chaitra	Tvashatri	Jom'ya
B-i-sh-a-k	Vayshaka	Vayshoka	Vayshakxa	Vaisakka	Indrogni	Agniya
Z-i-sh-t	Jirta	Jayshtxa	Jayshitxa	Jyerhtha	Shukra	Ravdra
A-a-so-f	Otoda	Oshoda	Oshoraxa	Ashadha	Vishvedevoh	Sorta
S-r-a-v-a	Sarvana	Srovana	Shrovana	Sratvana	Vishnu	Pitr'ya
B-x-d-r-b-d	Bhadrabata	Bxodrabata	Bhadrapada Bhadrapada	Aja	Sonta
A-s-v-j	Ashuja	Ashuja	Ashvayuja	Asvina	Oshana	Maytre
K-a-r-s	Kortika	Kortika	Korttika	Karttika	Agni	Shakra
M-n-k-s	Mankathira	Mirgashir-sha	Morgashir-sha	Margasirsha	Sovt'ya	Nirriti
B-v-sh	Yusa	Pausha	Pavsha	Pansha	Jiva	Vishnu
M-a-к	Moga	Marha	Mogha	Magha	Pitr'ya	Varuna
B-a-к-г	Balkuna	Lxalguna	Phalguna	Phalguna[3]	Bxagra	Pushan

Indian holidays are celebrated in these months

Jaytra for Indians is meant a festive prcession. So they call all the holidays "*Jaytra*". Most of the holidays are celebrated by women and children.

Holidays in *Chatra (Jaytra)* month;

The second day the month – *agdus* (it is celebrated by Kashmir's people).

The eleventh day of the month – *hindole* (The songs are sung the whole day in the temples).

The fourteenth day of the month- *bohand* (holiday for women).

The twenty-second day – *chaytra - chashati* (holiday was dedicated to Bhavagadgi, having a bath and donating).

Holidays in *Vayshakha (Vayshoka)* month:
The third day of the month – *gauretritya* (For the sake of Gaure, for women)
From the tenth to the sixteenth of the month - lighting fire.

Holidays in *Jayshtha (Jayayshtxa)* month:
The first day of the moth - one moon completes, another new moon appears (when moon is full, holiday day is celebrated for wives)

Holidays in *Oshoda (Oshora)* month:
Ohore - denotions are given all days of the month.

Holidays in *Shravana (Srovana)* month:
During the full moon, refreshments are organized for Brahmans.

Holidys in *Bxadrapada (Bxodrapada)* month:
The third day of the month- women's holiday.
The sixth day of the month – *gayhat* (the poor and beggars are provided with food)
The eighth day of the month - *dxruvagriha* (women celebrate this day to have a baby).
The eleventh of the month – *parvate* (the sacred string is prepared and worn).
The sixteenth day of the month – men and children celebrate this day by wearing holiday clothes (give alms).

Holidays in *Ashvayudja (Ashuja)* month:
The eighth day of the month - in honor of Mahonavame (sugar cane is absorbed, denotion is given, gaatling is sacrified).
The fifteenth day of the month - Holiday *Puhoy* (in honor of Vasudeva(Indians struggle with each other and play with animals).
The sixteenth day of the month- Holiday, denotion is given to Brahmans.
The twenty-third day of the month - *ashoka,* (ohoy) (entertaining, wrestling)

Holidays in *Kortika (Kartiki)* month:
The first day the month - debole, merry-making is done and a lot of lamps are lighted at night, presently it meets to Divali).

Holidays in *Morgashirsha* month:
The third day of the month - guvonabotrejo (Gaure) (Women's Holiday Day).

Holidays in *Pausha (Pavsha)* month:
The eighth (moonlight) day of the month-ashtaka (food is prepared and presents are given to Brahmans).
The eighth (dark) day of the month - *shakortam* (turnip is eaten).

Holidays in *Magha* month:
The third day of the month - *mohgatriga* (a holiday in honor of Gaure).
The twenty third day of the month – *monsartagu* (food is prepared with black mung bean and meat).

Holidays in *Pxalguna (Lxalguna)* month:
The eighth day of the month - *purortaku* (food is prepared with fat for Brahmans).
The fifteenth of the month – *shivaroti* (aromatic parfumes and basils are given as a present to Mahodeva).
The twenty third day of the month - *puvatton* (rice is cooked with butter and sugar).
The Hindus of the city of Multan celebrate the holiday in honor of the Sun, which is called *Somba purayotra,* and they pray for the Sun.
Almost all of the holidays above are considered as religious holidays, there are several holidays in each month, which are devoted for women and children.

Famous days of the Indians
Days are distinguished from each other according to given characteristics. For this reason, days are divided into famous (great) and ordinary days. *Sunday* is considered as a Great day in India, because this day is the day of the Sun, like Friday in Muslims. Furthermore Great days includes *avomasa* and

purnima days, since in this day the Sun and the Moon are joined, the moon has become full.

Four of these days are well-known: the third day of the Vayshakha– *Kshayretok*, the ninth day of Korttika – *Tretojuga* starts, the fifteenth day of Margho – *Dvopara* starts, the thirteenth day of Oshvayuja – *Kalijuga* starts.

There is no worthy reason to utter, they are taken to take the meaning. These days are designated to give denotions and celebrate holidays. In these famous days the time of gaining morally good deeds is called as punyakola.

Balabhadra said that in his comments about "Khandakhadyaka" said: "If someone is priestess a like *juga*, which means he has fully acknowledged the power of the Lord, avoids doing thins, keeps such a lifestyle till the end of his days on this Earth, all boons and good deeds collected by him are not ample to be comprehended with the person's good deeds, donations, ablutions, lubricating body with oil, prayings in *punyakola*. In all above described days aimed to be the time for doing good deeds day. Donations are made and ceremonies are organized to gain boons in these days, otherwise, these can be aimless period only for entertainment. There are also days of happiness in Indian culture – *bihu* and *shibu*, these are two equinoxes in autumn and spring. S*onta* is a sacrifice when oil and grains are thrown to the fire. It can be observed that Biruni accurately inserted exact days of ceremonies in his work. These are: Gemini zodiac starts entering time in 180, Virgo in 140, Sagittarius in 260, Pisces starts in 220 of the Sun.

The days of the Sun and lunar eclipses are considered to be awful time for Indians, even *vayshiy* and *shudras* commit suicides considering that it is the best time to die, while *brahmans* and *kshatriys* were not allowed to do that. There not only happy days and time, but also there are unhappy days and periods for Indians. Pointing to get rid of unhappiness and tragedy, they break dishes by dropping it to the floor21.

In the data of Biruni about India, the outlook of the initial

---

[21] Abu Rayhon Beruni.Tanlangan asarlar. T. II. – Tashkent: Fan, 1965. – B. 436.

Midlle century, hardworking and careful scholar is reflected. P.G. Bulgakov assessed Biruni's work by saying that: Eventhough the thousand-year-progress is separated us from Biruni, it does not deman us Greatness, but intensifies the Greatness with incomparable work in Middle century Muslim literature22.

Biruni's data about India is the result of deep analysis of Hind sources and his personal observations, moreover he commented reliability of every source by giving his ideas. Biruni's peculiar approach and detailed concepts about Indians social and spiritual life are more valuable than data about India given by Arabian geographers. Biruni gave real, original, clear information about different spheres of Indians.

Abu Rayhon Beruni described all the holidays of the Hindus, reflecting their medieval traditions, ethnography and social history.

Biruni is one of researchers who left priceless information about Indian peoples' history and culture in the Middle centuries. His works serve as a main source to scientists and researchers who deal with Indian history and ethnograph.

References

1. Abu Rayhan Beruni. Qadimgi xalqlardan qolgan yodgor-liklar. Tanlangan asarlar. T. I. Tashkent: O'zbekiston, 2020.
2. Abu Rayhon Berun. Tanlangan asarlar. T. I. Toshkent: Fan, 1968.
3. Abu Rayhan Beruni. Pamyatniki minuvshih pokoleniy. T. I. Tashkent: Fan. 2015.
4. Abu Rayhan Beruni. Tanlangan asarlar. T. II. Tashkent: Fan, 1965.

---

[22] Abu Rayhon Beruni.Tanlangan asarlar. T. II. – Tashkent: Fan, 1972. – B. 206.

5. Abu Rayhan Beruni. Tanlangan asarlar. T. V. Toshkent: Fan, 1973.
6. Abu Rayhon Beruni. Tanlangan asarlar. T. VI. Toshkent-Urganch-Khiva: Ishonch, 2006.
7. Boilot D. J. L' Oeuvre d'al – Beruni, essai bibliographique. Caire, 1955.
8. Bartold V.V. Raboti po istorii islama i arabskogo xalifata.T.VI. Maskva: Nauka, 1966.
9. Beleniskiy A. M. Kratkiy ocherk jizni i trudov Biruni. Moskva, 1963.
10. Bulgakov P. G. Jizn i trudi Beruni. Tashkent: Fan, 1972.
11. Biruni va ijtimoiy fanlar. Biruniy tug'ilgan kunining ming yilligiga. Toshkent: Fan, 1973.
12. Matvievskaya G.P., Rozenfeld B.A. Matematiki i astronomi musulmanskogo srednevekovya i ix trudi (VIII - XVII vv.). T.2. Moskva: 1983.
13. Muhammad Ibn Muso Xorazmiy. Tanlangan asarlar. Matematika, Astronomiya, Geografiya. – Toshkent: Fan, 1983.
14. Starr S. F. Unutilgan ma'rifat: Markaziy Osiyoning arab istilosidan to Amir Temur davrigacha bo'lgan oltin asri.- Toshkent: O'zbekiston, 2018.
15. Ghurrat al-Zijat or Karana tilaka. Institute of sindhology university of sind. Sind, -Pakistan. 1973.
16. I. Yu. Krachkovskiy. Izbrannie sochineniya. T. IV. Moskva-Leningrad, 1957.

Ph.D. Student,
Al-Biruni Institute of Oriental Studies,
Academy of the Sciences of the Republic of
Uzbekistan
kuranbayevaumida778@gmail.com

8. Indian Linguistic Tradition : A View from Russian Indology

Prof. Dr. Zilola Khudaybergenova

Linguistics originated in ancient times in connection with the awakening of a special cognitive interest in language, which was stimulated by the needs of emerging states and their activities in the spheres of administration and economy, the creation and dissemination of writing, the need to teach writing and train qualified scribes-administrators, as well as to solve a number of applied tasks arising from the activity of interpreting sacred texts and performing religious rituals, experiments in the field of poetics, etc.

The distinctive and extremely stable linguistic tradition of the Eastern world originated in ancient India[1]. She, like the Chinese linguistic tradition (but much more intensively) influenced the formation and development of linguistic thought in neighboring countries[2]. At the beginning of the 2nd millennium BC. Indo-European tribes of the Aryans, or Aryans (Indo-Iranians), invade Iran and India from the Northwest. As a result of the divergence, the Indo-Iranian languages split into two branches - Iranian and Indo-Aryan. The speakers of the languages of the first branch also settle in the territories of modern Afghanistan and Tajikistan. The self-name of the Indo-Iranian tribes, who lived earlier in the

---

[1] Баранников П. А. Возникновение и развитие обществ по распространению языка хинди в Индии // Письменные памятники и проблемы истории культуры народов Востока. Тезисы докладов II годичной научной сессии ЛО ИНА. Март 1966 года. Ленинград.

[2] Березин Ф.М. История лингвистических учений. М.: Высшая школа, 1984. 319 с.

northern Black Sea region, and then in Asia Minor, is arya (in the original meaning 'noble, loyal, friendly; representative of one of the three higher castes'). This word formed the basis of two proper names - Iran (aryanam 'the country of the Aryans / noble'), which has survived to this day and meant the territory of settlement of the first group of Aryan tribes, and Aryavarta (Aryavarta 'way, the country of the Aryans / noble'), which meant in Vedic mythology and in real life, the original territory of settlement of another group of Aryans in India. We know about the Indo-Aryans as the carriers of the Vedic culture (mid-1st millennium BC - mid-1st millennium AD), embodied in orally transmitted religious texts - the Vedas (Rig Veda, Samaveda, Yajurveda, Atharva -veda) [3].

Russian Indology : Formation and Development
The rise of Indology in Russia and St. Petersburg dates back to the first half of the 18th century. After the founding of the Academy of Sciences, one of its first academicians was T.-Z. Bayer, who came to Russia in 1726[4]. Being engaged mainly in Chinese, Mongolian, Kalmyk, Manchu and Tangut (Tibetan) languages, he was one of the first in Russia to start studying "Brahmin" language, i.e. Sanskrit, under the guidance of the Indian Sonkhbara who came to St. Petersburg. The fruit of these studies was two of his works on the literature and grammar of these languages. In the second article, for the first time in Russia, samples of the Sanskrit alphabet (Devanagari), printed from wooden plates, which were made according to the drawings of Bayer himself, are given, and brief information about the Dravidian (Tamul, Telugu) and some New Indian languages (Marathi, Gujarati, etc.) is given.). In the 30s. XVIII century. In addition to

---

[3] Алпатов В.М. История лингвистических учений. Учебное пособие. М.: "Языки русской культуры", 1999. – 368 с.
[4] https://dic.academic.ru/dic.nsf/enc_biography/7377/Байер

Bayer, D.G. Messerschmidt, who was interested in the Punjabi and Tamil languages, studied the Devanagari alphabet, as well as the alphabets of the Dravidian languages.

The study of Sanskrit in Russia in the initial period depended on the scientific interests of individual scientists, who were engaged in it only along the way with their main oriental studies. A similar picture was observed in the first decades of the existence of the Academy of Sciences. Here, first of all, we should mention F. Adelung (1768–1843), an honorary academician who tried to give an overview of literature in Sanskrit[5]. R.H. Lenz (1808-1836) left a noticeable trace in the study of Sanskrit. He was the first to lecture free of charge on Sanskrit literature and comparative linguistics at St. Petersburg University. P.Ya. Petrov (1814–1875) was the direct successor of R.H. Lenz in the study of Sanskrit. The result of his studies was the work "Adding to the catalog of Sanskrit manuscripts kept in the Asian Museum of the St. Petersburg Academy of Sciences."

From the first half of the 19th century. the main center for the study of Sanskrit becomes the Academy of Sciences. This period is associated with the name of Acad. O. N. Bötlingka (1815-1904)[6]. In 1887 he published the famous Panini grammar. His merit was the publication of Wopadeva's grammar, Hemachandra's synonymous dictionary with a German translation, the Upanishads, the ancient drama Mrichchakatika ("Clay Cart") in German translation, as well as a Sanskrit anthology. The culmination of O. N. Bötlingka's many years of activity was the creation of Sanskrit dictionaries

---

[5] http://funeral-spb.narod.ru/necropols/volkovskoe/tombs/adelung/adelung.html

[6] http://allpetrischule-spb.org/index.php?title=Бетлинг,_Оттон_Николаевич

published by the Academy of Sciences: complete (1852–1875) and short (1879–1889). These dictionaries marked the era in the study of Sanskrit and became widely known all over the world under the name "Petersburg dictionaries". They served as the basis of all European Indological science for a whole century and contributed to the development of comparative-historical linguistics.

Indological research at the Academy of Sciences was carried out in two directions. The first (earlier) was linguistic, which found its expression in the publication of the above-mentioned Sanskrit dictionaries, monuments of Indian grammatical literature and various Sanskrit texts.

The second direction in Indology was Buddhist. The founders of the scientific study of Buddhism are the Sinologist Acad. V.P. Vasiliev[7] (1818-1900) and indologist prof. I.P. Minaev[8] (1840-1890). The latter brought up a wonderful school of Russian Indologists, who became the most prominent scientists of their time and continued his work. Two of them became academicians-S.F.Oldenburg and F.I. Scherbatskaya.

In addition to northern Buddhism, which S.F. Oldenburg was engaged in all his life, he studied Indian folklore, fairy tales and jatakas, and worked on the publication of Sanskrit texts. S.F. Oldenburg paid special attention to Mahabharata, having completely worked through the entire epic under the leadership of an Indian in London. He was the initiator and permanent director of the publication of the world famous series "Collection of Original and Advanced Buddhist Texts" under the general title "The Buddhist Library", founded by

---

[7] Академик В.П. Васильев (1818-1900) Как исследователь истории и культуры Китая, Тибета и Монголии. К 200-летию со дня рождения. –М., 2018.

[8] http://www.rgo-sib.ru/rgo/39.htm

him in 1897[9].

At the turn of the XIX and XX centuries. began an intensive and comprehensive survey of Central Asian cultures. Centers of Buddhist culture were discovered (SF Oldenburg's expeditions to Turpan [1909–1910] and Dunhuang [1914–1915]), new documents in Sanskrit and Tibetan languages were discovered, and an intensive study of northern Buddhism began.

This is the path that Acad. F.I.Scherbatskaya (1866-1942)[10]. The scientific interests of F.I.Scherbatsky were steadily aimed at studying Indian philosophy, more precisely, Buddhist logic, as well as Buddhism itself from Sanskrit and Tibetan sources. Our close proximity to the countries of the Buddhist world and the enormous wealth of the Academy of Sciences in the field of Tibetan Buddhist literature also influenced his choice.

Thus, from the end of the XIX and beginning of the XX century. the study of Sanskrit at the Academy of Sciences was subordinated to the study of Buddhist philosophy and culture. However, along with this, the philological direction continued to exist. In this respect, the activities of the third student of I.P. Minaev - prof. ND Mironov, who for many years dealt with the issues of Vedic literature (based on the hymns of the Rig

---

[9] Сергей Федорович Ольденбург - ученый и организатор науки. –М., 2016.

[10] Аникеев И. П. Выдающийся русский индолог Ф. И. Щербатской // Вестник истории мировой культуры. 1958. № 3; Сидорова Е. Г. Интерпретация буддизма средствами философской компаративистики: вклад Ф. И. Щербатского в формирование языка межкультурного диалога // Восток. Афро-Азиатские общества: история и современность. 2008. № 3. С. 47-57. Щербатской Ф.И. Избранные труды по буддизму. М., 1988.

Veda) and worked on the description of Sanskrit manuscripts, some of which were collected and brought by the researcher himself. As a result of this work, I.P. Mironov prepared and published two catalogs of these manuscripts, which are available both in the St. Petersburg Branch of the Institute of Oriental Studies of the Russian Academy of Sciences and in the State Public Library.

After the October Revolution, the further development of the traditional sections of Russian Indology continued. The "Buddhist Library" gained even greater scope. The most prominent scientists from the countries of the West and the East united around it: prof. Sylvain Levy (France), prof. De La Vallais Poussin (Belgium), Vogihara (Japan), M. Walleser (Germany), F.I.Scherbatskaya and O.O. Rosenberg (Russia).

On the initiative of Oldenburg and Shcherbatsky, the publication of the series "Monuments of Indian Philosophy" was resumed, which they had conceived back in 1914 and approved by a resolution of the Academy of Sciences. For this, first of all, the works of Vachaspatimishra on all Indian philosophical systems, the main treatises of the Nyaya system, the seven treatises of Dharmakirti, works on the logic of Dignagia and Vasubandhu's work "Abhidharmakosha", containing the system of primitive Buddhism, were selected.

Already in the first years of Soviet power, there was an urgent need for textbooks for the study of Sanskrit. In 1923, on the initiative of F.I.Scherbatsky and under his editorship, a Russian translation of the textbook by G. Buhler was made. This textbook, presented from the point of view of the Indian grammatical tradition, is still used in the study of Sanskrit at St. Petersburg State University and other universities in the country.

In the plans of the Institute of Oriental Studies, reorganized in 1930, an emphasis was placed on a new topic, where in the first place were questions of the economy of the countries of the East. Among the issues requiring development on the basis of Sanskrit sources, in addition to traditional topics, were the publication of the most important Indian monuments on the history, economy and state structure of ancient India. At the same time, work began on Kautilya's treatise "Arthashastra", which was interrupted and resumed only in 1938 (the publication of the complete Russian translation of Arthashastra was published only in 1959). In the same 1938, a student of I.P. Shcherbatsky and Acad. A.P. Barannikov M.A.Shiryaev (1887-1952) began a new translation of the "Laws of Manu".

In 1939, on the initiative of A.P. Barannikov, who was at that time the director of the Institute of Oriental Studies, the Russian academic translation of Mahabharata, the most important epic monument of ancient India, was started. Work on the translation of the first book, Adiparva, continued with significant interruptions during the war, both under the conditions of the siege of Leningrad and during the stay of the Institute of Oriental Studies in Tashkent. The first book was published in 1950 under the editorship of A.P. Barannikov.

After a long break, the translation of the second book of the Mahabharata - Sabhaparva, was prepared, which was published in 1962, the work on the translation and study of the Mahabharata continued further. In 1964, the translation and study of the fourth book of this monument - Virataparva, which was published in 1967, was completed and prepared for publication.

It is especially worth noting the activities of V.S.Vorobyev-Desyatovsky (1928-1956), who, possessing rare abilities and talent, deep linguistic training and a broad scientific outlook, in a relatively short period of time was able to prepare a number of very valuable works and research. In the Sector of Oriental Manuscripts, V.S.Vorobyev-Desyatovsky was successfully engaged in the study of Central Asian manuscripts, continuing the tradition started by S.F.

Oldenburg[11]. He dismantled the Indian Foundation and published an article about it "Collection of Indian Manuscripts of the Institute of Oriental Studies of the USSR Academy of Sciences. "V.S.Vorobyov-Desyatovsky showed particular interest in studying the manuscript collection consisting of the collections of N.F. Petrovsky, P.K. Kozlov, S.F.Oldenburg and others, and containing unique handwritten materials of the 1st – 9th centuries. in Sanskrit, Saka, Kuchin and Tibetan languages. The work on the description and preparation for publication of a number of interesting materials remained unfinished. The study of the "hybrid" Sanskrit, which was distinguished by unusual inflectional forms, which he began with great enthusiasm, also ended. The work of V.S.Vorobyev-Desyatovsky on the description and study of Central Asian manuscripts is continued by M.I.Vorobyeva-Desyatovskaya. Together with MI Vorobyeva-Desyatovskaya the work on Buddhist Sanskrit manuscripts was carried out by E.N. Temkin and V.G. Erman.

Today at the St. Petersburg Branch of the Institute of Oriental Studies of the Russian Academy of Sciences, work continues on the academic translation and research of the most important monument of Indian culture - Mahabharata. To date, S.L. Neveleva and Ya.V. Vasilkov have published nine books of the Mahabharata (books III, VIII, X, XI, XIV, XVII and XVIII). The work on the XIIth book of the Mahabharata is carried out by the young scientist M.I. Petrova.

Indian Linguistic Tradition: Interpretation of Russian Indologists

The desire to preserve the purity of the language of the religious ritual, which received the name Vedic, was the basis for awakening a special interest in the problems of language in

---

[11] Документы по деятельности В.С. Воробьева-Десятовского. Письменные памятники Востока. 2016. №2. –С.112-125.

the 1st millennium BC. first of all, among the representatives of the highest caste - the priests-Brahmins, who performed complex cult rites in an already obsolete and not always understandable language even in their own circle, which was considered the language of the gods and to which magical power was attributed. The Vedic language, which served the Indian branch of the Aryans, by the middle of the 1st millennium BC. is practically out of use. There was a need for an accurate pronunciation of the sacred hymns - the Vedas, the normalization of Sanskrit - the same for the whole of India, and comprehensive comments on the ritual texts were also needed.

The problematic situation that developed in India under the influence of the needs of a religious cult differed from those that took place in the Middle East and China: here the priority was given to spoken speech, and not to writing; the letter came relatively late. Accordingly, primary attention was paid to the study of the laws of melody, rhythm, metrics, phonetics (and then the Chinese learned from representatives of Indian culture, joining Buddhism), as well as the elementary etymologization of words[12].

Questions of language are considered by the Hindus in the earliest monuments of Vedic literature - Vedangs. In one of the Vedangas (shiksha) issues of phonetics and pronunciation are highlighted: the ancient Indians made significant progress in the study of speech sounds and their classification based on articulatory signs. They already realized the non-identity of the concepts of the sound of speech and phoneme, they had the outline of the concept of the syllable phoneme. Articulatory classifications of sounds built on a clear logical

---

[12] Алпатов В.М. История лингвистических учений. Учебное пособие. М.: "Языки русской культуры", 1999. – 368 с.

basis were reflected in the sequence of graphic signs in the alphanumeric systems of Indian writing (brahmi - from about the 8th century BC, kharoshthi, nagari, devanagari, charade, etc.), which, most likely, they go back not to the still undeciphered Proto-Indian (mostly hieroglyphic), but to the West Semitic syllabic writing. Another vedanga (chanda) is devoted to the theory of poetry, in the third (nirukta) questions of etymology and lexicology are considered. Nirukta is a special discipline dealing with the explanation and etymological interpretation of words used in priestly ritual. Dictionaries were actively developed that catalog the names of the gods, the names of the actions they perform, the objects at their disposal, the signs of these objects, etc. Yaski's Nirukta is the first extensive lexicographical work of this kind that has come down to us, consisting of five parts and including synonymous series and thematic groups of object names, lists of verbs and verbal nouns, less systematized lists of nouns and adjectives, etc. In his work, Yaska paid special attention to etymology. At the same time, he included in his Nirukta grammatical information (grammatical classification of words, information from the field of word formation, the concept of case, the seven-membered paradigm of the name - without vocative).

The achievements of the ancient Indians in the field of lexicography are also noticeable. They wrote extensive ritual and mythological treatises written in Sanskrit, a language qualitatively different from Vedic, by the Brahmans (8-7 centuries BC), which set out the general programs of the ritual actions of the priests and the interpretation of the Vedic verses being performed at the same time. At the same time, they also turned to the Vedic language. Collections of glosses to obsolete words of the "Rig Veda" are the first actually linguistic experiments.

The development of grammar problems - vedanga vyakarana - reaches a particularly high level. The pinnacle of grammatical thought and a model for many imitations was the work "Ashtadhyaya" ('Eight Books') by Panini (5th or 4th century BC), which sets the task of strict regulation and canonization of Sanskrit, which developed alongside the Vedic language on a different dialectal basis and gradually supplanted it in religious use. Panini constantly draws attention to the main features of Vedic and the differences from Sanskrit. The description of the language follows a strictly synchronous principle. Attention is drawn to the extreme conciseness of the presentation (in order to make it easier to memorize the rules by heart). Panini's grammar, based on the previous linguistic tradition, contains over 4,000 rules (sutras). A sophisticated system of symbolizing linguistic units, rules and operations is used. It is written in an extremely formalized language, reminiscent of algebraic formulas, which, without special commentary, is incomprehensible even to people who kno/w Sanskrit well. For example, the sutra ató heh is commented as "in the plural after a, the personal ending of the 2nd person singular is omitted."[13]. Большое место уделяется фонетике. Much attention is paid to phonetics. Panini speaks in detail about combinatorial sound changes, concerns issues of stress.

Analyzing morphological phenomena, Panini singles out various classes of verb roots, types of endings in the noun declension. The concepts of root and suffix are analyzed on the basis of the word paradigm; Panini is familiar with the concepts of morpheme zero and internal inflection[14].

And today, from the standpoint of "active grammar" (ie, the speaker's grammar) and generative linguistics, Panini's original approach to the description of language is striking: it goes from communicative goal setting and transmitted

---

[13] Сусов И.П. Введение в теоретическое языкознание. Электронный учебник http://homepages.tversu.ru/~susov

[14] Березин Ф.М. История лингвистических учений. С.24.

meaning to the selection of lexical morphemes (roots) and then syntactic constructions. Phonetic information dissolves into the main body of grammar. They are presented from positions similar in spirit to modern morphonology. Special attention is paid to morphological analysis (without differentiation of inflection and word formation. For the first time in the history of linguistics, the concept of "fictitious" morphemes is postulated. The syntax is constructed primarily as a statement of a set of information about the functions of a noun in a sentence, etc., scattered in different places of work. In grammar contains a number of applications in the form of lists of words combined by grammatical features.

According to A.P. Barannikova [15], Panini for the first time in the history of Indian linguistics provides examples of the comparative method, comparing Sanskrit and Vedic language in the field of phonetics, morphology, word formation and, partly, syntax. But Panini only states the facts of the difference, but does not draw any theoretical conclusions from this.

It should be noted the predominantly theoretical orientation of Panini's work, which anticipates in its scientific level the achievements of modern formal logic, structural and generative linguistics. The method of analyzing a word by its morphological structure is still used today. Subsequent grammatical works in ancient and medieval India are mainly comments or revisions of the canonized grammar of Panini (Vyadi, Katyayana, Patanjali, and in the Middle Ages Chandra, Vararuchi, Hechamandra, Jayaditya, Vamana, Bhattoji Dikshit). Panini's principles served as a basis for describing a number of other Indo-Aryan languages (including

---

[15] Баранников А.П., Баранников П.А. Хиндустани (хинди и урду). Грамматический очерк / Под общей редакцией М.Н.Сотникова. М.: Издательство литературы на иностранных языках, 1956.

Prakrit).

Vararuchi (3-2 centuries BC) was the first in linguistics to put forward the idea that Sanskrit is the source to which all the facts of the Middle Indian languages are traced. In the grammar Illumination of the Prakrit he showed how Prakrit words and forms were formed from Sanskrit words and forms. According to A.P. Barannikov, Vararuchi gives a rudimentary form of comparative grammar; he applies the comparative historical method long before this method became widespread in Europe[16].

Vararuchi analyzes phonetics in great detail, studying the formation of each sound, phonetic changes, in particular assimilation. Moreover, Vararuchi considers phonetic changes in connection with morphological transformations, thus indicating the connection between phonetics and morphology.

Along with classical Sanskrit, Buddhist hybrid Sanskrit arises and spreads, which, along with Pali, was one of the main languages of the Buddhist religion, gradually (from the 6th-5th centuries BC to the end of the 1st millennium AD).) which suppressed the religion of Brahmanism, and then during the 1st millennium AD. dissolved on the territory of India in Hinduism as a renewed Brahmanism. The ancient Indians also turned to questions of the philosophy of language, initially in mythological legends and religious texts, and then in philosophical and grammatical works. They recognized language as the supreme deity ("Rig Veda"). In the Vedic pantheon, the gods were distinguished, in whose jurisdiction linguistic activity is: the goddess of Speech Vach, the goddess of the sacred speech of Bharati, the goddess of the true speech

---

[16] Баранников П. А. Возникновение и развитие обществ по распространению языка хинди в Индии // Письменные памятники и проблемы истории культуры народов Востока. Тезисы докладов II годичной научной сессии ЛО ИНА. Март 1966 года. Ленинград.

of Varuna. In the Hindu pantheon, Speech (Vac) began to be identified with Brahman - the impersonal absolute, the universal spiritual substance. Saraswati was assigned here the function of the goddess of knowledge, wisdom and eloquence. In general, the discussion of the problems of language occupied the representatives of practically all the main systems of Indian religious philosophy: Brahmanism, Jainism, Buddhism, Hinduism. The linguophilosophical ideas of the leading representative of the "grammatical school" of philosophy, Bhartrihari (5-6 centuries AD), set forth in the famous work "Vakyapadiya" ("About a word and a sentence"), were especially widespread in India. He examines the issues of correlation between a sentence and a judgment in a philosophical aspect, defining a sentence as a single indivisible statement that expresses a single indivisible meaning. Bhartrihari, like other grammarians, considers a sentence to be the basic unit of language, since only it is capable of transmitting a thought, and words are artificial, in reality expressing nothing by the constructions of scientists. Therefore, ancient Indian grammarians are not interested in the word, they believe that words serve only to describe linguistic material, but they themselves are not included in this material. Bhartrihari distinguished three aspects of words: writing, phonological structure, and nominative function.

This thinker identified Brahman as the highest reality, which has no beginning or end, with the Word (Word-essence), from which the entire Universe with its infinite variety of objects and phenomena unfolds. The universe is, in his opinion, both that which should be expressed (expressed, signified), and that which should be expressed (expressing, signifying), namely words, speech. Bhartrihari believed that knowledge is intertwined with the word already in a newborn, that from this interweaving all human activity is born and science, art and crafts take their origins. He distinguished three stages that the Word passes through in its development:

"visionary" (here speech is indivisible and eternal), "intermediate" (here the Word is a mental and not perceived by people essence, although it has a temporal sequence, as it were), and "exposed" (where articulated, sounding speech is observed). With an orientation toward the second stage, he formulates the concept of sphota as the central link in the entire "grammatical philosophy". Sphota is for him an indivisible linguistic symbol, a kind of state of consciousness communicated to the listener by means of speech sounds. The utterance is recognized as the main unit from which words are allocated, and not which is composed of words. They are distinguished by sphota of a sentence, sphota of a word, and even sphota of a phoneme (but not a sound).

Phonetics reached an unusually high development in ancient India, which was associated with the need to preserve the purity of the pronunciation of Vedic hymns. Long before the Greeks, the Indians distinguished vowels, consonants, and fricatives. They were familiar with the concept of a phoneme (sphota - see above), which they opposed to the sound of speech. The distinction between the sound of a language (phoneme) and the sound of speech was clearly drawn by Panini. Later, Indian linguists identified 8 varieties of each phoneme.

The description of sounds in the ancient Indian grammatical tradition was made on a physiological basis. Indian linguists described in detail the articulations of sounds, studied the work of the organs of the speech apparatus, and gave a clear classification of sounds according to the method and place of their formation. They first drew attention to the alternation of vowels, having developed the doctrine of the 3 steps of raising vowels. The basis (lowest) stage of alternation is the sounds [i] and [u], the first stage of ascent (guna) is formed by [a + i] = [ai] = [ē], [a + u] = [au] = [ō] , and the second step (vrdhi) [a] + the first step [ai + a] = [āi], [au + a] =

[āu][17].

In morphology, three sections were distinguished :
1. Classification of parts of speech.
2. Formation of words.
3. Changing words[18]:

There were 4 parts of speech: name, verb, preposition and particle. Name is a word denoting an object; verb - a word denoting an action, both taking place at the present moment and already accomplished. Seven cases were singled out: nominative, accusative, instrumental, dative, defensive, genitive, local. At that time they were designated by numbers: 1,2 ... Prepositions were considered as indicative elements of the language, and the particles were divided into comparative, connecting and insignificant. Having turned to the analysis of words, Indo-European linguists distinguished roots, suffixes and endings in words. There were three categories of roots:

a) simple (primary);
b) generators;
c) derivatives.

Also in ancient India dictionaries were compiled. One of the first dictionaries - nighantavas - lists of incomprehensible words used in the Vedas. In the 5th or 6th century. linguist Amara compiled a Sanskrit dictionary, which is still widely used by European Sanskritologists[19].

European scholars became acquainted with Sanskrit and the ideas of ancient Indian grammar in the late 18th and early 19th centuries, which had a significant impact on the

---

[17] Березин Ф.М. История лингвистических учений. С. 132.
[18] Алпатов В.М. История лингвистических учений. С. 168.
[19] Баранников А.П., Баранников П.А. Хиндустани (хинди и урду). Грамматический очерк / Под общей редакцией М.Н.Сотникова. М.: Издательство литературы на иностранных языках, 1956.

formation of comparative historical linguistics and its method. The founders of comparative studies believed that the ancient Indian language is the ancestor of all Indo-European languages, that it possesses the highest perfection that was lost in the development of descendant languages. Frequent appeal to the concepts developed by the ancient Indians and especially the analysis procedures is also observed in modern European and American linguistics. At the same time, it often cannot do without erroneous identification of the concepts put forward by ancient Indian science with similar concepts formulated in the European linguistic tradition, without sufficient consideration of differences in ethnocultural, general scientific and linguistic contexts. It should be noted the ethnocultural specificity of Indian science, which remained indifferent to the history and chronology of the emergence of grammatical treatises and dictionaries, which did not sharply change its guidelines. This explains the difficulty of dividing the history of Indian linguistics into ancient and medieval. The differences lie mainly in the emergence of a developed lexicography at the beginning of the Middle Ages and the formation, alongside the grammatical, of the lexicographic tradition. In the Middle Ages, the same, as in antiquity, can be traced, the motives for the subordination of linguistic studies to the practical needs of the restoration and re-creation of the ritual, now for the religious and yogic purposes of achieving the otherworldly.

Both in antiquity and in the Middle Ages, the language was understood by Indian thinkers as a type of activity (in contrast to European linguists, who saw in the language primarily a nomenclature of names). In the medieval period, attention to the word increased, since the teachings of Buddha Gautama / Shakyamuni (6th century BC) replaced the Vedic-Brahmanist ideology, which placed at the forefront the authority of the Vedic-Brahmanist ideology, in the depths of which the works of Panini and his contemporaries were formed. Buddha refused to bow before the authority of the

Vedas and replaced them with conversations and sermons of the teacher - sutras, which already have a different structure and cover almost the entire semantic-psychic sphere of human life, which put the meaning of the word in the center of attention. Representatives of classical grammar continued to interpret the texts of the Vedas, and semantic linguists began to interpret the teachings of the Buddha. Brahminist-minded Panini and his successors showed interest in the way of expression, in the form of the texts, and the representatives of Buddhist ideology - in the content side of the texts. This was due to the difference in the sets of terms. By the end of the 1st millennium AD. Buddhist religion lost its position in India due to the revival of Brahmanism in the face of Hinduism, which again strengthened the position of the Panini tradition. Both in antiquity and in the Middle Ages, the goals of describing the language, its intended purpose for specific addressees, were taken into account. Indian scholars have developed procedures for establishing and classifying in the analysis of the language of units of a finite set not found in direct experience, refusing to distinguish between their essence and phenomenon. They had an inherent belief that the superhuman author taught people language as a matrix, i.e. a curtailed form of knowledge, developed further by the efforts of people. Many medieval commentators on Panini's work are known who worked in line with his tradition: Patanjali, Katyayana, Buddhist Chandragomin (5th century), Jain Digambar Jainendra (5th century), Jain Shvetambar Shakatayana (8th century). They tried to make Panini's book even more concise[20]. Appears connected by their method with the grammar of Panini and at the same time, as if revising her grammatical treatises "Dhatupatha", "Gana-patha", as well as Chandragomin's "Unadisutra", where the author distinguishes between the morpheme and the word, claiming that the latter has a referent ... On the basis of Panini's model, Prakrit grammars (codified in the literature forms of Middle Indian

---

[20] Березин Ф.М. История лингвистических учений. С.24.

speech) are created: Vararuchi, Hemachandra (13th century). The object of grammatical description is the Pali language, which served southern Buddhism. The authors of works on the Pali language Kacchayana, Sanghanandin, Brahmadatta are guided mainly by Aindra's prepaninian grammar school. The first dictionaries appear. The Buddhist Amarasimha (5th century) laid down the principles of Indian lexicography (grouping words according to meaningful features, an ordered list of synonyms, a list of ambiguous words with interpretations, and the poetic form of dictionary entries for memorization). He was followed by the Hindu Halayudha, the Jain Hemachandra (11-13 centuries). Attention is drawn to the classification of vocabulary in accordance with the classification of world phenomena adopted at that time, the groping of indivisible one-sided units of content (analogous to the figures of content in L. Yelmslev), and the distinction between primary and secondary meanings of words. At the next stage in the development of Buddhist thought, the concept of mantra appears - an utterance as an atom of purposeful linguistic activity, as a unity of figures of expression (phonemes) and figures of content.

Subsequently, (taking into account the yogic use of language), which was the last fundamental achievement of medieval Indian linguistic thought, the understanding of meaning as a quantity determined by an extra-linguistic context, situation, pragmatic factors was formed, which was in good agreement with the general understanding of language as a mode of activity.

In modern India, its own linguistic tradition is still alive, although Indian scholars and especially their Western colleagues are striving to apply the methods of comparative historical, areal, structural, generative linguistics developed in the Western tradition to the study of Sanskrit and other Indo-Aryan languages.

University of Bartın
Republic of Turkey

9. Typological Analyzes of Grammatical Categories of Numbers and Cases in Hindi and Uzbek

Dr. Rahmatjonova Kamola Abdumutal Qizi

Abstract

Comparing the two languages, a new stage emerges not only in Hindi and Uzbek linguistics, but also in world linguistics. Becouse is easier to learn and teach the language. The present study considers of the grammatical representation of the category of number of two genetically and typological different languages Hindi and Uzbek. There are authentic material for illustration-studied items taken from modern fictions of the Hindi and Uzbek authors. Affinities and differences in the category of number of the two languages are considers in structural, semantics and function.

We know Hindi as the official language of India. About 400 million people in the world speak Hindi and 120 million have Hindi as their second language. It has been strongly influenced by Sanskrit; a lot of words in Hindi come from there. There are numerous other facts about Hindi that most of you wouldn't know.

The sentence structure in Hindi differs widely from English. In Hindi verbs and auxiliary verbs always go to the end of the sentence. For instance, the sentence, आप कैसे हैं in Hindi actually translates to '*How are you?*' in English; but if the word to word translation is considered, the sentence becomes 'You how are'. Similarly, मैं अच्छा हूँ, becomes *I fine am* instead of *I am fine*. However, although genetically and morphologically quite different, the structure of sentence in Hindi is similar to that in Uzbek. For example, मैं अध्यापक हूँ । in Hindi; *Men o 'qituvchiman (I am a teacher)*in Uzbek.

The aim of the topic is to make a contrastive - typological analysis of the grammatical categories number and case of noun in the Hindi and Uzbek languages.

Grammatical category – the system of form, which have unique meaning. Usually grammatical category has two types: morphological and syntactic grammatical category.

Such kind of a method does not exist in many languages. Despite some classical Indo-Aryan languages, such as Latin, Sanskrit and etc., in Indian language category of case is not syntax, but morphological class.[3]

Morphologic grammatical category – the system of two and more meanings and forms of these meanings, which can be, composed one with another. For example, the categories of tense of verb and nouns.[3]

Syntax grammatical category – form that serve to show the syntax relation by uniting the word by their meanings. For example, the category of case.[3]

In the grammatical system of all languages, the category of case takes very important place. The relation of subject with other words depends on the category of case. This category "is a system of forms that shows the relation and addiction of subject to other subject or verb".[3]

The category of case shows the feature of the language. This feature helps to indicate the meaning of the word and to explore the language itself if one considers carefully it shows the importance of the topic.

The object of the topic is number and case grammatical categories of the noun used in the authentic texts of Hindi and Uzbek languages.

The scientific novelty of the topic: the grammatical categories of number and case of the noun Hindi and Uzbek languages were studied for the first time within the contrastive - typological aspects, as a result, general and specify features of selected languages was determined linguistic facts of converging, relatively converging and divergent languages of

Hindi and Uzbek is founded;

In both languages, the commonality of the number grammatical category in terms of meaning and functions determined based on authentic materials;

The similarities and differences between the two comparable languages were analyzed on the example of the agreement category, and the actual results of the analyzes are reflected in the tables.

This topic is one of the first scientific researches in Uzbekistan, devoted to the comparative typological study of the Hindi and Uzbek languages, belonging to two different families, the Indo-Aryan language group of the Indo-European language family and the Turkic language group of the Altaic language family respectively.

At present, one of the most pressing issues in the study of different languages in the partial realm of world linguistics is the comparative study of two languages in a typological way. In addition, the present study focuses on foreign language problems - learning and comprehending - especially for the purpose of comparison of the different grammatical genres of the native language - Uzbek - remains an important task.

The purpose of the present study is to analyze the grammatical categories of nouns in Hindi and Uzbek languages based on a typological approach.

Based on above, grammatical categories are divided into types such as morphological and syntactic categories. A grammatical category in any language can be included in a group of grammatical categories only based on the internal nature of the language. A grammatical category that is morphologically considered in one language (e.g., a grammatical category specific to a noun in Uzbek) may be a syntactic category in another language.

In addition, it was found that in the Hindi language, noun-specific numbers and conjunctions fall into the morphological-syntactic grammatical categories. Moreover, in this language, the number is related to morphological and syntactic grammatical categories. For example,

No.	Grammatical categories of Noun	Hindi	Uzbek
1.	Gender	morphological grammatical category	-
2.	Number	syntactic grammatical category	morphological grammatical category
3.	Case	syntactic grammatical category	syntactic grammatical category
4.	Possessive category	-	syntactic grammatical category
5.	Definiteness	-	-

Therefore, there are three grammatical categories (gender, number and case) of Noun in Hindi[4] and there are three grammatical categories (possessive, number and case) of Noun in Uzbek[1].

The peculiarity of the grammatical category of numbers in the Hindi and Uzbek languages is the phenomenon of mutual isomorphism. In these languages, the singular form of nouns is equal to the morpheme Ø, that is, no pointer is involved to express the meaning of the singular.

In the following analyzes, partial and complete isomorphism of the grammatical category of numbers in the selected languages were observed in all three groups. In both languages, plural affixes (in Hindi -याँ, -एँ, -ए, while in Uzbek –lar (-s), a) do not occur because of the semantic nature of the base to which it is added. For example,

Indian Culture In Central Asia

In Hindi :

1. भोला ने आँखें कुछ ऐसी फेरीं कि उसे अब रघ्घू में सब बुराइयाँ ही बुराइयाँ नज़र आती ।[6]

2. मेरे पुराने दोस्त हैं ।

3. नवीन जी की *आँखें* सजल हो गई ।[7]

In Uzbek :

1. U ham osmonga – xira *yulduzlarga* qaradi. (He also looked at the sky – the opaque *stars*.)[8]

2. Martning oxirgi *kunlari* edi. (It was the last *days* of March)

3. Osmonda suzib yurgan bulut *parchalari* oftobni bir zumda yuz kuyga solayapti.[8] (*Pieces* of clouds floating in the sky instantly put the sun in a different state).

In addition, it is expressed with numeral words of number grammatical category of Noun in these languages.

In Hindi :

1. पन्ना के *चार* बच्चे थे *तीन* बेटे और *एक* बेटी ।[7]

2. *छः महीने* बाद वह कलकत्ता से घर आया ।[6]

3. *एक महीना* गुज़र गया।

In Uzbek :

1. *Bir kun* o'tdi, *uch kun* o'tdi, *o'n kun* o'tdi, na Salimjon, na qudalar , hech kim yo'lamadi.[8] (*One day* passed, *three days* passed, *ten days* passed neither Salimjon, nor the relatives, nor anyone came)

2. *Bir qop somon, o'n o'n beshta xoda, bir arava qamish* – uy, ho'kiz topish uchun necha zamonlar qozonni suvga tashlab qo'yish kerak bo'ladi.[8] (*A pair of straw, fifteen stalks, a card reed* – to find a house and bull will need put only water in the pot for some time).

3. *Uch-to'rt kishi* bo'lib asta kirsak, hovlining o'rtasida katta gulhan, hotini Malohatxon uning atrofida dodlab yuribdi.[8] (When we slowly entered in *groups of three or four*, there was a big fire in the middle of the yard, and his wife Malohatkhan was screaming around him.)

It may be noticed that in case of number + noun, there are different rules even in one language family. For example, in Hindi, we see if the number-qualifying noun is more than one, noun will be also plural. Like चार बच्चे char bachche, but in Persian, also from Indo-Aryan family of Indo-European family, qualifying noun will remain singular like Uzbek.

Although the types of case in Hindi and Uzbek differ in number (8 in Hindi and 6 in Uzbek), some agreements are found to be similar in meaning. In particular, words that come in the forms of subject, object (tushum), adverb of place and time, and exit are in the phenomenon of isomorphism due to their multifunctional nature. Although agglutinative traits predominate in one of the selected languages analytically, it has been observed that the functional structure of the consonant forms in the sentence is in most cases the same. For example,

No.	कारक	विभक्ति	In Uzbek
1.	कर्ता	Ø, ने	Ø
2.	करण	को	-ni
3.	कर्म	से, के द्वारा	bilan, yordamida
4.	सम्प्रदान	के लिए, को	uchun, -ga, -ka, -qa
5.	अपादान	से	-dan
6.	सम्बन्ध	का, के, की,	-ning
7.	अधिकरण	में, पर	-da
8.	संबोधन	हे, अरे	hoy, iya

In Hindi :

1. *मुलिया का* जीवन अंधकारमय हो गया ।[6]

2. मे रे लिए दुनिया में कोई देवता नहीं कोई गुरु नहीं कोई हाकिम नहीं।[6]

3. उसके *मुख* पर उल्लास था और *आँखों में* गर्व।[6]

In Uzbek :

1. *Qozonning zangi* chiqib qoraygan go'jaga qatiq ham rang kirgizolmadi.[8] (Milk couldn't add white color to the food in the *blackened dish*).
2. Uning *yuzida* xiralik va *ko'zlarida* g'urur bor edi. (There was sadness *on his face* and pride *in his eyes*).

In general, linguistics, the theoretical and practical study of a particular language has a number of problems, such as the systemic structure of language, its close connection with historical processes, the movement of language and speech units as a means of communication, which is one of the most pressing problems of both theoretical and practical linguistics.

It is found out only few important cases of both the said languages is analyzed though both have many more imminent as well as complex problems to be analyzed which may be taken up by the present researcher in future. The comparative study of the discussed cases and referred have roots in historical linguistics in the development of both the languages. The outcome of the present comparative study may bring forth the close affinity in both the languages despite the fact both belong to different language families. A number of pressing issues in the field of Hindi will inevitably be studied in a comparative aspect in future research. In brief, the migration and assimilation process expanded the word corpus and absorbed with the convenient changes syntactically.

References:

1. Abdurahmonov G'. O'zbek tili grammatikasi.–T.: O' qituvchi, 1996.
2. Shomatov O.N. Hindiy tili me'yoriy grammatikasi. 1-qism. – T.: Toshkent davlat sharqshunoslik instituti, 2010. – B. 112.

3. Hojiyev A. Tilshunoslik terminlarining izohli lug'ati. –T.: "O'zbekiston milliy ensiklopediyasi" davlat ilmiy nashriyoti, 2002.
4. Bhola:na:th Tiva:ri: – Hindi: bha:sha: – Ila:ha:ba:d, 1972. – P. 709.
5. Va:sudevanandan Prasa:d – A:dhunik hindi: vya:karaN oar rachna: – Bha:rti: bhavan, PaTna:, 2003. – P.∘406.

Examples for illustration are taken from:

6. Premchand – Ma:nasrovar – 1, Dilli: – P. 280.
7. Premchand – Ma:nasrovar – 2, Dilli:– P. 304.
8. Abdulla Qahhor. Dahshat. – T.: Adabiyot uchqunlari, 2018. – B. 109.
9. O'tkir Xoshimov. Ikki eshik orasi. – T.: G'. G'ilom nomidagi adabiyot va san'at nashriyoti – B. 109.

Tashkent State University of Oriental Studies, Tashkent, Uzbekistan

10. The Importance of Nyaya's Logical Methodology in the Modern Education System

Madalimov Timur

Abstract

In the second millennium BC, civilization was formed in ancient India, and the peoples living around the Ganges oasis began to switch to agriculture. From that time onwards, the ideological processes in Indian society were gradually changing. These changes are mainly observed in the fields of mathematics, logic, medicine and astronomy. Unlike mathema-tics, the science of logic was formed in India and was originally formed not as a science as a whole, but as an integral part of Indian philosophy. Therefore, Indian logic was formed in all philosophical schools. In particular, the logic of Nyaya differs from other philosophical schools

Keywords : logic, intuition, conclusion, analogy, doubt, reasoning

Introduction.

An important aspect to understand the general features of modern Indian philosophy is the relationship between philosophy and daily consciousness in India [13]. Nyaya is a science of logic and studies the nature of knowledge and the only reliable methodology for the philosophical examination of objects of knowledge. It is a tool for gaining accurate knowledge about oneself and determining the purpose of life. The study of Nyaya allows us to distinguish truth from falsehood, and ensures that false teachings and beliefs are prevented until knowledge reaches the stage of understanding and enlightenment. Today, as it was centuries ago, we are confronted by many sages with many doctrines, different social and political ideologies. It is doubtful whether every new teaching and teacher's conflicting views and ideologies are the right way to go. The seeker faces the same problem in trying to distinguish truth from falsehood. The teachings of the Nyaya system are aimed at creating a logical basis for learning and knowing the truth. Nyaya engages in critical inquiry. He studies all the doctrines - traditional and modern, and resolutely fights against all opposition and irrational beliefs. Wherever constructive thinking is focused on acquiring real understanding, logic is needed. This desire to seek truth is born in human nature, and logic allows us to practice constructive rational thinking. The goal of logic is to understand Self by providing the means to learn, listen, reflect, and judge. This ends with the elimination of doubts and leads to mature wisdom or affirmation of what is accepted according to tradition.

Metod and Material.

This is a qualitative research using the content, comparative-historical, characteristic analysis approach. About 10 articles on Nyaya logic have been used to explain its importance in modern education. In addition, the researcher analyzed and compared scientific papers on the relevance of the education system.

Research And Results :

A. Origin of Nyaya School

History Of The Development Of Logic In India Is Divided Into Four Periods:

1. The Logic Of The First Buddha Covers The VI-V Centuries BC;
2. The Logic Of Nyaya And Vaisheshika - III-II Centuries BC
3. Dharma And Dharmakirti School - VI-VIII Centuries AD
4. The Fourth Period Covers The VIII-XVII Centuries

Early Buddhist logic was largely devoted to philosophical epistemology, in which thinking was explained mainly through emotional cognition. The logic of Nyaya and Vaisheshika, on the other hand, took a radical turn in Indian logic, leading to the classical period of Indian thought. In ancient Indian philosophical schools, the path to the right knowledge was shown in different ways. For example:

In the philosophical school of Charvaka Lokayata- through intuition (pratyaksha);

mimansa-through verbal testimony (shabda);

In the schools of Vaisheshika and Buddhism- through intuition and conclusion (anumana);

Sankhya-intuition, conclusion, throughverbal testimony;

Nyaya-through intuition, conclusion, oral testimony, comparison;

Prabhakara- through intuition, conclusion, comparison, oral testimony, conjecture;

Bhakti and Vedanta-through intuition, conclusion, comparison, oral testimony, conjecture, non-existence;

Knowledge is classified by probabilities, intuition, inference, comparison, verbal testimony, conjecture, and non-existence.

The peculiarity of the indian school of philosophy is that its syllogisms differ from the classical logic of ancient greece. In the mimansa school, it is said that the correctness of knowledge is achieved through oral testimony (shabda). Oral testimony is the exemplary testimony of a trustee (apta), that is, one who has true knowledge and is the possessor of truth. According to mimansa, a trustworthy person should have the following qualities:

a. Free from superstitions and prejudices;

b. Lack of interest in information results;

c. Recognized as trustworthy by other authorities;

The opinion of the trustee is not discussed, only the need to have the above qualities when choosing him. But subjectivity is not allowed in the selection.

For example, the "scientists" who provide "evidence" to a tobacco company that tobacco is not harmful to health are not trustworthy people because they are funded by a tobacco company and their results have a positive impact on a proven product.

The main focus of Phabkara's philosophical teachings is on probability in knowing. Probability (sambhava)-the existence of something means the existence of its companion. For example, the conclusion that "if there is no (black) cloud, there is no rain" leads to the probable conclusion, "if there is a black cloud, there is rain." in the bhakti and vedanta schools, the specificity of knowledge is explained by the method of non-existence. Absence is the existence of one of the two opposites, the absence of the other. This is determined by the second law of formal logic, the law of Nazism: "two opposing opinions expressed at the same time cannot be true at the same time." for example, the absence of the sun indicates the presence of stars. It is not true that there are two opposing views (the sun and the stars) at the same time. The most optimized form of logic in ancient india is given in the nyaya school of philosophy. The teachings of the nyaya system are aimed at creating a logical basis for learning and knowing the truth. Nyaya engages in critical inquiry. He studies all beliefs - traditional and modern and fights sharply against all superstitions, based and irrational beliefs. Wherever constructive thinking is focused on acquiring real understanding, logic is needed. This desire to seek truth is born in human nature, and logic allows us to practice constructive rational thinking. The goal of logic is to understand oneself by providing means of learning, listening, reflecting, and judging. This ends with the elimination of doubts and leads to mature wisdom or affirmation of what is accepted according to tradition.

B. **Main purpose of Nyaya methodology**

The logical way to determine the truth in nyaya is by applying 16 categories of logic called padarthas or Themes.

1. Means Of Correct Knowledge
2. The Object Of Correct Knowledge

3. Doubt
4. Reason
5. Imagination
6. Demonstrate The Truth
7. Syllogism
8. Reason And Confidence
9. Discussion
10. Mentality
11. Dispute
12. Objection
13. Bad Thoughts
14. Unfair Reasons
15. Useless Connector
16. Identifier

According to Nyaya, we learn information in four ways:

1. Empirical knowledge, experience - pratyaksha
2. Discursive thinking, conclusion ---- anumāna
3. Analogy - upamana
4. Oral testimony of a reliable source - shabda

There Are 4 Types Of Suspicion

1. Perception of common features or lack of perception of difference.

   For example, in the dark, a wire can be confused with a man or a rope with a snake.
2. Conflicting testimonies of witnesses or differences of opinion of two or more persons on one or another subject
3. False feelings

   Hearing the noise of the leaves of the bush, looking with suspicion that there may be an animal or a human
4. Insensitivity error

   There are 5 logical steps in a syllogism to establish correct knowledge:

1. A guess (problem) is a statement of something that needs to be proven
2. Cause is the evidence used to prove this hypothesis

3. An example is a generally accepted example of something similar
4. Narration is a comparison.
5. Conclusion- shows that the previous four stages of sylogism correspond to the same idea.
1. Presumption- john is dead
2. Cause-because he is human
3. Example - all people die just like socrates napoleon and king henry
4. Apply- john is also human
5. Conclusion - he is dead

The conclusion consists of three parts
1) large foundation (sadhya)
2) small base (paksha)
3) medium base (hetu)

The researchers then introduced five additional components : however, they do not actually form any part of the main argument, but they can be used to supplement the argument during opposition. In other words, they can be used to argue against or harass an opponent in a debate.

They are as follows :
1. Check - check the thesis
For example, is there a fire all over this hill, or is there just a fire somewhere?
2. subha (samsaya) - to question the cause of the thesis:
For example, what you think of as smoke may simply be dust.
1. Ability - to determine the correctness of the use of this example to make the conclusion true
For example, where there is a fire, is there smoke all the time? Doesn't gas emit smoke?
2. Objective - to identify an unattended, neglected object
3. The removal of all doubts (saya-vyudas) is to make sure that the antithesis is not correct.
For example, there is no doubt that where there is smoke,

there is fire.

The task of the thesis is to establish the relationship of the essence with the attribute to be displayed.

The function of cause is to indicate that the attribute to be displayed is the cause; because it provides the means by which things are proven. He can accomplish his goal by approving or rejecting the sample

The function of the sample is to show that these two properties are on the same substrate - the object to be represented and the means of representation. It consists of simple examples and includes the reasons given

The example can be positive or negative. A negative example is a familiar example that does not have a property to be set up and that the absence of this feature is absolutely rejected for a given reason. Thus, it creates a similarity or difference as a means of demonstrating what needs to be proven, and allows it to be followed by an additional example through similarity.

C. Difference between Nyaya logic with other

When we talk about nyaya logic, there are some differences between this logic and the ancient greek logic. The science of logic has had its place in the system of sciences since ancient times. Although aristotle is considered the founder of the science of logic, this science was formed long before that - in the vi century bc in ancient india. The formation of the science of logic as a separate science is associated with the name of aristotle (384-322 bc). He was the first to define the scope of issues in which logic is studied. Aristotle describes logic as a science that "identifies unknown knowledge from known knowledge," "separates true thought from erroneous thought." he emphasizes that the task of logic is to determine the true thought, the truth. In aristotle's doctrine of logic, reasoning takes the lead. He analyzes perception and reasoning, which are forms of thinking, as components of inference. Consideration is the result of mental analysis and can be true or false. Reflection refers to whether or not something is relevant to something. Any statement will not be considered. Only firm, descriptive ideas are considered. The thinker shows that the structure of reasoning has a logic, a logical cut, and a logical link: not s - p or s - p. It distinguishes between affirmative and negative judgment in content, and general judgment, partial judgment, and vague judgment in scope. Aristotle analyzed simple, necessary, and possible types of considerations in terms of modality.

Aristotle analyzes concepts as components of reasoning, paying particular attention to the relationship between general and individual concepts.

Aristotle classifies categories (concepts) as follows: 1) essence; 2) quantity; 3) quality; 4) attitude; 5) place 6) time; 7) status; 8) possession; 9) movement; 10) exposure. He developed the theoretical basis for deductive, that is, syllogistic, conclusions, explaining the derivation of new considerations from existing considerations when referring to syllogism. The axiom of syllogism, general and special rules, figures, modes of silligism, entimema, epixeremia, polysyllogism, sorit are described in detail in the work "first analytics". He knew figure i was perfect. Aristotle did not consider the issue of direct inference separately.

In his teaching, drawing conclusions is considered a form of proof. He analyzed the scientific (apodectic), dialectical, rhetorical, sophistic methods of proof, developed eristics - the rules of successful debate, and perestroika - argued that aimless reasoning is harmful. He considered inductive proof to be weaker than deduction. He described the analogy (paradigm) as the inference from partiality to partiality. Aristotle's doctrine of logic had a great influence on the further development of the science of logic. The transition to a new stage in the development of the science of logic in the post-aristotle period is associated with the name of the representatives of the stoic school.

A. Comparision Central Asian methodology and Nyaya

The methodology of logic in central asia has its own characteristics. It is based on the religion and teachings of islam. It is called theology, and islamic teachings are described. In addition, the sciences of jurisprudence and hadith developed during this period. The hadith then transmits its relation to the level of sahih, hasan, weak or gharib (strange). Then he would comment on the hadith narrators, the chain of transmission, and the evidences of the hadith. As an example of the aforementioned opinion, we read in detail in the hadith of abu isa al-tirmidhi in —al-jami` as-sahih in the chapter —purification‖ that —one who is settled on a journey and in one place is subjected to it [12].

in particular, the great scholar who grew up in central asia entered the islamic world with the hadiths of the hadith scholar imam al-bukhari. In his works, farobi gave extensive information about the science of logic, its subject, structure, tasks, stages and forms of the thought process, logical rules, methods and practices. Including. When it comes to the etymology of the subject and concept of the science of logic, farobi refers to the ancient greek thinkers. According to him, the greeks used logic in three senses: as a human point of view that expresses thought through language: as a word that guides objects to be conquered by the human intellect; understood as an inner spiritual force endowed with man to know the world. Complementing these definitions, farobi defines logic as "the science that guides and improves the human intellect according to certain rules." to further clarify this definition, in farobi's works, logic is considered to be the science of the head, the science, and even the art, which studies the laws of reason as a science. Only the laws of reasoning can reveal the truth to us. According to farobi, without them, we will not know when our opinion is true, when it is false, or when we have made a mistake. Furthermore, we cannot find the contradictions that underlie the truth and their solutions. In farobi's works, forms of thinking such as understanding, judgment, and inference are explained in a very comprehensive and detailed way. Especially. The syllogism, its origins, figures and modules have been studied extensively. According to farobi, concept is a category of universal nature that provides knowledge about things that are perceived emotionally. In addition, in the system of logic of farobi there is a wide range of methods and practices of concept formation, as well as the relationship between them. In his logic, farobi pays great attention to the doctrine of syllogisms. A syllogism is defined as the specificity of conclusions that are logically derived from two or more interconnected bases. Farobi singles out five types of syllogistic art, such as philosophy, dialectics, sophistry, rhetoric, and poetics. When it comes to the structure of a syllogism, it can be divided into large base, small base, and result. The syllogism also divides the term into three terms: large, small, and medium, and defines each separately. Concerning the logic of farobi, we can say that his work was able to introduce the logic of aristotle to the general scientific community, as well as to create a new trend in history called the "arab school of logic."

Iv. Conclusion :

The logic of nyaya is still relevant today and applies to modern fields of education. In this way we achieve:

First, logical thinking teaches students to argue every sentence

Second, nyaya logic helps to dispel dogma in students

Third, through the above logic, new innovations emerge in students.

References

1. K.k.mittal. Materialism in indian thouyht new dehli, 1974, p.10
2. Aurobindo sri. Birth centenary library, vol.16, pondichery, 1972, p.232.

3. Aurobindo sri. The future evolution of man, the divinasefeupron earth. Madras – london, 1974, p.182.
4. Gandi m. My religion. Ahmedabad. 1955. P.4.
5. Gandim.k. Truth is god. Ahmedabad, 1957, p.11.
6. Gandi. M.k. messenger of god. Yong india 1919-1922. Madras, 1922, p. 1167.
7. Tendulkar d.g. mahatma, sife of mohandas karamchand gandi 9n 8.
8. Radkhakrishnan s. Occasional speeches and writings, series 3, july 1959/ may 1962, delhi, 1963, p. 258-259.
9. Lal b/k/ contemporary indian philosophy. Delhi roranasi – patna, 1978, p. Xix.
10. Radhakrishnan s. East and west. Some reflections. London, 1955, p.115, 120.
11. The philosophy of sarvepalli radhakrishnan, p.80.
12. Madalimov, t., karimov, n., is'haqov, m., sulaymonov, j., & alimova, r. (2019). Contribution of abu isa tirmidhi to the science of hadith. *International journal of innovative technology and exploring engineering (ijitee, 9*(1), 593-599.
13. Madalimov, t., mullajonov, i., pulatov, sh., qodirov, m., & valiyev, l. (2020). Some characteristics of modern indian philosophy. *International journal of multi- disciplinary research and publications, 2* (11), 47-49.
14. Madalimov, t. A. (2019) "problems of knowing the nyaya philosophy school in ancient india," central asian problems of modern science and education: vol. 4 :iss. 2
15. Мадалимов, т. А. (2020). Main features of the logic of the ancient east. *Science and education, 1* (4), 236-241

Teacher,
Chirchik state pedagogical Institute of Tashkent region,
Uzbekistan

11. Morphological Analysis of Turkic Words in The Work of "Ain-I-Akbari"

Salimbekov Nodirbek Ulug' Bekovich

The historic cultural exchange between Central Asian and the Indians is traced back to the ancient times. Although geographically apart, the people of these regions with different cultures, ethnic backgrounds and languages have been affecting and influencing each other. Language families tend to share distinctive characteristics, like how they construct words (morphology) and sentences (syntax). A language family will also have a core of shared word roots, though sometimes these roots can be hard to recognize as people's pronunciation changes over time. In addition, languages frequently borrow new vocabulary from other languages. History is the witness to the interactions between Turkic and Indian societies and these intermingling can be seen in various aspects such as art, architecture, literature, cuisine, costume and the language etc.

The Baburids, who dominated the history of India for the better part of two centuries and who lingered on with reduced power for another century and half, were far more successful as a ruling family than any of the dynasties of the Delhi Sultanate.

In this article, we analyzed the Turkic words which we found in the work of 'Ain-i-Akbari' in 3 ways: semantic, typological and analysis of Turkic suffixes '-chi'.

Ain-i-Akbari the third volume of the Akbarnamah, written by Abul Fazl, the court historian of Emperor Akbar (1556-1605). While Akbarnamah is a book of history, Ain-i-Akbari embodies Ains or rules and regulations framed and put into effect for proper administration by Akbar. It is regarded as an administrative manual and is like a modern gazetteer.

Though a part of the Akbarnamah, Ain-i-Akbari is itself a voluminous work. The regulations embodied in the Ain-i-

Akbari provide information about Akbar's government, and several departments, its different ranks etc. Histories produced in India under Muslim rule were all chronicles giving accounts of wars, conquests, and dynastic changes, mostly in chronological order.

The Ain-i-Akbari is divided into five books. The first book called manzil-abadi deals with the imperial household and its maintenance, and the second called sipah-abadi, with the servants of the emperor, military and civil services. The third deals with imperial administration, containing regulations for the judiciary and the executive. The fourth contains information on Hindu philosophy, science, social customs and literature. The fifth contains sayings of Akbar, along with an account of the ancestry and biography of the author.

Since the ancient time of the language, till the end of the Baburid dynasty, that is until the middle of the XIX century, the interaction between the Turkic peoples and the Indian people in various spheres continued, and as a result, the Turkic language influenced the language of the Indians. After the invasion of the Turkic peoples from Central Asia to India, Hindi words were used in the works created in the Persian language. This means that representatives of the ruling circle began to use any form of Indian [or Panjabi] language[1]. According to Chatterdji, Persian words have changed their meaning in India. Muhammad Abdul Ghani in his work 'The Persian language and the history of literature in the palace of the Mughals', made a list of Hindi words, and Persian words which have slightly changed the meaning[2].

Even if the work 'Ain-i-Akbari' is written in Persian, there are several Turkic words are used. We have identified 22 Turkic words. 'Humayunnamah' is also written in India, in Persian language, like 'Ain-i-Akbari'. It tells us two things; 'Humayunama' was written more than half a century after the death of Babur in the period of its dissolution, although Gulbadan himself and the people of the palace understood Turkic and spoke, but the position of this language was not the same as before. Secondly, according to tradition, works were written in Persian. Because of these reasons, the 'Humayunama' is written in Persian[3].

When analyzing the Turkic words identified in the work of 'Ain i Akbari' in terms of semantics the following were identified and some of them are giving as a sample: *'qushbegi'* an expert of hunting animals of the king, *'qurbegi'* person responsible for the military system, *'beg'* ruler, *'yulma'* name of meal, *'yuzbashi'* centurion, *'uymaq'* an alliance of sibling families in various fields resulting from the disintegration of the ancient descendants of the Mongol and Turkic peoples, *'tamgha'* medal, *'qarawal'* guard, *'navruz'* Nawruz festival, *'bitakchi'* palace writer, *'banduqchi'* a person who watches over weapons.

When we studied work of some scientists who worked on this field, we will have a clearer picture. Especially, Kholmonova analyzes semantically the Turkic words in the 'Boburnama', the verb 'Beg' is actively used in the ancient Turkic language, and she says that, it means the ruler, the geniuses and introduces into the lexemes that express the concept of social closeness to the person[4]. The word 'aymok' is included in the group of words related to the relative generation but it has following meanings also: 1. people 2. country 3. class, glad, tribe[5].

It is also worth noting that the spelling of the Turkic words quoted in 'Ain i Akbari' cannot always be called correct. we can conclude that most of words were phonetically changed over time.

The Turkic words identified in the work of 'Ain-i-Akbari' are an expression from the words associated mainly with the life of palace. The reason for the fact that these words are related to the life of the palace is associated with the peculiarity of the work 'Ain-i-Akbari', that is, in the work more connected with the activities of the king, with the palace officials, with the commanders, with tax collection.

Indian Culture In Central Asia

The words identified were analyzed thematically into the following groups:

Root words: *'akhtachi'* horseman, *'ataliq'* A private tutor, an instructor, *'beg'* A title affixed to the names of Mogals, corresponding with lord, master, *'bitakchi'* palace writer, *'budagh'* a piece of generation tree, *'kushka'* abrasion, *'mankli'* a man with a mole, *'nawruz'* Nawruz festival, *'qarawal'* guard, gamekeeper, *'sayurghal'* to make a gift, *'tamgha'* The royal insignia, seal, diploma, *'turan'* Turan (name of place), *'tuzuk'* State; dignity, regulation, ordinance, *'uymaq'* an alliance of sibling families in various fields resulting from the disintegration of the ancient descendants of the Mongol and Turkic peoples, *'yulma'* Yulma name of dish, *'yuzbashi'* centurion

Derivative words: *'banduqchi'* gunman, gunsmith, *'parwanchi'* deputy minister, executive of the decree

Hybrid words: *'akhta begi'* horseman of the king, *'bar begi'* chief servant of the khan's palace, *'qush begi'* an expert of hunting animals of the king, *'qurbegi'* person responsible for the military system

These words are adopted to the language of the population and are distinguished by the fact that they are involved in the formation of compound words and terms with words in the local language. It should also be noted that at the beginning of the Middle Ages, the languages like Arabic, Persian, Turkic was not used as a source for Indian languages, it is an important concept that the source was the new Persian language of Eastern Iran which was used by the rulers who ruled in India[3].

The state language was a Persian, but the native language of the rulers of that time was Turkic. But Babur also used Indian words, although he wrote 'Baburnama' in Turkic. A. Ibrahimov is giving the number of Hindi words in Baburnama[4].

Scientists have expressed different opinions on the issue of how many Turkic words are in the Indian language. According to S.K Chatterji, Turkic words in the Indian language are less than a hundred. Fellon gives 70 Turkic words in his dictionary but in Platts dictionary contains about 80 Turkic words. But Bhaulanath Tiwari says that the number of Turkic words in the Indian language is not less than one twenty five.

In this place, it should also be noted that BhaulanathTiwari considering that most of Turkic words in Hindi are related to the military sphere. Like: *'chaqmaqi'* flintstone gun, *'top'* gun, *'haraval'* vanguard, *'topchii'* gunner, *'qaraaval'* guard, *'chaqmaq'* flintstone, *'tamga'* medal, *'elchi'* ambassador, etc.

The classification of words with '-chi' suffix

Those 22 words which collected from the book, 4 of them are formed with suffix '-chi'. It is noteworthy that this suffix was added mainly to words borrowed from Arabic, and later to words in Persian and Turkic, and even there were cases of word formation with this suffix in Hindi.

Here are giving sample of words: *'bitakchi'* palace writer; *'parwanchi'* deputy minister, executive of the decree; *'bandukchi'* gunman, gunsmith; *'akhtachi'* horseman

This indicates that the suffix '-chi' has been completely assimilated into Hindi. This suffix is also used in modern Hindi as a word-forming suffix.

An analysis of the Turkic words found in the work shows that although the Turkic words are rarely used in the work 'Ain-i-Akbari', they have a place in important and active sectors of the palace.

Akbar's close friend, scientist, poet Abdulfazl's way of life and the works he created, first of all 'Akbarnamah' and 'Ain-i-Akbari' were written on the basis of reliable sources in particular, in the history of India, economy, politics, religion etc., it is of incomparable importance in the study of the Baburids Kingdom.

It can be said that although Turkic words are rare in Hindi, they are widely used in colloquial and literary language. In general, the two languages chosen belong to different language groups in terms of genealogy and typology. In this respect, the distinctive features between languages are obvious, such distinctive features can be seen in the phonetics and syntax of languages. At the same time, there are many linguistic facts that bring them closer together. This has been considered in the example of the Turkic languages in Hindi. Most of the Turkic words studied are mainly related to at that time (XV-XVII century) military field. One of the main reasons for this may be related to the historical events of the period when Turkic languages entered the Indian region.

In conclusion we can say, these words which we found from the work, some of them, they do not stand aside and are actively used in modern Hindi too. By their function and meaning they are used in everyday life.

References
1. Chatterdji S.K. 'Vvedenie v indo-ariyskoe yazikoznanie', Moskva, 1977, p.193.
2. Abdul Rashid 'Farsi mein hindi alfaz', Delhi, Maktebe Rabita, 1996
3. Ibrahimov A. 'Humayunnoma leksikasi hussida (about the lexicon of Humayunnama)', Tashkent, 2010
4. Z. Kholmonova 'Boburnoma leksikasi (the lexicon of Baburnama)' Tashkent, 2007, 78-pages
5. Sevortyan E. V. 'Etimologicheskiy slovar tyurkskixyazikov (Etymological dictionary of the Turkic languages)' Moscow, 1974 p.110

Researcher,
Tashkent State University of Oriental Studies,
Tashkent, Uzbekistan

12. India and Central Asia : Cooperation for Regional Security and Stability

Dr. Tuychiyeva Rano Almamatovna

Annotation

This article describes the history of India's cooperation with the countries of Central Asia, the main factors that led to its development or decline, as well as the current state of bilateral relations. The study focuses on data and analysis of areas of security and stability in interregional relations.

Keywords : India, Central Asia, regional security, stability, defense system, bilateral and multilateral relations, border issues, Afghan problem and etc.

Introduction

The countries of the region are pursuing an active foreign policy to achieve peace and sustainable development in Central Asia. Making Central Asia a zone of peace and good neighborliness has also been identified as a priority of Uzbekistan's foreign policy. At a time when today's sources of global threat are increasing, ensuring security in Central Asia has become one of the most important tasks facing the countries of the region. Areas of trade and economic, transport and transit-logistics, security and stability, completion of issues related to state borders, fair use of water resources, strengthening cultural and humanitarian ties, friendship and good neighborly relations between nations are being developed between the two countries.

The Action Strategy for the five priority areas of development of the Republic of Uzbekistan for 2017-2021, adopted by the President of the Republic of Uzbekistan, states that the formation of security, stability and good neighborliness around Uzbekistan is a priority of our foreign policy in the near and medium term. and increased efficiency. In recent years, we have witnessed the growing geopolitical and geostrategic importance of the Central Asian region, its significant mineral and raw material resources, and the conflict of strategic interests of the world's major powers in the region.

Territorial security problems in the Central Asian subregion, as well as around the world, are characterized by terrorism, extremism, proliferation of weapons of mass destruction, drug trafficking, environmental degradation, global warming, deforestation, pandemic outbreaks and other threats. The risk of wars over the distribution of water resources is also growing. Additionally, the countries of the region have not yet been able to find adequate answers to many old and new problems of an internal, endogenous nature. These include domestic political and socio-economic instability, inter-ethnic tensions, conflicts between regional elites and government structures, poverty, widening income gaps and growing social imbalances, high youth unemployment, rampant corruption, low efficiency, willingness to raise its head in the face of any political instability, and active use of social problems to discredit secular ruling regimes such as radical Islamism, drug trafficking, and the rise of religious extremism are emerging as major threats to regional security today.

The geopolitical features of Central Asia encourage the world powers to cooperate with the countries of the region, both in terms of developing their economic ties and militarily and strategically. Despite the fact that the region is located at the crossroads of Afghanistan, Pakistan, Iran and other Asian countries, creating instability for the region, the development of cooperation with the republics of this region is expected to provide other Asian countries with important guarantees for global and regional security.

Don MichaelLein Gill describes the efforts made by states to connect with Central Asia, calling this a clear manifestation of Helford McKinder's Heartland theory. According to him, the Heartland is a very important geographical area, whoever takes control of this region will be able to control the rest of the world. If we look at the Heartland theory and the maps provided by Mackinder, the Central Asian region is at the very center of the Heartland. In addition, McKinder's "Geographical Turn Point of History" clearly describes the strategies for entering and influencing Central Asia in international affairs and the benefits that can be seen from it[1].

Methods and Analysis

In particular, India's relations with Central Asia date back to the ancient millennia, and in recent years, countries have exchanged ideas, cultures and goods through the Silk Road. With the collapse of the Silk Road, the beginning of the European "era of discoveries," as well as the growing influence of the Russian and Chinese empires on Central Asia, the region fell short of India's strategic vision for some time. During the British Empire's "Great Game" of the 19th century, India's foreign relations were largely limited to areas bordering modern Central Asia[2]. After India gained independence, the country's foreign policy was mainly focused on solidarity with its close neighbors, major powers in the international system, and other African-Asian colonies. Thanks to the country's strong diplomatic, defense and economic cooperation with the Soviet Union, warm relations between India and Central Asia began to be restored. In the 1990s, when the five Central Asian republics of Kazakhstan, Kyrgyzstan, Tajikistan, Turkmenistan and Uzbekistan gained independence, India was faced with challenges such as

---

[1] Don McLain Gill. India Needs a "China Strategy" in Central Asia. 2020. https://www.geopoliticalmonitor.com/india-needs-a-china-strategy-in-central-asia/

[2] Peter Hopkirk, The Great Game: On Secret Service in High Asia. John Murray, London, 2006.

adapting to the post-Cold War international order and domestic economic reforms. Over the decades since then, India's relations with the region have developed slowly, despite having a number of advantages.

According to Frederick Starr, after the collapse of the former Soviet Union, border weakness, political instability and economic hardships paved the way for the spread of terrorist groups in the CA republics. New Delhi, on the other hand, was also concerned that neighboring countries were supporting extremist groups, as this would also pose a direct threat to India's national security, especially as the Kashmir problem deepens. Moreover, India was in the process of consolidating its geopolitical position in the international arena. This, in turn, required the country to join international efforts to address global issues such as terrorism and religious conflicts[3].

Ayjaz Wani, on the other hand, although Pakistan was the first to recognize the independence of the CA states and established diplomatic relations with them, has lagged far behind India in the development of bilateral relations in recent years. One of the main reasons for this is that the CA states have expressed distrust of Pakistan because of its role in supporting the movement of terrorist groups[4].

As India began to adapt to the post-Cold War regime, its foreign policy developed and focused on relations with India's "neighboring neighborhood," including Central Asia. Former Indian Prime Minister Narasimha Rao, who visited the region

---

[3] S. Frederick Starr. Reconnecting India and Central Asia Emerging Security and Economic Dimensions. Central Asia-Caucasus Institute & Silk Road Studies Program – A Joint Transatlantic Research and Policy Center. 2010. Pp.8-10

[4] Ayjaz Wani. India and China in Central Asia: Understanding the new rivalry in the heart of Eurasia. Observer research foundation. 2020.https://www.orfonline.org/research/india-and-china-in-central-asia-understanding

four times in the 1990s, in addition to agreements between the parties to expand trade, investment and aid to the region, stressed common threats - religious fundamentalism, ethnic chauvinism, terrorism, drugs, violence and crime - must be tackled together[5].

The current serious threats to India in the region were exacerbated by the Taliban's takeover of control of Afghanistan in 1996, the crossing of the India-Pakistan nuclear threshold in 1998, and the growing American and Chinese influence in Central Asia. Over the next decade, as India's economy grew, its demand for energy and the need to diversify resources outside the Gulf increased. During this period, Central Asia also sought to provide energy to rapidly developing countries in Asia, such as India and China, to eliminate their dependence on pipelines passing through Russia. However, the existence of serious financial, political, security and technical constraints between India and the region, the difficulty of communication by any planned means, has frustrated oil and gas diplomacy. For example, the Turkmenistan-Afghanistan-Pakistan-India (TAPI) project, supported by the Asian Development Bank (ADB), was proposed in the mid-1990s, but the intergovernmental agreement was officially signed in 2010. In the ensuing period, instability in Afghanistan and the situation between India and Pakistan came to a halt again[6].

However, it can be said that in 2001-2010, India's

---

[5] Emilian Kavalski, 'India's Bifurcated Look to "Central Eurasia": The Central Asian Republics and Afghanistan', in David Malone, C. Raja Mohan and Srinath Raghavan (eds), The Oxford Handbook of Indian Foreign Policy. Oxford University Press, New Delhi, 2015, pp. 424-437.

[6] Angira Sen Sharma, 'Uncertainty Still Looms Large Over TAPI', Indian Council of World Affairs, September 28, 2012, https://icwa.in/pdfs/IBunsertanitystill.pdf

relations with the CA republics reached a new level. Since the early 2000s, India has traditionally expanded the supply of pharmaceuticals, tea, clothing, leather goods, cosmetics, cotton fiber, textiles, rice, electronics, fertilizers and more. New Delhi has begun to become one of the largest trading partners in the region. The trade volume between India and CA reached $ 500 million. However, there are some issues that hinder the further development of this sector, the main of which was the problem of trade routes. India, for its part, has based its demand on natural gas and energy resources in the negotiations (over the past 30 years, India has become one of the world's largest consumers of energy. In 2002 alone, it consumed 26 billion cubic meters of natural gas. the figure reached 37 billion cubic meters, and in 2010 it reached 51 billion cubic meters[7]). Therefore, India's relations with the Central Asian states, which are rich in energy resources, have become important both geostrategically and economically.

In 2002 alone, India signed more than a dozen trade agreements with the CA republics. The region has also become one of the world's strategic zones where the interests of Russia, China and a number of major Middle Eastern countries intersect politically. In addition, the region has emerged as a region rich in oil, natural gas, gold, copper, aluminum, iron and other important natural resources. The geographical proximity of foreign players such as Russia, China, the United States, and even Afghanistan and Pakistan has had a significant impact on India's bilateral relations in the CA. The phrase "New games in Central Asia" soon appeared in the analysis of the world's major politicians[8].

---

[7] Central Asia Atlas Of Natural Resources. Central Asian Countries Initiative for Land Management Asian Development Bank Manila, Philippines 2010. Pp.38
[8] Ayjaz Wani. India and China in Central Asia: Understanding the new rivalry in the heart of Eurasia. Observer research

Regional competition was mixed with religious radicalism and terrorism. This has led to a climate of mistrust in South Asia towards the CA. At the same time, the moderate movement of Turkey in the MO, the radical actions of Iran and Saudi Arabia, the support of the Taliban movement in Afghanistan by Pakistan and its direct threat to the CA began to negatively affect the development of India-Central Asia relations. Nirmala Joshi noted that India's efforts to strengthen relations with Central Asia over the years have strengthened its domestic political-strategic, economic, peace and security system on the basis of "expanded neighborhood", joint solution to terrorism and Afghanistan, strengthening its energy supply and trade and economic ties. was done according to their development needs[9].

As a result of attempts to increase its influence in the CA, the Russia-China-India triangle emerged in the region in the 2000s, writes Don MichaelLein Gill. During a visit to New Delhi in February 2002, former Russian Foreign Minister Igor Ivanov noted that "the development of this triangle in the CA region is slow but steady"[10]. India's influence in the CA has grown from year to year, and it has also relied on its historically close friend Russia in its activities in the region. In particular, in July 2002, a joint Indo-Russian Working Group

---

foundation. 2020. Pp. 3-4.
https://www.orfonline.org/research/india-and-china-in-central-asia-understanding

[9] Nirmala Joshi. Reconnecting India and Central Asia Emerging Security and Economic Dimensions. Central Asia-Caucasus Institute & Silk Road Studies Program – A Joint Transatlantic Research and Policy Center. 2010. Pp.15-17

[10] Don McLain Gill. India Needs a "China Strategy" in Central Asia. 2020.
https://www.geopoliticalmonitor.com/india-needs-a-china-strategy-in-central-asia/

was established, which aims to take practical measures to combat terrorism, religious extremism and organized crime in Uzbekistan and Afghanistan.

In April 2002, during the official visit of the Minister of Defense of India to Tajikistan, an agreement was signed on the construction of an Indian military base in Farkhor. This military base was also of great importance to Pakistan (Pakistan is very close to Tajikistan, separated only by the Vahan corridor, which belongs to Afghanistan). According to the agreement of the three countries (India, Pakistan and Tajikistan), the military base will operate without compromising its national security, taking into account the sovereignty of Tajikistan[11].

Results and Discussions

Rhea Menon and Sharanya Rajiv focused on India-Kazakhstan relations, noting that the two countries have been actively visiting each other since 2001, mainly on security and countering modern threats in the region. they write. The main tasks in the fight against bilateral military-technical and international terrorism are reflected in the Memorandum of Military-Technical Cooperation signed between the Governments of the Republic of Kazakhstan and the Republic of India[12]. At a 2003 meeting of the two countries' defense ministers, former Indian Defense Minister George Fernandez

---

[11] Вызовы безопасности в Центральной Азии /Ин-т мировой экономики и междунар. Отношений РАН; Фонд перспективных исследований и инициатив и др.; отв. ред. И.Я. Кобринская.–М.: ИМЭМО РАН, 2013. – 148 с.

[12] Rhea Menon, Sharanya Rajiv. Realizing India's Strategic Interests in Central Asia. December 01, 2019 https://Carnegieindia.Org/2019/12/01/Realizing-India-S-Strategic-Interests-In-Central-Asia

said: "... we will focus on counter-terrorism in our cooperation. That is what the current situation demands. " After that, the India-Kazakhstan Joint Counter-Terrorism Working Group was established and active practical work was launched[13]. At the initiative of Kazakhstan, the Conference on Interaction and Confidence Building Measures in Asia was established, which includes not only India and Kazakhstan, but also Kyrgyzstan, Tajikistan, Uzbekistan, Afghanistan and Pakistan.

The Indian strategy aimed at strengthening military-technical and military-political influence in the region has remained strong in recent years. India has been actively involved in the construction and equipping of hospitals for Tajik servicemen. He initiated the opening of a joint high-level military research center in neighboring Kyrgyzstan and the organization of training for Kyrgyz soldiers to serve in UN peacekeeping missions. According to Ayjaz Wani, India has also found a good language with Uzbekistan on security issues. At the same time, India's resentment and desire to fight extremist religious organizations in Pakistan, which is trying to spread religious extremism on its territory, has helped India[14].

It should be noted that by this time, terrorist groups threatening Central Asia from Afghanistan and Pakistan began to have an equally dangerous impact on India. Despite India's growing military-political influence in the region and high-

---

[13] Roman Muzalevsky. Unlocking India's Strategic Potential In Central Asia. Strategic Studies Institute and U.S. Army War College Press, 2015. Pp. 18.

[14] Ayjaz Wani. India and China in Central Asia: Understanding the new rivalry in the heart of Eurasia. Observer research foundation. 2020. https://www.orfonline.org/research/india-and-china-in-central-asia-understanding

level propaganda on instability in Afghanistan and Pakistan, it has had a more "soft" foreign policy relationship with the CA than its other foreign partners. Roman Muzalevsky concludes in his research that "... that is why India could not compare itself not only with the Russians, Chinese and Americans, but also with the European Union, Iran and Turkey as a competitor in the CA region ..." [15].

Today, efforts to reconnect New Delhi with the region are starting anew. Over the past decade, Central Asian states have been looking for practical partners, especially in the economic and security spheres. Both sides are interested in combating radicalization and terrorism, curbing illegal trade and exploring opportunities for economic cooperation. India's deep ties with the region provide an excellent environment for both sides to take advantage of existing opportunities and find new and innovative ways to develop current cooperation. India has also explored the possibility of connecting to Central Asia through Iran's Chabahar port and land corridors through Afghanistan, and agreements on the project have been signed.

The first India-Central Asia Dialogue, held in Bishkek in June 2012, was an important step for the country in establishing long-term cooperation with the region. The main purpose of this conference is to hold an annual forum of conversations between academics, scientists, government officials and businessmen in India and CA, as well as to jointly build universities, hospitals, information technology centers and their electronic networks in the CA area, develop mutual trade and tourism. improvement of air communication, organization of joint scientific research, strategic partnership on defense and security issues and reaching new agreements in a number of other areas. At the conference, former Indian

---

[15] Roman Muzalevsky. Unlocking India's Strategic Potential In Central Asia. Strategic Studies Institute and U.S. Army War College Press, 2015. Pp. 67.

Foreign Minister Edapakat Ahmad also announced the "Linking to Central Asia" project, which sets out India's strategy in Central Asia. Within the framework of this project, work has been started on the construction and improvement of modern hospitals, universities, information technology and electronic site development centers.

In addition to the economy, regional security issues in Central Asia are among the main concerns of India in the region, and their relevance is growing day by day. The rise of Islamic radicalization has become a major security issue for regional governments. It is estimated that between 2,000 and 4,000 Central Asian terrorists migrated to join the group after the start of the civil war in Syria and the emergence of the Islamic State (ISIS). In addition to men in the region, who make up 5-10 percent of foreign fighters, these migrants include families, especially women and children[16]. Given the experience of successfully pursuing ISIS domestically and limiting its influence, India's plan for Central Asia also includes the fight against terrorism and radicalization. In addition, India has expanded its civil nuclear cooperation with the region to secure energy interests[17].

Over the past period, factors such as the US presence in

---

[16] Edward Lemon, Vera Mironova, and William Tobey, 'Jihadists from Ex-Soviet Central Asia: Where are They? Why Did They Radicalize? What Next?', Russia Matters, 7 December, 2018, https://www.russiamatters.org/analysis/jihadists-ex-soviet-central-asia-where-are-they-why-did-they-radicalize-what-next

[17] Rikar Hussein and Asim Kashgarian, 'Analysts: Central Asin States Must Learn From IS-Linked Citizens', Voice of America, 17 June 2019, https://www.voanews.com/extremismwatch/analysts-central-asian-states-mustlearn-linked-citizens

Afghanistan, the deep-rooted religious extremism and terrorism in Pakistan, and China's growing influence in Central Asia have created a number of problems and obstacles in the development of Central-South Asian relations. In particular, three main factors of conflict - the Kashmir issue, the situation in Afghanistan and instability in the Xinjiang region - have had a significant impact on the definition of trends and relations in the Central Asia-India direction. The escalation of problems such as terrorism, religious extremism, drug trafficking, border conflicts, cyber threats, illegal migration and human trafficking, which revolve around such major conflicts, has exacerbated the security situation in the two regions.

In particular, Mezb-i-Harak-Jihad, Dukdas-al-Irshad, and other non-governmental religious extremist organizations operating in Pakistan conduct various trainings every year that call on more than 100 young people from Central Asian countries to carry out terrorist attacks. by organizing courses and carrying out their destructive propaganda work. In particular, over the past few years, Uzbekistan has established strong ties with terrorist forces in Pakistan and has been fighting insurgents in the southern part of the country bordering Afghanistan, which has become a hotbed of terrorism. Drug trafficking, which is inextricably linked to terrorism, is also one of the most pressing issues facing the region.

The growing level of danger of the problem for Central Asia can be seen in the position of the countries of the region in the Asian ranking of drug exports and imports[18]. The amount of drugs entering Uzbekistan from Afghanistan has increased by 11% over the past five years. About 50-65% of black drugs exported from Afghanistan are transported

---

[18] https://www.unodc.org/unodc/en/data-and-analysis/ wdr2021.html

through the Central Asian republics. Today, drug trafficking is also booming in India and Pakistan, and clandestine groups working in the field are able to find permanent partners in CA countries. As a result, drug-related crime is on the rise across a very large network. Attempts to commit prohibited crimes due to the large amount of profits from them are leading to an increase in corruption and economic imbalances in countries[19].

Historically, Afghanistan has actually been a bridge to CA for India. During the country's stabilization, India's trade and economic ties with Afghanistan have been strengthened, and Kabul has been a good bridge to further expand ties with the CA countries. While there is significant cooperation in the trade, economic, political, cultural and social fields, New Delhi has primarily sought to strengthen energy cooperation with the CA to meet its growing energy needs. But the future of the initiatives will depend on what political and security scenarios emerge in Afghanistan in the coming years. Most importantly, all countries should take political initiatives to minimize the conflicting features of regional policy in the region.

Prime Minister Modi's official visit to Central Asia in June 2015 was not only a symbolic but also a smart strategic step for Indian diplomacy. Now the Indian government is focusing on rebuilding ties with the Central Asian region in a modern way. The first, through regional ties, is the resumption of long-delayed projects, with Prime Minister Modi visiting Iran in 2016, India's bridge to Central Asia. During this visit, both sides signed an agreement on the development of the port

---

[19] Галишева, Н.В. (2018). Центральноазиатский вектор внешнеэкономической политики Пакистана: основные проблемы и перспективы. Вестник РУДН. Серия: Международные отношения.
http://journals.rudn.ru/international_relations

of Chabahar[20]. While these steps have given new life to India's vision of Eurasian relations, New Delhi needs to combine skilled diplomacy with practical efforts to ensure the sustainability of these projects in the face of U.S.-Iran conflict. The second is through strengthening multilateral cooperation platforms with Central Asian states and other external forces. On the economic front, the Eurasian Economic Union, which includes India and Central Asian states Kazakhstan and Kyrgyzstan, set up a Joint Research Group in 2015 to explore the possibilities of a Free Trade Agreement[21].

India's accession to the Shanghai Cooperation Organization in 2017 shows that there have been significant changes in the country's approach to the entire region. Recognizing this as a positive step, India began to see the region not as part of mechanisms involving bilateral or other external forces, but as a high-potential partner with the potential to communicate in general. India's accession to the SCO has also given its member states the task of cooperating primarily in the fight against terrorism, drug trafficking, extremism and religious discrimination in the region. India then offered its practical assistance in solving the following problems :

a. Establishment of a joint working group on combating terrorism in the MO;

---

[20]'India Takes Over Operations of Part of Chabahar Port in Iran', Economic Times, 7 January, 2019, https://economictimes. indiatimes.com/news/politics-and-nation/india-takes-over-operations-of-part-ofchabahar-port-in-iran/articleshow/67424219.cms?from=mdr

[21]'Joint Statement Between the Russian Federation and the Republic of India: Shared Trust, New Horizons, 24 December 2015', Ministry of External Affairs, 24 December 2015, https://mea.gov.in/bilateral-documents. htm?dtl/26243/Joint_Statement

b. Development of information and intelligence exchange mechanisms;

c. Training and provision of modern weapons for the military forces of the MO;

d. Assistance in eliminating the root causes of terrorism, unemployment, poverty, poverty and other factors;

e. An issue that has a positive impact on the fight against terrorism - cooperation with the countries of the CIS on the establishment of stability in Afghanistan[22].

Although many of India's ambitions in Central Asia have not yet been realized, the region has become an important focus of India's expanded neighborhood policy. In addition, India has begun to pay more attention to projects in the framework of its "Connect to Central Asia" initiative, India-Central Asia Dialogue, North-South International Transport Corridor and the Shanghai Cooperation Organization to develop relations with the Central Asian region.

India's growing interest in the CA region means that India is trying to strengthen its position not only in the Asian region but around the world. Speaking about the importance of the region, the country's 12th Prime Minister Inder Kumar Gujral said that "Central Asian countries are India's closest foreign partners"[23].

Rhea Menon and Sharanya Rajiv also say that "as India looks beyond its borders, Central Asia provides India with the right platform to expand its political, economic and cultural

---

[22] Stobdan P. The Strategic Dimension India and Central Asia 2020. Manohar Parrikar Institute for Defence Studies and Analyses, New Delhi KW Publishers Pvt Ltd New Delhi. Pp.34-35

[23] Nirmala Joshi. Reconnecting India and Central Asia Emerging Security and Economic Dimensions. Central Asia-Caucasus Institute & Silk Road Studies Program – A Joint Transatlantic Research and Policy Center. 2010. P.85.

ties and play a leading role in Eurasia"[24].

India's interests in the region included the implementation of energy security, trade and infrastructure development programs. At the same time, the CA is taking the initiative to establish strong cooperation with the republics on security in the region. The CA has to compete with foreign players such as the US, Russia and China in achieving its strategic goals. In particular, Pakistan's entry into the region is also motivating India to operate in a highly competitive environment. In particular, the unstable and complicated situation in Afghanistan is becoming a serious problem for Central and South Asia, expanding the scope of common security problems in the two regions. This situation confronts the countries of the two regions with issues that need to be addressed jointly and tasks that need to be fulfilled. Terrorism, drug trafficking, arms and human trafficking, ethnic and social conflicts, political instability and others have been added to the list of growing threats in the two regions. In the context of the current situation and the sharp dynamics of events, the relations between the two regions, in particular India's relations with Central Asia, are attracting the attention of many experts and leading politicians in the international arena and are at the center of heated discussions.

The North-South International Transport Corridor project, developed by India, China and Russia and connecting 7,200 km from north to south of the Eurasian region, fully meets the interests of not only these countries, but also Central Asian countries, in particular Uzbekistan, in trade and economic spheres. This trade corridor covers the area from India to Russia, the Persian Gulf and the Caspian Sea, according to

---

[24] Rhea Menon, Sharanya Rajiv. Realizing India's Strategic Interests in Central Asia. December 01, 2019 https://Carnegieindia.Org/2019/12/01/Realizing-India-S-Strategic-Interests-In-Central-Asia

which goods and products are transported from the ports of Kandla and Jawaharlal Nehru in northern India to the Iranian port of Bander Abbas. It is then transported by road and rail to Moscow and St. Petersburg, Russia. As a continuation of the project, the construction of a new railway connecting the northern part of the Caspian Sea and Uzbekistan, Kazakhstan, Turkmenistan and Iran is expected. This project will reduce the time spent on transportation of goods in the countries of the region by 30%, and reduce prices by up to 40%.

India also aims to connect Jammu and Kashmir to the Great Silk Road system via the Greater Kashmir Railway, which connects Pakistan's Free Kashmir region. The restoration of the Great Silk Road across Kashmir will be the basis for positive economic and geopolitical changes not only in the region but around the world. The reopening of traditional trade routes will help harmonize the interests of the Silk Road partners, create a free trade zone and, most importantly, strengthen intercultural ties and resolve ideological conflicts peacefully.

Speaking on India's Central Asia policy, Weitz, in his "Averting a new Great Game in Central Asia" said: "New Delhi has made a significant contribution to ensuring sustainable development in the region, expanding trade and investment opportunities, tackling terrorism, drug trafficking and religious extremism, and ensuring energy security in order to develop cooperation without harming any third country"[25]. It should be noted that while CA is not a direct neighbor of India, the region is of great strategic importance to New Delhi. As we can see, over the years, both sides have worked hard to strengthen relations.

---

[25] Weitz, R. (2006). Averting a new Great Game in Central Asia. The Washington Quarterly, 29 (3), 155–167.

Indian Culture In Central Asia

Experts say the main factor weakening India's role is its geographical remoteness from the region. While it will take time to resolve its long-standing problems and conflicts with Pakistan, as well as consolidate regional instability, loud official statements alone are not enough. All this makes India a "small player." In our opinion, these statements are also true to some extent, but most of the world's political forecasters overestimate the development potential of India-Central Asia relations. This is due to the fact that since the establishment of formal relations, the interests have not weakened, on the contrary, the scope of cooperation has expanded, jointly developed long-term plans, successful joint projects have emerged. An atmosphere of mutual understanding and cooperation on key international and regional issues has been formed. This is a clear indication that close human relations have emerged between the countries as a result of hundreds of years of mutual cultural, political and economic influences.

Over the past years, in the framework of cooperation between India and the SCO, the dynamics of growth and development has been observed in the modern relations of the country with its members in all areas, especially in the field of security. Bilateral and multilateral cooperation between India and Central Asia is being reshaped through official visits of heads of state and, of course, the Shanghai Cooperation Organization and active official meetings, and is being implemented through new approaches and advanced initiatives. This is undoubtedly a clear indication that the interests of the two regions are converging. We can confirm that the last decade has been the beginning of close cooperation between India and the Central Asian Republics in the fields of security and defense.

From the above figures, it can be seen that with a good understanding of the close connection of geoeconomics with geopolitics, along with economic cooperation between India and CA countries, great attention is paid to military training and efforts to develop strong defense ties by strengthening strategic and security cooperation. Security cooperation between India and the CA also includes conducting joint military-defense research, coordinating counter-terrorism measures and closely consulting on Afghanistan, whose security is of paramount importance to both sides.

Another major reason why India is trying to strengthen its position in the CA is its traditional foreign policy rivals - China and Pakistan - in their efforts for success in the region. "While competition with China in the region is focused on the economic sphere, tensions with Pakistan are related to security issues in the CA," said Yogesh Joshi and Ankit Mukherjee[26]. Here, India faces two challenges: the country needs to increase its capacity and potential as a worthy competitor to China in the region, and reduce Pakistan's influence. A number of experts have been using the phrase "the fate of the late" in reference to India's policy in the region. Two French researchers working in Washington discuss several reasons for the current situation in their book, Central Asia on a World Map: Indian Ideas and Strategies[27].

According to Naboka A.V., by this time, the convergence of views and interests on fundamental issues had formed between the Central Asian republics and India: a) secularism and commitment to democracy, and the struggle against religious fundamentalism; (b) Recognizing the threat of cross-border terrorism, arms and drug trafficking, religious extremism and ethnic and religious discrimination to regional

---

[26] Yogesh Joshi & Anit Mukherjee. From Denial to Punishment: The Security Dilemma and Changes in India's Military Strategy towards China, Asian Security. 2019. Pp. 25-43

[27] Sébastien Peyrouse, Marlène Laruelle. Mapping Central Asia. Indian Perceptions and Strategies. Routledge, 2016. 262 Pages

security and stability; (c) Observance of the principles of the territorial integrity of States and the inviolability of state borders; d) development of economic, scientific and cultural cooperation; d) Ensuring a peaceful and peaceful neighborhood in Afghanistan, etc[28].

"Central and South Asia: Regional Interdependence" held in Tashkent on July 14-15, 2021. In his speech at the international conference "Threats and Opportunities", President Mirziyoyev said: "... I am confident that active and open dialogue between the countries of Central and South Asia will create unique opportunities for the full realization of our huge trade, economic, cultural and civilizational potential[29]". It also called on the participating States to join forces in the fight against threats to security and stability, to fight terrorism, extremism, transnational crime, in particular cybercrime, and to develop a joint drug action plan with the United Nations Office on Drugs and Crime. one of the main directions in which it is necessary to unite forces is to combat the threat of terrorism. This event itself confirms that the strengthening of cooperation between the Central Asian and South Asian regions has become a very important factor in ensuring peace and stability in these regions.

Conclusion

In conclusion, the importance of Central Asia for India is very high in the distant and recent past, even today, and this importance will undoubtedly remain strong in the future. With

---

[28] Набока А.В. Роль Международного Сотрудничества В Обеспечении Безопасности В Центральной Азии. DOI:10.20542/2307-1494-2016-2-87-100.

[29] President of the Republic of Uzbekistan Shavkat Mirziyoyev. "New Uzbekistan Strategy". Speech at the international conference "Central and South Asia: Regional Interdependence. Threats and opportunities"// https://president. uz/uz/lists/view/4484

the increasing threats and threats of religious extremism, terrorism and aggressive nationalism to the integrity and security of the Indian nation, the strategic value of Central Asia for the country has further increased. In India's strategic thinking, Central Asia has become an important part of its expanded neighborhood. For India, stability and security in the region came first. Afghanistan is inextricably linked to India's problems in Central Asia, which is characterized by the fact that Tajikistan, Uzbekistan and Turkmenistan share common borders with the destabilized region. In the immediate context, India's concerns are related to the unstable security scenario that is emerging in the region. The threat of non-traditional threats poses a serious threat not only to the integrity of India and Central Asian states, but also to the existence of democracy and open societies. However, it is clear that the integration of South and Central Asia will bring great economic benefits to all parties, which will lead to positive results for stability and security in the region. Strategically and contextually, both India and Central Asia will continue to adhere to this concept.

References
1. Angira Sen Sharma, 'Uncertainty Still Looms Large Over TAPI', Indian Council of World Affairs, September 28, 2012, https://icwa.in/pdfs/IBunsertanitystill.pdf
2. Ayjaz Wani. India and China in Central Asia: Understanding the new rivalry in the heart of Eurasia. Observer research foundation. 2020. https://www.orfonline.org/research/india-and-china-in-central-asia-understanding
3. Central Asia Atlas Of Natural Resources. Central Asian Countries Initiative for Land Management Asian Development Bank Manila, Philippines 2010.

4.Don McLain Gill. India Needs a "China Strategy" in Central Asia. 2020. https://www.geopoliticalmonitor.com/india-needs-a-china-strategy-in-central-asia/

5.Edward Lemon, Vera Mironova, and William Tobey, 'Jihadists from Ex-Soviet Central Asia: Where are They? Why Did They Radicalize? What Next?', Russia Matters, 7 December 2018, https://www.russiamatters.org/analysis/jihadists-ex-soviet-central-asia-where-are-they-why-did-they-radicalize-what-next

6.Emilian Kavalski, 'India's Bifurcated Look to "Central Eurasia": The Central Asian Republics and Afghanistan', in David Malone, C. Raja Mohan and Srinath Raghavan (eds), The Oxford Handbook of Indian Foreign Policy. Oxford University Press, New Delhi, 2015.

7.Frederick S. Starr. Reconnecting India and Central Asia Emerging Security and Economic Dimensions. Central Asia-Caucasus Institute & Silk Road Studies Program – A Joint Transatlantic Research and Policy Center. 2010.

8.https://www.unodc.org/unodc/en/data-and-analysis/wdr2021.html

9.'India Takes Over Operations of Part of Chabahar Port in Iran', Economic Times, 7 January 2019, https://economictimes.indiatimes.com/news/politics-and-nation/india-takes-over-operations-of-part-ofchabahar-port-in-iran/articleshow/67424219.cms?from=mdr

10. 'Joint Statement Between the Russian Federation and the Republic of India: Shared Trust, New Horizons, 24 December 2015', Ministry of External Affairs, 24 December 2015, https://mea.gov.in/bilateral-documents.htm?dtl/26243/Joint_Statement

11. Nirmala Joshi. Reconnecting India and Central Asia Emerging Security and Economic Dimensions. Central

Asia-Caucasus Institute & Silk Road Studies Program – A Joint Transatlantic Research and Policy Center. 2010.

12. Peter Hopkirk, The Great Game: On Secret Service in High Asia. John Murray, London, 2006.

13. Rhea Menon, Sharanya Rajiv. Realizing India's Strategic Interests in Central Asia. December 01, 2019 https://Carnegieindia.Org/2019/12/01/Realizing-India-S-Strategic-Interests-In-Central-Asia

14. Rikar Hussein and Asim Kashgarian, 'Analysts: Central Asin States Must Learn From IS-Linked Citizens', Voice of America, 17 June 2019, https://www.voanews.com/extremismwatch/analysts-central-asian-states-mustlearn-linked-citizens

15. Roman Muzalevsky. Unlocking India's Strategic Potential In Central Asia. Strategic Studies Institute and U.S. Army War College Press, 2015.

16. Sébastien Peyrouse, Marlène Laruelle. Mapping Central Asia. Indian Perceptions and Strategies. Routledge, 2016. 262 Pages

17. Stobdan P. The Strategic Dimension India and Central Asia 2020. Manohar Parrikar Institute for Defence Studies and Analyses, New Delhi KW Publishers Pvt Ltd New Delhi.

18. Weitz, R. (2006). Averting a new Great Game in Central Asia. The Washington Quarterly, 29 (3), 155–167.

19. Yogesh Joshi & Anit Mukherjee. From Denial to Punishment: The Security Dilemma and Changes in India's Military Strategy towards China, Asian Security. 2019.

20. Вызовы безопасности в Центральной Азии /Ин-т мировой экономики и междунар. Отношений РАН; Фонд перспективных исследований и инициатив и др.; отв. ред. И.Я. Кобринская. – М.:ИМЭМО РАН, 2013.

21. Галишева, Н.В. (2018). Центральноазиатский вектор внешноэкономической политики Пакистана: основные проблемы и перспективы. Вестник РУДН. Серия: Международные отношения.
http://journals.rudn.ru/international_relations

22. Набока А.В. Роль Международного Сотрудничества В Обеспечении Безопасности В Центральной Азии. DOI:10.20542/2307-1494-2016-2-87-100.

Uzbek State University of World Languages, Uzbekistan

13. Expression of Good Wishes and Curses in Uzbek, Russian and Urdu languages (Based on the Materials of the "Yulduzli Tunlar Bobur" by Pirimkul Kadyrov)

Umarova Mohira

Annotation : This article is intended for those, who study comparative linguistics and linguoculturology. This thesis addresses the issues of expressing acts of curses and good wishes in the Uzbek language and their translation into Russian and Urdu.

Keywords : expression, god wishes, curses, Russian, Urdu, "Yulduzli tunlar", translation, linguoculturology.

Good wishes and curses play significant communicative role in different people's cultures.

I.V. Krokova wrote: "A curse, as a typological unit of language, is an independent statement in speech, which refers either to the class of expressives or to declarations and is motivated and caused by a pragmatic context.Curse expressions, in their canonical form, appear as performative statements which built according to the standard model "I curse you". It is considered an explicit performative expression of desecration tactics, exile tactics and ill-intentioned tactics. These speech statements aim to achieve certain perlocutionary effects - to cause moral or physical harm to the addressee by performing a verbal act of alienation or stating the fact of alienation from oneself or society. The use of curse statements in speech transforms the conversation from cooperative way into the conflict, which entails a verbal aggression and varies in intensity degrees and manifestation forms.Cursing is a common occurrence in the invective forms of communication, which are vivid examples of the speech organization in accordance with the statement pragmatics. The general functional focus of curses - wishes of trouble and misfortune expressed in words".[1]

Good wishes are small speech formulas used in everyday conversations for one reason or another. In all world nations they are derived from spells, prayers; which were possibly influencedto supernatural forces and the outer world, according to ancient men's concepts.The main function is read in the word "well-wishes" - the wish of good, blessing to another person. Words and actions related to the expression of positive and sincere feelings, wishing for blessings play significant role in creating, maintaining good relationships between people. Additional functions of well-wishes are embodiedaccording to the type of communicative situation (meeting, farewell, compliments, wedding, childbirth, apology, etc.) We can say with certainty that well-wishes are part of our life, without which relationships, harmony, well-being between close people would be impossible to maintain.

O.V. Meshkova writes about the inclusion of well-wishes in our communicative space: "Good wishes accompany a person throughout his life: from small phrases such as "good night ","grow big","be healthy" to detailed wishes in greeting cards, toasts, etc.for a happy life" [Meshkova 2010]. Demand and importance of well-wishes in various areas of our life indicate the need to study these language forms from the standpoint of stylistics, rhetoric, psychology, as well as theoretical and practical significance of the results of such studies.

Let's refer to some definitions that exist in modern Russian linguistics. N.I. Formanovskaya speaks of benevolence as a wish-action directed to another person, and suggests to consider it as a concept in the basis of speech etiquette

---

[1] Speech act of the curse and lexical and grammatical means of its implementation. Scientific library of dissertations and abstracts.

[Formanovskaya 2011]. V.V. Pleshakova defines well-wishes as "statements with a communicative task of wishing any good to someone else" [Pleshakova 2006]. N.S. Grebenshchikova understands under benevolence "wishing the person physical, spiritual and social well-being: health, salvation of the soul, peace, joy" [Grebenshchikova 2004]. O.V. Meshkova considers good wishes as "verbal formulas, which main task is to wish good to self or to another person" [Meshkova 2010].T.A. Agapkina names benevolence as a text containing the wish of good, and the ritual of pronouncing it [Agapkina]

As analysis object we selected the novel of Uzbek writer Pirimkul Kadyrov "YulduzliTunlar", its translation into Russian "Babur" (translated from Uzbek by Y. Surovtsev) and the version in Urdu language " بابر"(translated from Russian by M. Salim).

Before reviewing examples of translationof well-wishes and curses expressionsin the novel, I would like to note that translation into Urdu was done from Russian language variant,therefore we identified some inconsistencies of the translated text with the original novel.Basically,the translation into Urdu corresponds to the Russian translation, but, taking into account the capacity of Urdu language, in our opinion, the translation directly from the Uzbek language would have been more beautiful.Urdu language has equivalents of translated words, which etymology dates back to the Arabic and Persian languages; these words would sound more melodic and would better correspond to the original language.

Examples :

1.Men <u>yuzi qora</u>, sabab bo'ldim o'limga! Men!

О, я проклятая, виновата в его смерти! Я!

ہاۓ کتنی منحوس ہوں ! میں ہی <u>قصوروار</u> ہوں ان کی موت کی! میں!

[Hae kitni manhus hun! Main hi qusurwar hun un ki mot ki! Main!]

In the original version, curse expression "**yuziqora**" is translated into Russian as "CURSED". The translation corresponds to the original in a certain sense. This expression in Urdu language literally translates as: "Oh, I'm so cursed (unhappy) I am to be blamed for his death! I am! ". It is obvious here that translation corresponds to the original.

2. "Padariga la'nat"– deb Tohir qo'lidagi bolta bilan ko'prik qanotlarini qarsillatib sindira ketdi.

«А, будь проклят!»- воскликнул Тахир и опять стал кружить перила.

-"بہار میں جائے"- طاہر نے کہا.

["bahr mein jaye"-Tahir ne kaha]

In the original version, the word – curse "padariga la'nat" is translated into Russian as "ah, damn". Here, the Russian translation does not quite correspond to the original, as the expression "padarigala'nat" is translated as "cursing his father" or "let his father be cursed". It is shown here that translator into Russian language simplified the expression.

In Urdu language, this expression literally translates as "hell with it, darn it". There was a phraseology used in the translation, and the translator completely changed the meaning of the expression.

3. "Ma'zur tuting amirzodam," –dedi. "Harom o'lgur ot yiqildi".

«Помилуйте, повелитель, - никак не сдвину поганца».

"معاف فرمائیے حکمران. کمبخت گھوڑا کسی طرح ٹس سے میں ہی نہیں ہوتا"

[maaf farmaiye, hukmraan. Kambakht ghora kisi tarah tis se mein hi nahin hota!]

Translation from Uzbek language into Russian literally sounds as: "let the bastard die". The translator managed to preserve the general meaning of the curse. While translated into Urdu language, the same expression literally sounds as "the injured horse is absolutely motionless/does not react". Here again the translator used expression as locution, which resulted in distortion of the meaning.

4. Jim yot o'laksa! Hozir kirib, bir jarohatingni o'ngga yetkazaman.

Помолчи ты, завтрашний труп! Вот выйду к тебе и к единой ране добавлю десять

چپ ره زنده لاش، خاموش ہو جا، ورنہ اندرا کے ایک زحم کے دس کرونگا.

[chup rah zindalash, khamush ho ja, varna andr aa ke aek zahm ke das karunga]

Exact meaning of the word "o'laksa" in Russian language is "barely alive". But the translator conveyed meaning quite differently. In Urdu, this curse translates as "living corpse"- « завтрашний труп » The translator retained the meaning given by the author of the novel to this phrase.

5. Iloho Rustamday o'g'il ko'ring, begim …

Да ниспошлет вам Всевишний сына, могучего как Рустам...

خدا آپ کو رستم جیساطاقتور فرزند عطا کرے، بیگم صاحب!

[khuda aap ko rustam jeisa taaqtur farzand aata kare, begum sahiba]

Translation into both languages corresponds to the original composition. Translators added the word " могучего"- "mighty" to convey the meaning of using the comparison with hero Rustam in both Russian and Urdu translations.

6. Imomi zamonimiz ming yil umr ko'rsinlar" – deb olqish aytdi.

Пусть здравствует тысячу лет наш светлейший имам!

ہمارے مقدّس امام کو عمر ہزار سالہ تک نصیب ہو !

[hamare muqadas imam ko umr hazar sal tak nasiib ho!]

The translators correctly conveyed the meaning of well-wishes when translating into both languages. In Urdu language as well as Russian language the translators used the word "saint" to convey meaning of how deary imam is to them.

Thus, in equal cultural spaces, well-wishes and curses act as text complexes that have verbal organization and discursive practice. Comparison of the above excerptions showed that when translating into Russian language Uzbek national flavor of well-wishes and curses expressions often times is not quite accurately conveyed. During translation, words and phrases are omitted, the "sophistication" of expressions and its flamboyance gets lost. Moreover due to the fact that translation of novel into Urdu was done from Russian instead of the original Uzbek language, the potentials of Urdu language were not fully utilized.

Literature:

1. Qodirov P., "Yulduzli tunlar. Bobur" – T.: 2016. – 208 b.
2. Кадыров П., "Бабур" – М.: 1983.-215 с.
3. "Sharq tarjimashunosligi; tarixi, hozirgi kuni va kelajagi", 2. (Ilmiy maqolalar to'plami), -T., 2014
4. T.Halmirzaev "Urdu-rus lug'ati" 2012
5. Khamidov H. Badiiy tarjimada tilak, duo va qarg'ishlarning berilishi 122-128
6. "ظہیر الدین بابر" جملہ حقوق بحق . "رادوگا" اشاعت گھر . تاشقند محفوظہ ۱۹۸۲ س.
7. O'zbek tilining izohli lug'ati. – M.: "Rus tili", 1981.

Tashkent State Institute of Oriental Studies, Uzbekistan

14. The Relationship between two Greatest People of 20th Century in India : Gandi and Tagore

Dr. Muhammadjon Kadirov

Introduction

Famous Indian writer, Krishna Kripalani, created a scientific biography of a great humanist, Rabindranath Tagore. Being his secretary, he lived near the ingenious poet for many years. Not only was he married with Tagore's granddaughter, Nondita, but he also became a member of his family. K. Kripalani started to actively participate in the construction of national culture, once India had been conquered by nations. From 1954 to 1966, he worked as a secretary of the *Sahitya Academy* (Literary Academy), the aim of which, was to provide assistance to the development of Indian literature, which according to Nehru, represented a unity in diversity, for it went on in all languages of contemporary India. For the time being, K. Kipalani leads an organization called *"National book trust"*, which accounts for the organization of mutual acquaintance of people's literatures in the Republic of India.

Method

This is a qualitative research using the content, comparative-historical, characteristic analysis approach.

Research and Results

One of the most significant contributions to Indian literature is the biography of Rabindranath Tagore, entered in 1980 as the second supplemented edition. (the first one had been published by the centenary since his birth in 1861).

In 1861, when Tagore was born, India was manipulated by British people. The country was ruled by foreigners, and the British queen was proclaimed an emperor of India. It seemed that this sparkling brilliant would embellish the imperial crown until the very end. Indeed, it was the thought of rulers. What is surprising was that many Indian people shared and welcomed this faith.

The greatest uprising in 1857 was ruthlessly suppressed, and primordial ruling classes were either eradicated or trampled into dust. A new class was on the rise, the bourgeoisie class with new views and culture, and English administration supported it in any way.

The majority of faculties conditioned these transformations, including events within the world's scope, which affected India. However, the power of nature as well as that of people are bleak on their own, and if they are not suppressed and directed, they can turn out to be destructive rather than creative. Two people, among those who could contribute to the creation of a new fate of India, surpass others: these people are Gandi and Tagore.

GandiMoxandasKaramchand, named by Moxatma as *"The great soul"* (1869 – 1948) – is a distinguished leader of national liberation movement in India. He was the one who developed a nonviolent tactic of resistance against colonizers. He acquired legal education in England. From 1893 to 1914, he lived in the South Africa, where he led mass movement against racial discrimination of Indian people. Gandi witnessed the influence of L. N. Tolstoy, with whom he was in correspondence. While returning to India, he got closer to the party of Indian national congress, and became one of the recognized leaders of movement towards both independence (*svaradj*) and economic autonomy (*svadeshi*). He advocated for equality of "untouchables" and for the development of crafts (spinning and weaving), wherein he saw an underlying means of economic solution of India. During the period, when English people triggered bloody clashes between Indians and Muslims, he advocated for the unity of dwellers of India. For this reason, he was killed by a member of religious-communal organization called *"RashtriyaSvayamsevakSangh"*.

Gandi's contribution is well-known: he contributed more than anyone in the history of India. Tagore's contribution is less noticeable, yet deeper, for he released and nourished hidden sources of creativity in the fields, wherein a politician was powerless.

Although Tagorewas first and foremost a poet, he is more than just a poet within the European sense of the word, as well as Gandi, who is more than just a politician and patriot. Tagor was the person who was called in India *Kavi*, prophet, seer. His ingenuity enriched everything he touched. Like the sun itself, in honor of which, he was called *robi* (in Bengal), the derivative from *rovi* (in Sanskrit), which means the sun, he emitted light and warmth, animated intellectual and spiritual ground of his country, unraveling unknown horizons of thought, and moved the bridge between South and West.

Tagore stood out among contemporary writers not only because his poems and proses, translated into research volumes by scientists, were enjoyed by sophisticated intellectuals, but also because mediocre illiterate people in crowded schools of Calcutta or in remote locations of Bengal honored them with love.

The great aspiration of the multifaceted genius, Tagore, towards the development of Indian art, dancing, music, crafts, painting, his respect for local national art schools, encouragement of both classic and national traditions in his school in Santiniketan became an incentive, which lets these conventions survive and flourish these days.

His whole life, from the birth to the death, a distinctive feature of his nature was duality: on the one hand, it was an intense self-absorption, on the other, it was a masculine participation in solving world problems.

The poems, he writes, "gushed and rushed like a waterfall". Being is becoming that life always moves on and updates, and that death – is the thing that helps to update. These poems are called "*Infinite life*" and "*Infinite death*". The life is filled with death, and immortality lies in death. "Each year, got along by me, I would die."

"I felt bliss, resembling the one felt by Shiva, when it washes unclean stain of being with ultimate emptiness and enjoys its invincibility." This abstract philosophical play was, to a significant extent, the history of spiritual experience of the author. An ordinary girl from despicable caste, ragged and illiterate, brought this proud Indian scientist to the gates of true wisdom.

Two worlds are presented in dramas and poems "*Nature's retribution*": on the one hand, there are wanderers and Christians busy with usual domestic stuff, on the other, there is a hermit completely immersed in self-moving infinity of his imagination. Love brings a bridge over abyss between these two worlds, where the hermit and plodder meet one another, and visible insignificance of momentum and visible emptiness of infinity fade… "*Nature's retribution*" can be considered a foreword regarding all my creativity. Or, to be more accurate, the play concerns the topic, to which all my subsequent compositions are dedicated – the treatment's joy of infinity in ultimate", Tagore wrote.

"I think that's enough of me", Rabindranath wrote in private letter dated in October of 1891 – to live and die intrinsic to a person, with love and trust to this world, and look at it neither as dreams of the creator nor as devil's smirk. And another letter dated in 16th June of 1892: There is nothing more wonderful and greater than fulfilling a daily duty of life easily and naturally.

In the letter sent on February of 1893, he wrote the following:

"What a miserable, God – forgotten our country is, where there is a lack of a simple will to act! The ability to think and feel was exhausted, passions weakened. Daring adventures, true full – blooded life is unknown to anyone. Men and women glide silently like shadows, eat, drink, do their daily work, smoke, sleep and chat non – stop. We talk about everything like children, and our feelings easily slide into sentimentality. There is a lack of an adult, a serious desire for struggle and full-blooded life! " [7]A very important poem, in which he condemns nationalism as "the pride of nations", was written on the last day of the last century. The Boer War brought deep disappointment to the claims of Western democracies, Tagore saw in her bloody massacre a dangerous omen of future world slaughter "The last sun of the century."It hurts him that his Western comrades in the pen, instead of raising their voices in defense of the entrusted humanity, rush into the general battle:

Poets rave - their voices

You can't tell from the growling dogs.[8] Tagore and a number of other leading figures in the field of education implemented the plan for a national education system and created a council, which was headed by the famous Indian philosopher - yogiAurobindo Ghosh. For this council, Tagore read a series of lectures on literary criticism, which later appeared under the title "Sahitya" ("Literature"). Leading the masses, dissatisfied with foreign rule, he hoped to use the awakened passion for freedom for a constructive program of the country's revival.Tagore outlined this program in a series of excellent speeches and articles in which he formulated the basic principles of the future theory of nonviolent resistance, so famous later thanks to Mahatma Gandhi.

His poetry of this period, which reached a climax in passionatesincerity in the simplicity "Gitanjali" was created by the blood of the heart. Tagore's spiritual insight is born of a deep experience of grief and loneliness.

The most amazing thing is that grief made him love this land, this life even more. He sought inspiration not in the loneliness of his soul, but in every manifestation of being.

The understanding of the true fate of his country, which the hero of the novel ("Mountain"), is expressed by Tagore in a beautiful hymn addressed to India, created at the same time.

Two years later, Tagore returned to this idea and gave a public lecture in Calcutta, which he then published in his book "A Course of Indian History".In the same year, 1912, she sounded in the famous song, which has now become the official anthem of India.

All suffering and pain, loss and failure, battles and disappointments both in worldly affairs and in creativity are dissolved and exalted in songs that poured out from his overflowing and purified heart in 1909 and 1910.Many of these songs, which made up the book "Gitanjali" ("Sacrificial Songs"), were subsequently translated into English by him and brought him worldwide fame.

In October 1912, accompanied by his son and daughter-in-law, Rabindranath sailed to the United States.There Tagore first began to write serious prose in English, these were lectures that were later given at Harvard University and published under the title "Shadhona" ("Understanding of Life").

He pointed out that "the West is proud of the fact that it subjugates nature, as if we live in a hostile world, where in the struggle we have to get everything we need, defeating the order of things hostile to us ... India, on the other hand, seeks to establish the harmony that exists between man and the universe."[9].

In November 1912, while Tagore was in Illinois, the first edition of Gitanjali was published in London.

The New Age newspaper wrote: "Any of us could write as many of these texts as we want, but nobody could be led to believe that it is good English, good poetry, good philosophy and a good guide to life."

Some argued that"the British have been very successful in the cultivation of Indians, since Indians can now write so well in English."[10].

One American newspaper wrote: "The award of the Nobel

Prize for Literature to an Indian has created a lot of chagrin and a lot of surprise among white writers. They cannot understand why this award went to a man with dark skin."

The Globe newspaper (Toronto, Canada) wrote: "For the first time, the Nobel Prize went to someone whom we cannot call 'white'.It will take some time before we get used to the idea that someone named Rabindranath Tagore might receive a worldwide prize for literary achievement.Weren't they told us that the west and east will not leave their places? The name sounds funny. The first time we saw it on the pages of newspapers, it seemed to us that it was invented as a joke. "[11].

In January 1913, Rabindranath came to Chicago. He gave lectures "The Ideals of the Ancient Civilization of India" and "The Problem of Evil".He then traveled to Rochester to attend the Religious Liberals Congress, where he spoke on racial conflicts.Here he met with the German philosopher Rudolf Aiken, who had come to the congress from Germany, and an ardent admirer of Gitanjali.

Rabindranath was in Shankinikston when the news came that he had been awarded the Nobel Prize on November 13, 1913.Tagore turned from a personality into a symbol of Western acceptance of Asian culture and its potential revival.He was the first to capture in the minds of the Western intelligentsia the fact, now generally recognized, that the "wisdom of Asia" is alive, that it should be treated like a living being, and not like a curious museum exhibit.

The true events are recalled by the Swedish academician Andres Esterling: "T. Sturge Moore, an English writer, a member of the

Royal Society, proposed him (Tagore) for consideration as a candidate for the award.The minutes of the Nobel Committee show that this proposal was received with interest and surprise" [10].

The dispute was settled in Tagore's favor thanks to a written review by Werner von Heidenstam, who himself three years later received the Nobel Prize."Now that we have found the ideal poet of true scale, we have no right to pass him by.For the first time, and perhaps the last, we had the opportunity to discover a great name before it appears in all the newspapers, we should not be petty and miss the opportunity by waiting until next year."[11]

There are no two regions on earth more different in terms of climate and social structure than the tropical plains of Bengal and the snow-covered mountains of Scandinavia.But the poems written in the Ganges delta found in the heart of the Scandinavian the same sensitive, sincere and deep echo as in the hearts of Tagore's compatriots. And this is proof not only of the worldwide significance of the poems of "Gitanjali", but also of Tagore's correctness in his firm conviction that a single heart beats in the chest of humanity, despite the barriers erected by nationalists, priests and politicians.

Tagore wrote to Sturge Moore: "The literature of a country is created not only for domestic consumption.Its value lies in the fact that it is absolutely necessary for foreign lands. I think that the West was lucky that it received the spirit of the East through the Bible.She has increased the richness of your life because she is so alien to your temperament. With the passage of time, you may discard some of her doctrines and teachings, but she did her job - she created an opportunity for intellectual choice, an opportunity that is so necessary for all life growth. Western literature does the same for us by adding extraneous elements to our lives.Some of them complement and others contradict our trends. This is what we need" [12].

Sooner after finishing the work of "Falguni" (The art of spring), on March of 1915, Tagore met Gandi for the first time, who assured his activity in South Africa and returned to motherland, but still did not decide what he was going to do and where he would settle. He dissolved his colony called "Phoenix" and a school in South Africa, after which he sent the students to India. Andrews, who became the so-called connecting link between these two greatest people, suggested to place these students (there were around 12 children) in Santiniketan as long as Gandi arrived and initiated his new ashram. Tagore readily agreed, and the students arrived in Santiniketan several months ahead before the arrival of Gandi. Perhaps, it was interesting to watch two groups of children living side by side: Tagore's students are careless like Ariel (The soul of wind, the character of "Buri" by Shakespeare), singing, dancing and noisy, while little sacred students of Gandi are too wise and judicious for their age. Yet, all of them got along with one another, and Tagore appreciated and liked Gandi's students as his own ones.

Six days spent by Gandi in Santiniketan created a foundation of friendship between two titans of modern India. However, those same days revealed a contrast in terms of their personalities, particularly their different outlooks. The contrast was stark and compelling especially for fans of both people. Yet, deep and intimate relationship lied under the contrast, felt only by them and several friends, who stood out with the same increased susceptibility like Andrews and Jawaharlal Nehru. The so-called students or "trusted followers" of both drew their attention only to external manifestations of meeting. In a peculiar for himbusiness and practical manner, Gandi looked around, got acquainted with everyone, saw weak points and tried to demonstrate Tagore how to apply his own ideas in practice better. "You believe in simplicity and independence" – he told directly to inhabitants of ashram. "Wonderful, I also believe in these virtues. But how can you achieve independence without leading your household on your own? And how can you achieve simplicity if you live according to someone else's work?" He stated that they must do without wage labor, must account for clean maintenance of ashram like they do for their own bodies, by executing all household necessities, including cooking, washing dishes and so on. Students, as well as teachers, readily responded to Tagore's call. When they asked Tagore for permission, he smiled and said the following: "It would be interesting to try". Overall, on 15th March of 1915, a new life commenced at school, not for a long time though[13].

Before leaving Santiniketan, Gandi pointed out one drawback and frankly told about it to Tagore. In canteen, special seats are intended for boys from Arahman caste. Tagore, who did not desire the sarcasm in denunciation of caste system, anyway followed it in his own sanctuary. And that surprised Gandi. As a result, Tagore cancelled such practice, and currently it is not tolerated in Shantiniketan. And thereafter, he replied to Gandi by saying that he would be happy if his Arahman students voluntarily chose common table to eat on, instead of urging them to do so.

These two small episodes let us see main features when it comes to the contrast between two greatest people of modern India. One of them was an ascetic, who dreamed about making politics sacred, while the other one was a poet, who aspired to make sanctity wonderful.

On 3rd May of 1916, he sailed away to Japan in escort of Andrew, Pearson and young Indian artist Mukula. The poet travelled on a Japanese vessel, and he was impressed by discipline, support and friendship provided by the captain and his team.

The travelers stopped for 2 days in Tangun. Tagore wrote about females of Burma the following: "They are like flowers, blossomed everywhere on branches and ground. An eye does not see anything but them." By describing their grace and dignity, he wrote on a diary the following: "Females here freed themselves from the slavery of household chores, and therefore, achieved such perfection and independence. They do not have to apologize for their existence. They are liked by their feminine grace and honored by wonderful dignity of power. For the first time I noticed that work provided a female with a genuine grace when I saw our santals[14]".

Gandi was arrested on his way to Deli on 8th April of 1919. On 12th April, Tagore sent him an open letter, caliing him Maxatma: "Our powers, in panic and anger, finally showed the claws. In this crisis, you, the greatest leader, stood side by side with us. You returned to your motherland in a difficult for it moment... in order to lead it on a righteous way of clash. Freedom never comes to people through charity. We need to conquer it before applying it[15]".

After the death of Tagore, the national government of freed India took all responsibility for the existence of *Vishvabharat*as a national university. As a result, the first prime minister of India, Jawaharlal Nehru, became the president of this university, who in a true sense, combined both Gandi and Tagore in his own character.

Conclusion.

After 20 years, when Maxatma arrived in Santiniketan for the last time after 4 years after the death of Tagore, he said the following: "I started from aspiring to find contradiction between me and Grudev, and the law being a splendid discovery, that would be missing[16]." The splendid discovery was mutual.

When Tagore passed away, Jawaharlal Nehru was on a circular jail of Dehra Dun and sent a letter to Tagore's relatives on 27th August of 1941 which said the following: I used to meet a number of big people around the globe. Yet, in my soul, I do not have any doubt that two greatest people, whom I was honored to meet, were Gandi and Tagore. I think that they were outstanding characters in the world over the last quarter of century. I am sure, with time, this will be recognized..."

I wonder that, India, despite its current situation (or thanks to it) must have accompanied these two greatest people during life of one generation. And this also convinces me to believe in deep viability of India. That is why I am full of hope, and minor misfortunes and momentary discords seem insignificant and frivolous in front of greatest immutability of idea – which is itself India – from ancient times till these days. China is the same. India and China – how can they disappear?

References :
1. See: I. D. Serebryakov. The greatest humanist. Krishna Kripalani. Rabindranath Tagore. Moscow, "Young Guard", 1983. P.269
2. National uprising against English colonizers, which stirred up large regions of India during the years between 1857 and 1859. It is also called as the uprising of Indian mercenary troops, constituting the core of the rebels. (A translator's note from English language L. N. Asanova).
3. Krishna Kripalani. Rabindranath Tagore. Moscow, "Young guard", 1983, p.73
4. In the same place, p.75
5. In the same place, p.76
6. In the same place, p.102-103
7. In the same place, page 113
8. In the same place, page 129
9. In the same place, page 149.
10. In the same place, page 150.
11. In the same place, page 152.
10. In the same place, page 156.
11. In the same place, page 157.
12. In the same place, page 160.
13. See: Krishna Kripalani. Rabindranath Tagore. Moscow, "Young guard", 1983, p.165
14. In the same place, p.168.
   Santals–ancient tribes, inhabiting on a territory of West Bengal and Bihar.
15. In the same place, p.173.
16. In the same place , p.208

Associate Professor,
State University of Oriental Studies, Tashkent
Uzbekistan

15. Mahatma Gandhi's Teaching and its Relevance in the Modern World

Djamalov F.O.

Abstract

People were inspired by Mahatma Gandhi and his ideas about non-violence. His teaching is more relevant than ever in the current world. This article reveals the essence of this doctrine and its relevance to this day.

Keywords : *Gandhi, nonviolence, India, philosophy, tolerance, teaching, leader of the nation, relevance.*

In life, there is always a place for heroism,selfless service to the Motherland,and, self-denying, to give yourself, your thoughts, and life to the cause of peace and creation.Humanity knows many such examples.If you look into antiquity,it is above all the greatest philosopher Socrates, the Renaissance in the East represents "the second teacher after Aristotle"-encyclopedist Abu Nasr Farabi,and in the 20th century is the "father of the nation," great personality,political and public figure of India-Mohandas Karamchand Gandhi or known Mahatma Gandhi.

As a fighter for the independence of India, he is known to the world as a man who proposed its peaceful implementation. The theory of "Gandhism" is a philosophical concept of nonviolent struggle. It received the name "Satyagraha",which literally means"sat"-truth,"agraha"-hardness. This is a truth firmly maintained by the ideology of Mahatma Gandhi for more than 30 decades.He was faithful to it until the end of his 78-year life.Achieving independence, the desire to see India and its people free from the yoke of colonization-was the main desire of this great man. Rabindranath Tagore called him "the great soul" for his good feeling and lofty ideals.

Mahatma Gandhi propagandized the movement towards independence of the country and wanted the people to develop a sense of their own national pride and for officials to independently refuse honors,titles issued by Great Britain, from buying English goods in favor of purchasing their own national ones.Propagating the philosophy of nonviolent struggle, he constantly called on his fellow citizens to take peaceful action: mass strike and disobedience. The first such strike, the action of 1919, began peacefully, gradually got out of control and began a clash of protesters with the police. Accordingly, Gandhi, as the instigator, was arrested and sentenced to prison. While in prison, he critically began to rethink the essence of his theory,the ways to implement it. After his release, he did not return home,wishing peace to his family,wife and children, and continued to fight for independence,living in a hovel for the poor.While Gandhi was in prison, by sharing his food with children,he told them the importance of independence, the need to put an end to the brutality of the British.In parallel, he made this appeal to the political elite.Preaching his philosophy, he promoted on the one hand, the moral renewal of society,and on the other,he achieved that the principles he put forward began to change the stereotypes of people's thinking, influence the alignment and reorientation of political forces in the country [1, 68].

Mahatma Gandhi was a real yogi. His life became an example and inspiration for many people. The truths that he propagated among the population may seem simple, but the wisdom that is embedded in them is relevant in the current world. Here are some of the great practitioner's instructions:

1. Change. "You have to be the change you would like to see in the world."

You have to start with yourself. If we want change, we have to be an example. If you succeed, people will follow you. Anyone can blame government, society, and God for failures. Anyone can complain, but only a few are able to see the problem in themselves and begin to change.

2. Ask the right questions. "The strength of the question is that it lies at the heart of human progress."

Ask the right questions to the right people. The quality of life is directly dependent on the quality of the questions asked. You can't get the answers you want without asking questions. You cannot make progress without an inquiring and lively mind.

3. Always act. "There is an impulse to action — let's see what happens now. You can break one big plan into small steps and take the first step right now."

This is a more philosophical version of the usual "do not put off until tomorrow what can be done today." Tomorrow will never come, and yesterday is the past. We live in the present. So, we should act "here and now." In addition, we can nev-er be 100% sure that tomorrow will come at all. «Our future depends on what we do now. »

4. Forgive. "The weak cannot forgive. Forgiveness is a trait of strong people."

The fact that a person quickly forgives does not indicate his weakness. On the contrary, it is a sign of his spiritual power. Only the weak can never forgive and hold a grudge, anger or envy which can corrode them from the inside making them even weaker.

5. Watch your beliefs. "Your beliefs will become your thoughts. Your thoughts will become your words. Your words will become your actions. Your actions will become your habits. Your habits will become your values. Your values will become your destiny."

What are you thinking? What do you believe? How do you see yourself and your future? Do you believe in your potential? Whenever in doubt, remember this saying: "You are what you believe. Follow your thoughts, believe in your success and you will definitely succeed — let it not be the first time, but the tenth."

Nowadays, tolerance cannot be achieved without recourse to the worldview and activities of Mohandas Karamchand Gandhi. Nevertheless, the word "tolerance" occurs only occasionally in his works, although Gandhi himself was an exemplary tolerant person throughout his life. This paradox reflects the complexity of his philosophical concept. According to Gandhi, the affirmation of tolerance actually amounts to the establishment of a hierarchy between our position and the position of others[2, 51].

"I do not like the word tolerance", he writes in a letter to his supporters in 1930 while imprisoned in Yeravda Mandir, "but I could not think of a better one." Tolerance implies a gratuitous assumption of the inferiority of other faiths to one's own, whereas Ahisma teaches us to to entertain the same respect for the religious faiths of others as we accord to our own, thus admitting the imperfection of the latter. This admission will readily be made by a seeker of Truth who follows the law of love."The Smart Power Journal brings to our attention two letters in which the great politician and human rights activist of the XX century Mohandas Karamchand" Mahatma " Gandhi (1869-1948) anticipated these tenets of Pomeranian putting them into practice and bringing them almost to the absolute.

As at Wardha
C.P.
India.
23.7.'39.

Dear friend,

Friends have been urging me to write to you for the sake of humanity. But I nave resisted their request, because of the feeling that any letter from me would be an impertinence. Something tells me that I must not calculate and that I must make my appeal for whatever it may be worth.

It is quite clear that you are today the one person in the world who can prevent a war which may reduce humanity to the savage state. Must you pay that price for an object however worthy it may appear to you to be ? Will you listen to the appeal of one who has seliberately shunned the method of war not without considerable success? Any way I anticipate your forgiveness, if I have erred in writing to you.

Herr Hitler
Berlin
Germany.

I remain,

Your sincere friend

M.K. Gandhi

Picture 1. Letter to the Hitler

Mahatma Gandhi wrote these letters to Adolf Hitler. The combination of humility and dignity is striking. The combination of a willingness to meet the monster and reach out to him, so as not to miss even the smallest chance to save the humanity and individual people — and a firm unwavering adherence to their ideals and principles. Mahatma Gandhi says:

God has no religion... and God has no canons, no five pillars and no rules about wearing colorful clothes. He does not care whether we eat apples before the Savior, whether we cook milk and meat on different plates and whether we take food in the daytime during Ramadan. He does not require prayer, circumcision or the belief that the world is based on suffering. All this was invented by the people themselves: they blinded the gods, painted icons and applied ornaments to the white stone. They wrote hundreds of books, developed thousands of rules and restrictions. And nothing has changed in 2000 years. We have learned languages, we use the telephone, we have developed smart chopsticks and we keep cord blood but we continue to kill, rob, lie and hate, regardless of Jesus, Krishna, Muhammad and Buddha. We fight on the streets and in subway cars. We have hundreds of enemies and half a friend. We play hide-and-seek and fake votes. We wear masks and artificial valves. And we completely forgot why we live, breathe and produce milk. And we do not even know that we came to this Earth with a single task-to find happiness!

Thanks to a broad popular front of non-violent resistance, India finally gained peaceful independence from Britainin 1947, and Mahatma Gandhi prepared the first Constitution of India.

This event was followed by another, on a religious basis: violent opposition between Muslims and Hindus. As a result, the country was divided into India and Pakistan. Again, Mahatma Gandhi called for friendly relations, but when nothing happened to stop the feud, he went on a hunger strike. This action gave a positive result and the conflict stopped, although not for long.

Mahatma Gandhi constantly appealed to the conscience of people, urged them to be tolerant of each other,fight against caste inequality,wanted to stop the infringement of the untouchables through laws,he defended them demonstratively,on a legal basis,because he was a lawyer,which did not like the extremist forces in the face of influential elites. They three times made an attempt on this man, who wanted freedom for his people. Unfortunately, the third attempt took his life.

It should be noted that even under the bullets directed against him, he thought about the independence of India, the freedom of his people.Even as he was dying, he asked God to forgive someone whohad committed a sinister murder by shooting him directly in the heart. Gandhi always claimed during his lifetime: "Only the strong can forgive!"In this regard, the following words of Russian President Vladimir Putin deserve attention: "Modern leaders want to solve everything by force,and it is a pity that there is no one like Mahatma Gandhi among them."

Or take the words of another leader of the nation, who promoted the signing of the Peace Treaty on cooperation between India and Pakistan in Tashkent in 1966, Prime Minister Lal Bahadur Shastri. As it is known, born also as Mahatma Gandhi on October 2, to the question of Anil Kumar Shastri's grandson «Why does he not tell anyone that he was born on the same day as the Mahatma", replied that he "has no right to stand on the same level as such a great man". A Nehruvian Socialist and lifelong Congressman, Shastri continues to inspire India's farmers and soldiers as he was the man behind the iconic slogan of *"Jai Jawan, Jai Kisan"[1]*.

---

[1] "English: Hail the Soldier, Hail the Farmer"

Noted by many to be a soft-spoken and humble, Lal Bahadur Shastri was an important figure during the freedom struggle and became prominent after the Independence. Under the first Prime Minister of India Pandit Jawaharlal Nehru, he was the part of his cabinet and ran various portfolios in the Government such as Railway Ministry and Home Ministry. Shastri became the Prime Minister of India in June 1964. It is important to mention that Lal Bahadur Shastri, who was the Prime Minister during 1965 Indo-Pak war, stopped receiving his salary after India had faced food scarcity. In 1920, he joined the Indian Independence Movement. He also participated in the non-cooperation movement. In 1930, he participated in the Salt Satyagraha, for which he was imprisoned for more than two years. He became a loyal follower, first of Gandhi, and then of Jawaharlal Nehru. As a large part of his salary was always donated to various Gandhian causes, he used to run his household expenses on a limited budget. During his time as the Home Minister, he set up the first committee to tackle corruption. Shastri died on January 11, 1966 in Tashkent, where he signed a peace treaty with the then President of Pakistan Ayub Khan. Nowadays, one of Tashkent's most bustling streets is named after him and there is also a monument in the central part of the city dedicated to him [3, 88-89].

The main problems of modern society are the problems of popularizing the philosophy of consumption, violence and aggression, which leads to a number of other global socio-economic problems: the unfair distribution of income in the world, increased intolerance, militarization, the emergence of local conflicts that threaten to turn into a world war, the growth of environmental problems, etc. Our world, in which there is so much violence, now needs the teachings and instructions of Mahatma Gandhi.

The world will always need charity and loving kindness until wars and strife disappear from the face of the earth. And if we understand this, then the relevance of compassion and love as the basis of harmony throughout the world is obvious. And it becomes quite clear that the happiness of each individual depends on the rest of the world, on all other people. As stated in the views of the great soul.

Distribution of the new "My life" edition about Mahatma Gandhi to Uzbek libraries is undoubtedly a great event in our spiritual life.

First of all, Mahatma Gandhi was a great mastermind, humanist and a glorious leader of the Indian nation. With admirable qualities, a great love and devotion to his people he showed an immense patriotism on the way of bloodless strike for gaining national independence of India. His doctrine of "ahimsa", non-violence, is especially popular among enlightening world community.

Gandhi has made a decent contribution not only to his country but also the world in preventing oppression and violence. Voting on 15 June 2007 the United Nations General Assembly to establish 2 October as the International Day of Non-Violence, made Gandhi`s teachings recognized across the globe.

Using equality and truth against violence and oppression Mahatma Gandhi has justified a great power and opportunities a man can have with unwavering firmness.

It is known that India is a multinational, multiethnic and multilingual country. This diversity, showing a great legacy of any country on the one hand, creates numerous acute problems and tensions on the other.To reasonably resolve such a subtle and daunting task, Mahatma Gandhi gave his all in the struggle to unify India.Gandhi taught that religions throughout the world call for spiritual cleanness, rightfulness and brotherhood. Particularly, he has highly appreciated the attitude of Islam to humaneness.

Mahatma Gandhi was a real leader of the nation. He was privileged to devote his whole life for serving the people from the childhood to the rest of his days. He was closely familiar with wishes and problems of the common people.

Reading the "My life" we experience from the bottom of the heart what challenges die author has faced during his life and political activities. In spite of those difficulties he did not give up on his faith and the way chosen. The strong belief in his nation, nobleness and the future of India supported him in the most acute and challenging situations. His firmness and stamina can amaze anyone.

The author said, "There is no event or situation unknown for die people, because I openly lived in public".

Walking throughout India, Mahatma Gandhi tried to be the hope for aspirations of millions of poor, needy, widowed, orphaned and wounded people. Respectful and popular not only in the country but also in the globe he always lived a simple and austere life. By *Saying* "A person gained the same level as mine in social life must fully serve for others as a role model"*he was quite spiritually right.*

The most important and of special attention, despite putting a great country like India on the path of independent progress and defining its ways of development, this great man was always unsatisfied with achieved results. We know what a big attention Mahatma Gandhi has been attaching to the contemporary science, culture, healthcare, history, restoration of spirituality and youth education. Thus, I would like to note that today ongoing comprehensive reforms in Uzbekistan are also primarily directed to the implementation of highly prioritized tasks like ensuring human interests.

Of course, we can speak much about this thoughtful book of the great man taken a decent place in the world history. He left an indelible impression in readers' hearts with his right spirit, multifaceted and model activities, historical evidences and rich humane qualities.The most significant, the book of Mahatma Gandhi "My life", re-edited by a leading editorial office "Uzbekistan", will serve to inform us more about experienced, industrious, tolerant, sincere and noble Indian people, about their ancient history and rich culture [4, 67].

Today, there are monuments to Mahatma Gandhi in the United States, Great Britain,Kazakhstan,Tajikistan,Russia, and Mongolia.This is no accident.Progressive humanity honors his bright memory,and the forces of terrorism and extremism hostile to the world will not calm down even today, having stolen his ashes in 2019.I remember many of his sayings,especially this: "The world is big enough to meet the needs of any person, but too small to satisfy human greed."

References:

1.Djamalov F.O. Theory of nonviolence of Mahatma Gandhi: Vitality, relevance, needs// "Fuqarolik jamiyati" - no. 1 (61). Tashkent-P. 67-70
2.Sultanova E.S. Great soul// Collection of scientific articles- Tashkent-P. 50-53
3.Djamalov F.O. "Find the goal-resources will be found!" (collection dedicated to the 150th anniversary of the birth of Mahatma Gandhi), - [b. m.]: Publishing solutions, 2020. - 108 p.
4.Mirziyoyev Sh.M. "The owner of great soul"// What Gandhi means to me. An anthology – Delhi, 2020

Student,
University of World Economy and Diplomacy,
Tashkent, Uzbekistan

16. Homonym Verbs in Hindi

Saidnazarova Nodira Otaxon Qizi
Sodiqova Mavjuda Qobulovna

Annotation

This topic is about an overview of the types of homonyms in Hindi and a comprehensive lexical and morphological analysis of homonymous verbs in Hindi, and highlights similarities and differences between them.

The sum of all the words in a language is called the vocabulary. Words that occupy a worthy place in the vocabulary of any language are constantly in paradigmatic and syntagmatic relations with each other. Accordingly, they can be divided into several groups.

It is legal for words to be grouped differently in terms of pronunciation, spelling, and meaning. One of these is the phenomenon of homonymy.

The word omonim is derived from the Greek word "homos" which means "the same" and "onoma" or "onyma" is "name". Homonyms are words that are similar in pronunciation and spelling but differ in meaning. For example: रचना - I   a work, creation, creativity (*feminine*[1], noun); रचना-II to create, to compose (*transitive*[1] verb);   सीना-I sew (*transitive* verb) ; सीना- II breast (*feminine*, noun).

Two aspects of homonyms distinguish it from other forms of formation:

1) From the acoustic-articulatory point of view, homonymous words have the same properties, that is, their pronunciation is similar, almost the same:

चटकना - I crack, be opened (*intransitive*[1] verb) ; चटकना - II slap (*masculine*[1], noun)

2) Graphically, they have the same system, for example:

रसना–I tongue (*f.m.* noun); रसना– II to leak (*intrans.* verb)

According to research on the types of homonyms, homonyms can be divided into the following types:

1. Lexical[2] homonyms - homonyms between words are called lexical homonyms: आरी – I *f.m.* saw (noun) ; आरी - II tired, exhausted (adjective); सोना - I *m.* gold (noun) ; सोना - II *trans.* sleep (verb).

It is known that a word is called a lexeme. The main point of reference of the phenomenon of homonymy is the expression of the word, its appearance.

In homonymy, the harmony of sound and graphic expression is important. It is also important to note that homonyms can be divided into noun homonyms, verb homonyms, and adjective homonyms, depending on which parts of speech they belong to. The homonymous meanings of homonyms in Hindi can also refer to the same part of speech (अंत - end (noun); अंत – heart, soul (noun), two different parts of speech (जड़ – root; base (noun); जड़– dead, lifeless (adjective), and three different parts of speech (रोना– to cry (verb), रोना– crying, weeping (noun– the sound of crying), रोना– crying (adjective – crying baby). Homonymy within the same part of speech is more common in nouns and verbs.

If the homonymous meaning of the homonymous words belongs to two different parts of speech, then when in adding suffixes to those words, the homonymous relationship between them disappears: रचना– a work (to write a work), रचना– to create, to compose;

Compare: ये रचनाएं – these works , वह रचता है – he creates.

It is important to distinguish between homonyms and polysemous words. No matter polysemous word how many meanings there are, these meanings are interconnected. Because homonyms are different words, there is no connection between their meanings. Homonyms are two or more words that have the same form, while polysemous words are formed from the use of their own and figurative meanings.

2. Grammatical homonyms- Grammatical homonyms are homonyms between suffixes, phrases, or sentences. There are two types of grammatical homonyms:

a) morphological homonyms - homonymy between suffixes. For example: the suffix - ई is a homonymous suffix that can make two different word groups:

पहाड़ (mountain) + ई = पहाड़ी (पहाड़ी आदमी) - mountainous

बेरोज़गार (unemployed) + ई = बेरोज़गारी – unemployment. In these words the suffix - ई formed a group of nouns , धन (wealth - noun) + ई = धनी (rich - adjective) , जंगल (forest) + ई = जंगली (wild), in words such as, the suffix –ई formed a group of adjectives.

The suffix - ता is also:

मित्र (friend) + ता = मित्रता (friendship), in this word - ता formed a noun suffix, कर + ता = करता - in this word - ता is a suffix that forms an indefinite adjective of a verb.

b) Syntactic homonyms are homonyms between phrases or sentences:

राज भाई आया है ? (in this sentence राज is subject)

राज, भाई आया है ? (in this sentence राज was used as the person to whom it is addressed). The meaning in these sentences can only be distinguished from the tone.

3. Phraseological homonyms are homonymy between phrases, idioms and proverbs:

अच्छे रहना[3] – I to be healthy, to be in good health ; II to succeed, to profit

अखज करना– I to choose, to accept ; II to insist on one's opinion

इधर उधर को हाँकना - I to boast (boast in vain); II to talk about different topic (not talking about the same topic).

अख्तियार करना - I to accept; II to like;

As a result of research on homonymous verbs, it has been observed that homonymous meanings of homonymous verbs in Hindi are within the same part of speech or within different parts of speech. There are many examples of homonymous verbs, one meaning of which belongs to the verb and the other meaning belongs to the nouns or adjectives. In this case, it was found that the verbs belonging to the noun have more meanings, and the adjectives belonging to the adjectives have less.

For example: घटना - *I intrans.* to happen, to occur, to accomplish *verb*; II *intrans.* to shorten, to decrease, to reduce, decline – *verb;* III *f.m.* event, incident, situation – *noun.*

Ex: असहमति के कारण अक्सर बुरी चीजें घटती हैं । - Bad things often happen because of disagreements.

पिछले साल वेतन काफ़ी घटी थी । - Last year, salaries were significantly reduced.

इस घटना ने उन्हें बुरी तरह प्रभावित किया । - This incident affected them badly.

ताना – I *m.* objurgation, reproach; reproof – *noun*; II *trans.* to melt – *verb*

Ex: वह हमेशा अपनी गलतियों के लिए ताना सुनता है । - He always hears reproof for his mistakes.

लोहार लोहे को ताकर तरह-तरह की चीज़े बनाता है । - A blacksmith melts iron and makes various things.

मस्ताना – I drunken; intoxicated – *adjective*; II *intrans.* to get drunk – *verb*

Ex: वह प्यार से मस्ताना था । - He was intoxicated with love.

वह मस्ताया था क्योंकि उसने बहुत पी लिया था। - He was drunk because he drank a lot.

In the process of morphological analysis of homonymous verbs, it is clear from the above that one of the homonymous meanings of some homonymous verbs belongs to another part of speech. These homonymous verbs also differ in their form, use in sentences, and functions in speech.

In the process of grammatical analysis of homonymous verbs in Hindi, verbs were studied in terms of transitive and intransitive, and it became clear that homonymous verbs can be divided into the following 3 types:

1. Both homonymous meanings are transitive verbs.
2. Both homonymous meanings are intransitive verbs.
3. Mixed verbs, one of meaning is transitive and the other is intransitive

Some examples of this result:

1. Both homonymous meanings are transitive verbs:

उतारना - I *trans.* to take off ; to empty, unload; II *trans.* to pass across

Ex: बच्चे ने स्नान करने के लिए अपने कपड़े उतारे। - The boy took off his clothes for bathing.

उस ने नाव में सवार सभी यात्रियों को समुद्र तट के दूसरी ओर उतारा । - He passed across all the passengers (travelers) in the boat to the other side of the beach.

चीतना - I *trans.* to draw; II *trans.* to think, to conceive; to contemplate; to remember.

Ex: उन्होंने अपनी सबसे प्रसिद्ध चित्र दो साल तक चीता। - He painted his most famous painting for two years.

इस समस्या के समाधान के बारे में माँ ने बहुत देर तक चीता। -The mother thought for a long time about the solutions to this problems.

पुजाना - I *trans.* to gain respect, to earn the respect; II *trans.* to treat (wound).

Ex: प्रेमचंद ने अपने अमूल्य रचनाओं से लोगों के बीच आदर पुजाया था। - Premchand has earned the respect of the people with his priceless creativity.

प्राचीन काल में चिकित्सकों ने कई घावों को जड़ी-बूटियों से

पुजाया था। - In ancient times, physicians treated many wounds with herbs.

2. Both homonymous meanings are intransitive verbs:

उझकना - I *intrans.* to watch, to observe; II *intrans.* to jump, to jump off.

Ex: राम बहुत देर तक लोगों को उझका । - Ram watched the people for a long time.

श्याम दीवार के पीछे देखने के लिए दीवार से उझका ।[4] - Shyam jumped off the wall to see the back of the wall.

चसना - I *intrans.* to stick, to adhere; II *intrans.* to die, to pass away.

Ex: आज रमेश ने देखा कि कल की परीक्षा की घोषणा दीवार पर चसी थी।- Today Ramesh saw the announcement of yesterday's exam stuck the wall.

पिछले साल कोविड के कारण दुनिया भर में कई लोग चसे। - Last year, many people died around the world because of Covid.

गहगहाना - I *intrans.* to be satisfied, to be pleased; to be surprised; II *intrans.*to ripen well.

Ex: माँ अपने बेटे की अद्भुत क्षमता से गहगहायी थी। - Mother was surprised her son's unusual ability.

आज के सेब बहुत स्वादिष्ट हैं, वे बहुत गहगहाया था। - Today's apples are so delicious, they ripened well.

3. Mixed verbs, one of meaning is transitive and the other is intransitive:

कमाना - I *intrans.* to work, to earn; II *trans.* to reduce, to decrease

Ex: श्याम पिछले महीने में दलाली करके हजारों रुपयों कमाया था। - Last month Shyam worked as a broker, earning thousands of rupees.

सरकार ने पिछले महीने बाजार में कीमतों काफी कमायी थी। -

The government had significantly reduced prices in the market last month.

कूकना - I *intrans.* to sing, to warble; to chirp; II *trans.* to restart, to wind (watch).

Ex: रानी के दुःख के कारण बगीचे में पक्षी भी उदास कूके। - Birds in the garden also sang sadly because of the queen's grief.

घड़ीसाज़ ने घड़ी की मरम्मत की और उस ने उस को फिर कूका। - Watchmaker repaired the watch and restarted it.

ठठाना - I *trans.* to beat, to hit, to thrash; II *intrans.* to laugh.

Ex: सूरन ने चोर को बहुत बुरी तरह ठठाया। - Suran hit the thief very badly.

नाटक देखकर सभी दर्शक ठठाये। - Everyone in the audience laughed when they saw the play.

In conclusion, it became clear that homonyms are words that are the same in pronunciation and spelling, but differ in meaning. They have the following types:

1. Lexical homonyms are homonymy between words.
2. Grammatical homonyms are homonymy between suffixes
3. Phraseological homonyms are homonyms between phrases, that is, compounds that have a figurative meaning.

Homonymous verbs in Hindi can be classified according to their expression and analysis as follows:

1. When homonymous verbs are morphologically analyzed, they can be divided into homonymous verbs, one meaning of which is a verb and the other meaning is part of speech other than the verb.
2. In the process of grammatical analysis of homonymous verbs in Hindi, when verbs are studied in terms of transitive and intransitive, it became clear that homonymous verbs can be divided into 3 types:

1) Both homonymous meanings are transitive verbs.
2) both homonymous meanings are intransitive verbs.
3) mixed, that is, verbs, one meaning of which is transitive and the other is intransitive

Thus, the analysis shows that each homonymous verb differs from each other, has its own characteristics and forms, using in sentences is different also has different functions in speech.

References

1. Dr. N. Sreedharan. Learn hindi through English. Sura Books. 2008.
2. G'.Abdurahmonov. Hozirgi o'zbek adabiy tili. Toshkent. O'zbekiston. 2010. 110-118 pages.
3. भोलानाथ तिवारी, हिंदी मुहावरां कोश [Dictionary of hindi idioms] नई दिल्ली 1991. प॰ 20–40.

Websites:
4. https://rekhtadictionary.com.
Dictionaries:
5. В.М. Бескровный «Хинди – русский словарь». Москва, 1959.

[1]**Researcher,**
[2]**Senior Hindi teacher,**
Tashkent State University of Oriental Studies,
Uzbekistan

17. Analysis of lexemes from Persian affixes in Hindi

Ismatullayeva Mo'tabar Xushvaqt Qizi

Abstact
The article provides general information on the linguistics of affixes, the scientific and theoretical views of Russian and Uzbek Indian scholars on Persian affixes in Hindi, as well as the research of Indian linguists on this topic. In the course of covering the article, the scientific and theoretical views of many Indian scholars have been studied, and the theories of some of them have been cited as examples. Several examples of Persian affixes in Hindi have been given, and grammatical models have been developed based on them.
Keywords : affixes, Persian affixes, Dakxini languages, affixal method, word formation system,

Introduction

Affixation is a morphological process whereby a bound morpheme, an affix, is attached to a morphological base. Diachronically, the English word *affix* was first used as a verb and has its origin in Latin: *affixus*, past participle of the verb affigere, ad- 'to' + figere 'to'fix'. Affixation falls in the scope of Morphology where bound morphemes are either roots or affixes. Prefixes (affixes that precede the root) and suffixes (affixes that follow the root) are the most common types of affixes cross-linguistically. Affixes mark derivational(-*er* in *teach-er*) and inflectional (-*s* in *teacher-s*) changes, and affixation is the most common strategy that human languages employ for derivation of new words and word forms. However, languages vary in the ways they express the same semantics, and if in English the noun *biolog-ist* is derived from *biology* through the addition of the suffix -*ist*, in Russian (and other Slavic languages) the same derivation does not involve the addition of an affix but subtraction of form: *biolog-ija* 'biology' → *biolog* 'biologist'. Most languages make an extensive use of affixes (most European, African, Australian, and Amerindian languages are of this type),whereas others (e.g., Vietnamese), hardly do. In languages that use affixes, there is a general preference for suffixes over prefixes[1].

In English there are about 25 prefixes which can transfer words to a different part of speech.[2] *E.g.* - head *(n)* - behead *(v)*, bus *(n)* - debus(*v*), brown *(adj)* - embrown(*v*), title(*n*) entitle(*v*), war(*n*). - prewar *(adj)*. If it is so we can say that there is no functional difference between suffixes and prefixes. Besides there are linguists who treat prefixes as a part of word-composition. They think that a prefix has the same function as the first component of a compound word. Other linguists consider prefixes as derivational affixes which differ essentially from root - morphemes and stems. From the point of view of their origin affixes may be native and borrowed. The suffixes -ness, -ish, -dom, -ful, -less, -ship and prefixes be-, mis-, un-, fore-, etc are of native origin. But the affixes -able, -ment, -ation, -ism, -ist, re-, anti-, dis-, etc are of borrowed origin. They came from the Greek, Latin and French languages. Many of the suffixes and prefixes of native origin were independent words. In the course of time they have lost their independence and turned into derivational affixes[3].

The role of A.S. Barkhudarov is very important among linguists who have done extensive research on the use of Persian affixes in Hindi. A.S. Barkhudarov in his work "

---

[1] Affixation (Oxford Bibliographies in Linguistics, version 2014). Stela Manova. p.1.

[2] Мешков Д. «Словооброзование современного английского языка» М, 1976 р. 346.

[3] Карашук П.М. «Словообразование английского языка» М, 1977 р. 283

Словообразование в хинди " focuses on the method of affixation of word formation in Hindi. The difference between this scholar's research on affixes and our scientific work is that the scholar has given only general information. In his research on word formation in Dakhini, Professor O.N. Shomatov also focused on the Iranian suffixes widely used in Dakhini and studied their peculiarities[4].

In V.M. Beskrovny's two-volume "Хинди - русский словарь" singled out words made with Persian affixes, as well as affixes that served to enrich the vocabulary of the Indian language. On the subject of word formation in Hindi, Z.M. Dimshits describes the method of affixation as follows: "Affixation is a method of productive morphological word formation in Hindi". He explains the difference in the type of making :

1. Suffixation is the main affixal method in the Hindi word formation system. It is divided into two: root- suffixation in which the word does not change, for example :

a) बलवान – powerful (बल, -"power"), खेती– farming (खेत - "field");

b) root- suffixation in which phonetic changes occur in words, for example: लुटेरा–thief (लुट– "theft"), चुटपन–childhood (छोटा–"small"), लड़कपन– childhood, youth (लड़का–"child, young, child"), खिलाड़ी–player (खेल–"game"), ऐतिहासिक – historical (इतिहास - history);

2. Prefixation, for example: अंजान – unaware (ज्ञान –

---

[4] Шаматов А.Н. Классический дакхини (Южный хиндустани XVII в.). -М.: Наука, 1974.

"knowledge"), बेघर – homeless (घर – "home");

3. *Prefixal-suffixal* or a mixed word-formation method, based on the use of both suffixes and prefixes, for example: बेशर्मी, – shameless (शर्म–"shame"), अन्मेलपन,– irrelevant (मेल–"communication"), अंतरनगरीय – among cities (नगर – "city");

4. *Infixation*, internal inflection, a method characterized by the shortening, lengthening, or exchange of vowels (and sometimes consonants) in base words. An example of this type is the construction of transitive verbs from intransitive verbs: बँटना – to share → बांटना – divide ; फिरता– to walk → फेरना – to take a walk; भिगना – to get wet → भिगोना – wet; छुटना – to be free → छोड़ना – to free. ⁵"

An uzbek linguist professor O. N. Shomatov writes, "The Arab-Persian conquests began in the first centuries of the second millennium AD with Central Asia, Afghanistan, and Iran, as well as with the Arab conquest of Sindh and Islam in the 7th and 8th centuries. 'Secret consists of units assimilated during the course of historical relations[6].

Hindi hybrid words derived from Persian have a special place in the historical context of Hindi. From the 12th to the 13th century, Persian and Turkish influenced the languages and dialects of northwestern India for several hundred years. The main reason for this was the emergence of Muslim states in northern India.

---

[5] Шаматов А.Н. Классический дакхини (Южный хиндустани XVII в.). -M.: Наука, 1974. 195.b.

[6] Annotated dictionary of the Uzbek language. T II. -T.: " National Encyclopedia of Uzbekistan " State Scientific Publishing House, 2006. -B. 119

According to the Russian Indian scholar V.M. Beskrovniy, the role of Persian words in the formation of the Hindi language is important. According to him, a new hybrid word was formed as a result of the addition of special affixes to Persian words or special Persian elements to Hindi words in the vocabulary of Hindi. In his two-volume Indo-Russian Dictionary, V.M. Beskrovniy singled out lexical units made up of Persian affixes, as well as affixes that served to enrich the vocabulary of the Hindi language.

Professor O.N. Shomatov in his research on word formation in Dakhini, Shomatov also focuses on the Iranian suffixes widely used in Dakhini and classifies them as follows. For example:

1. [-ई] ~ The suffix is a productive suffix in classical dakhini. Also participates in the formation of nouns and adjectives.

a) Artificial words- abstract nouns are often formed from adjectives that are etymologically specific to the Arabic + Persian languages. There are about 30 such words.[7]

*[हारी] ~ without holidays \→ [हार]~ oppressed, crushed \\per.

*[इस्तिग़नाई] ~ wealth \→ [इस्तिग़ना]~wise\\arab

Nouns derived from Arabic + Persian can also serve as a basis for such words.

* [सबूरी] ~ patience \→ [सबूर]~ patience \\arab.

*[दोस्ती] ~ friendship \→ [दोस्त]~ friend \\per.

This suffix is productive because it can make abstract nouns from artificial words. It is made on the basis of the following template.

[noun (name) root + verb base + suffix [ई]

---

[7] Шаматов А.Н. Классический дакхини (Южный хиндустани XVII в.). -М.: Наука, 1974. –С. 80.

* [तमादारी] ~ racketeering \\→ [तमादार]~ biased \\ arab+per.

* [दस्तगीरी] ~ to own \\→ [दस्तगीर]~ owner, master

Words based on the following formula are rare:

[preffix or preffixoid + noun (name) basis + suffix [ई]

*[बे-अदब-ई] ~ uneducated/ rude

b) Compound words are formed from etymologically specific words of Persian + Arabic languages.

For example:

*[नफ़सानी] ~ noticeable → [नफ़सान]→[नफ़स]~ emotion, sensitivity

[-दार] The suffix is now productive. A noun makes an adjective or a noun through a phrase:

For example:

[ख़बरदार] ~ be aware

[सरदार] ~ leader

2. [-गी] The suffix noun is a noun from adjectives. Originally, this suffix is a variant of the Persian suffix [-ī].

In classical dakhini, this morpheme becomes an independent word-forming unit. Because it affects the bases of nouns (nouns) on the one hand, and can be combined with the bases of Indian words on the other hand, it is also widely used in the construction of hybrid words.[8]

*[परेशानगी] ~ sadness → [परेशान]~ sad \\ per.

*[उस्तादगी] ~ teaching → [उस्ताद]~ teacher \\arab.

In this regard, we also refer to the scientific and theoretical views of one of the Russian Indian scholars AS Barkhudarov. In his "Slovoobrazovanie v hindi", the scholar also focuses on Persian affixes in his research on the use of affixes in Hindi.

---

[8] Шаматов А.Н. Классический дакхини (Южный хиндустани XVII в.). -М.: Наука, 1974. –C. 86.

The scholar classifies Persian suffixes into Hindi as follows:
1. *Pure suffixes*
2. [-दार] The suffix makes a noun meaning "ownership" (a person's name based on occupation, type of activity, social status) and adjectives. The scope of this suffix is expanding in Hindi, and even though it is one of the most productive suffixes in Persian, it is much more common in Hindi.[9]

• The suffix [-dāra] is often added to Hindi words:
• [काँटेदार] – thorny; covered with thorns
• [कीचड़दार] – laundry, covered with laundry

The works of Indian linguists who have conducted scientific and theoretical research on the use of affixes in Hindi have also been studied in detail. Among them are the works of Indian linguists Dhirendra Varma, V. Prasad, Kamtaprasad Guru, Ramrajpal Dwivedi (Hindi Vyakarnik Shabdkosh (A Glossary of Hindi Grammar)) and others.

Masalan, Ramrajpal Dwivedi o'zining "Hindi Vyakarnik Shabdkosh" (A Glossary of Hindi Grammer) ya'ni "Hindiy tilining grammatik terminlari" nomli asarida ham preffiks hamda suffiks terminlariga ham ta'rif berib o'tgan.

Masalan: "Ramrajpal Dvivedi "Preffiks" terminini "परसर्ग", "Suffiks" terminini esa "उपसर्ग " hamda "प्रत्यय" deb nomlaydi. Ammo ba'zi bir hind tilshunos olimlar "प्रत्यय" atamasini ko'proq umumiy ma'noni anglatuvchi "affiks" ma'nosida ishlatganlar".[10] For example, Ramrajpal Dwivedi in his Glossary of Hindi Grammar describes both prefixes and suffixes.

For example, Ramrajpal Dvivedi calls the term "prefix" "

---

[9] O'sha asar. – b. 111.

[10] रामरजपल द्विवेदी, हिन्दी व्याकरणक शब्दकोश, सूर्य भारती प्रकाशन, दिल्ली, 2000

परसर्ग " and the term

"उपसर्ग ". However, some Indian linguists have used the term "

प्रत्यय"" to mean

"प्रत्यय"", which has a more general meaning.

In addition to the above, another Indian linguist, Kamtaprasad Guru, has also conducted research on the use of affixes in Hindi. The scholar classifies the Persian affixes used in Hindi as follows:

- [आ] The suffix creates the name of the executor of the activity (action):
- [दान] "to know"- [दाना] "educated"
- [रिह] "to be free" - [रिहा] "released"
- [आन] suffiksi hozirgi zamon sifatdoshini yasaydi, masalan
- [पुरस] "to ask" - [पुरसान] "questioner"
- [चसप] "paste" - [चसपान] "adhesive"
- [इनदा] suffix . Creates the name of the activity (action) executor, e.g.:

  [कुन] "to do" - [कुनिनदा] "doer"

  [जी] "to live" - [जिनदा] "liver"

  [चुनना] – in Hindi is added to the verb "to choose", and these suffixes [चुनिनदा] form the word "choose".

  [इश] suffix. Makes an abstract horse, e.g.:

- [कोश] "to strive" - [कोशिश] "striving"
- [नाल] "to complain" - [नालिश] "complaining"
- [ई] suffix makes an abstract noun.

For example :

  [रफ़तन] "to leave" - [रफ़तनी] "leave"

Persian affixes that have changed during the process of adaptation to Hindi:

This model focuses only on changes in the structure of affixes in the process of adaptation to Hindi. Contains the following affixes.

a. Affixes that change to only one sound:

№	Hindi	Persian
1.	-दार daar	-dor
2.	-बान baan	-bon
3.	-गाह gaah	-goh
4.	-कार kaar	-kor, gar (korgar)
5.	-इस्तन, स्तन istan, stan	-iston
6.	-ज़ार zaar	-zor
7.	-दान daan	-don
8.	-बाज़ baaz	-boz
9.	-बर्दार bardaar	-bardor
10.	-खन khan	-xon
11.	-साज़ saaz	-soz
12.	-नामा naama	-nome[11]

Persian affixes

A significantly large group of Persian affixes modify adjectives, verbs, nouns and adverbs. They decorate Hindi-Urdu speech with a variety of phonemes used by Hindi and Urdu poets and writers. There is a large list and some

---

[11] To'rayev S. "Linguistic analysis of lexical units made of Persian affixes in Hindi." Tashkent 2016. p. 53.

examples are as follows. Urdu words are in angle brackets "<--->" with the English meanings underneath.

Suffix words

1. गी: < ज़िंदगी> < बंदगी>

   ज़िंदा, (alive)- life, बंदा (servant) service

2. मी < गर्मी < नर्मी >

   गर्म hot)-heat, नर्म (soft)-softness

3. गार < madadgar>< मददगार khidmatgaar> ख़िदमतगार

   मदद (help)-helper, ख़िदमत -(service)-

4. बर: < दिलबर >< पाई घमबर >

   (carrier) दिल (heart)- lover(message) = messenger

5. बान or वान : < बागबान >< कौचवान>

   (driver)(Garden) –gardener(coach driver)

6. मंद < दौलतमंद >< अकलमंद >

   (wealth)= wealthy (wisdom) = wise= wealth thy

7. ची : < तबलची > < ख़ज़नची > (drum)= drummer(treasure)= treasurer

8. अक < धोलक >< ऐयनक>

   (small drum) (eyes= eye glasses)

9. आना : < सालाना > <zaanaana>

   (year=yearly)(lady= for ladies)

10. बेखबर, बेरहम: < बेखबर, bakhabar>< बेरहम Berahem>

    (without) (with information) (without kindness)

11. ईन: < रनगीन> <नामकीन>

    (with or full) (colorful) (salt=saltish)

12. नाक :< खातरनाक>< शर्मनाक sharamnak>

    (danger = dangerous) (shame=shameful)

Now we can see some examples of Persian prefixes:

1. बद : < बदचलन >< बदसुरत >

(bad) (character) (looks ugly)

2. खुब : < सुबसूत >< खूबसीरत >

(good) (beautiful) (has a good character)

3. कुम: < कुमज़ोर >< कुमाकल >

(less) (weak) (unwise)

In summary, the twins, Persian-Arabic made significant contributions towards Modern Urdu/Hindi, enriching the vocabulary with diverse senses, meanings, phonemes, and words, impacted the grammar also. Besides this linguistic hybridization, the plentiful literature of the twins also had a major impact on the literature of Urdu/Hindi. [12]

Conclusion

Affixal word formation refers to the formation of a new word using the affixes that exist in a particular language - the addition of minimal elements of the language to the base.We have observed that the word formation of a noun phrase includes the following lexical-semantic groups of nouns. These are abstract names, personal names, specific place names, and subject names.

The -ई suffix, which is considered to be the most productive of the abstract horse-forming suffixes, joins the stem, adjective, and verb stem to form a horse. An analysis of horses formed with the suffix ई showed that most of them were words made up of personal names. Depending on their meaning, they can be divided into the following types: , property, names that mean characters.

The most productive of the suffixes that make up a person's name is [dāshtan]

Nearly 46 Persian affixes and affixoids were involved in

---

[12] Abdul Jamil Khan. The politics of language. Urdu / Hindi: An artificial Divide. Algora Publishing New York. 2006. p. 149

the construction of names. The main contributors are suffixes, which are the most effective suffixes in the construction of nouns in Hindi.

References

1. Affixation (Oxford Bibliographies in Linguistics, version 2014). Stela Manova. p.1.
2. Мешков Д. «Словооброзование современного английского языка» М, 1976 p. 346.[1]
3. Карашук П.М. «Словообразование английского языка» М, 1977 p. 283
4. Шаматов А.Н. Классический дакхини (Южный хиндустани XVII в.). -М.: Наука, 1974.
5. Шаматов А.Н. Классический дакхини (Южный хиндустани XVII в.). -М.: Наука, 1974. 195.b.
6. Annotated dictionary of the Uzbek language. T II. -T.: " National Encyclopedia of Uzbekistan " State Scientific Publishing House, 2006. -B. 119
7. Abdul Jamil Khan. The politics of language. Urdu / Hindi: An artificial Divide. Algora Publishing New York. 2006. p. 149
8. Шаматов А.Н. Классический дакхини (Южный хиндустани XVII в.). -М.: Наука, 1974. –С. 80.
9. To'rayev S. "Linguistic analysis of lexical units made of Persian affixes in Hindi." Tashkent 2016. p. 53.
10. Abdul Jamil Khan. The politics of language. Urdu / Hindi: An artificial Divide. Algora Publishing New York. 2006. p. 149

**Master of the department
"Languages of South and Southeast Asia" at
Tashkent state University of Oriental studies**

18. The Role of Indian Women In Social Life
(On the example of Mira Sikri's work)

U.T. Maxamadkhodjaeva

"A woman is a man, a great man. She is a society educator. The happiness and unhappiness of the country depends on the woman. A woman with the right upbringing gives appropriate care to a man; a man with good upbringing makes the country prosperous. All happiness and prosperity begin with the woman; happiness must begin with her."

Imam Khomeini

Woman! There is a great power at the heart of these five letters that often seems simple to us. She is a miracle created by Allah, a delicate creation. She is the possessor of immense talent and intellect, so she can conquer the world out of the corner of her eye. The contribution of such beauties to the literary process is invaluable. An important social problem in Indian literature - the plight of Indian women - has long been a concern for many Indian writers, especially woman writers. An important social problem in Indian literature - the plight of Indian women - has long been a concern for many Indian writers, especially their writers.

Writers such as Mamta Kaliya, Subhadra Kumar Chaukhan, Ushadevi Mitra, Amrita Pritam, Mannu Bhandari, Mira Sikri, Susham Bedi, Dipak Sharma, Sara Ray, Shivrani Devi have addressed this problem through their works. In their novels and stories, they talked about the role of Indian women in the family and society. These famous Indian writers defend women because the constant disenfranchised, discriminated status of Indian women in society has always been one of India's national problems. "Throughout the centuries of Indian history, women have experienced all the hardships of life in a feudal society with a caste system and religious traditions.1"

---

[1] Салимова Ф.С. Женщины независимой Индии.

Poets and many other writers also praise the woman, draw her picture with delicate images, and turn the path of life into a book. However, no one can understand a woman's pain, her sorrows as a woman herself. For there are many secrets hidden in the depths of her soul, and many pains that afflict her heart. It is inevitable that the pouring out of these heartaches and sufferings will be an unforgettable story and the basis for the creation of great works. Such kind of woman is Mira Sikri, a wonderful Indian writer who aims to illustrate her subtleties with her pencil.

Writer Mira Sikri was born in 1941 in Gujranwala, India. She is very talented and the author of many books. The books "पैंतरे" (Maneuver), "ग़लती कहाँ" (Where is the error), "अनुपस्थित" (Existing) are in the hearts of readers. Her ability to see reality in a variety of ways further expands the world of the readers' imagination and perception.

In the author's works, the image of women's individuality is disappearing within the backward traditions of a male-dominated society. Mira Sikri is one of the writers who started writing about the issue of women long before the issue of feminism and gender entered society. The main issue he raised was how men use women for their own benefit. His works were published in literary magazines and quickly gained public attention. The images he created are imbued with the spirit of humanism. Mira Sikri, who used imaginary illustrations in the creation of the work, portrays weak heroes who do not attract much attention in life and society, including the saintly brahmana, his simple wife or widow who lives according to tradition.

One of Mira Sikri's stories is "Unexpected Hunger" ("anahōnī kī bhūkha"). The protagonist of the story is described as a girl who has suffered life blows. It depicts a girl driving a car and being taken to the wrong place and disgraced. Until then, it is a pity that the girl's imaginary

Ташкент. 1979. –С. 4

experiences are compared to a woman and seen as a rag that is discarded when worn out. What did the character of the story imagine? The fear in her, the distrust in Indian men, is clearly depicted.

बिन्दु को घर के दरवाज़े तक छोड़कर आ गई। भय-सा लग रहा है। कभी इसके साथ अकेली गई भी तो नहीं-दिन में भी। और बिन्दु ने भी तो उस दिन कहा था"—बचकर रहना ,ख़तरनाक आदमी है। "वह विनीत भाव से गाड़ी का दरवाज़ा पकड़े खड़ा है। दरवाज़ा खोलता है" -आइये "कहकर मुझे बैठने का संकेत करता है। क्या यह औपचारिकता है या सभ्य देखने की सायास चेष्टा। याद करने की कोशिश करती हूँ कि कभी इसने बिन्दु के साथ इस तरह की औपचारिकताएँ बरती हैं।

""I left Bindu at the door," he said. There is a slight sense of dread. He didn't even walk alone with her all day. Bindu also said that day, "Be careful, dangerous man." He opened the car door and motioned to me, "Come on." Is it a formality or an attempt to look decent? Sometimes I remember trying to do such formalities with Bindu.[2]"

Bindu, a friend of the hero of our story, warned her by telling her what kind of man he was. After that, the fear inside her increased even more. In this situation, the author points out that the girl is helpless, that she cannot get out of this situation.

अकेला घर। कोई भी व्यक्ति वहाँ नहीं होगा। न पत्नी ,न माँ ,न बहन। ऊपर से रात। सन्नाटा और मैं। कॉप जाती हूँ। फिर भी निडर दिखने के प्रयास में अनायास मुंह से निकल जाता है" – अगर बहुत ज़रूरी काम न हो तो पहले मुझे छोड़ दीजिये। "

Lonely house. There seems to be no one there. Not his wife, not his mother, not his sister. Silence and me. I'm trembling. I held myself back and said, "If it's not a very important job, drive me first.[3] "

---

[2] ममता कालिया, बीसवी सदी का हिंदी महिला साहित्य-लेखन, साहित्य अकादमी, नई दिल्ली, 2015, पेज 171

[3] ममता कालिया, बीसवी सदी का हिंदी महिला साहित्य-लेखन, साहित्य

In the story, the author reveals the inner experiences of the protagonist, saying that her whole being, feelings, thoughts and dreams have become a mirage.

The protagonist of Mira Sikri is a complex and multifaceted character who is looking for enlightenment and waiting for a happy destiny.

क्या मेरा संदेह ठीक है ? कुछ ऐसी-वैसी स्थिति आ गई तो मैं गाड़ी से कूद पड़ूंगी ,शोर मचा दूंगी ,पर क्या कोई सुन पाएगा ? दोषी तो मुझे ही ठहराया जाएगा।

"So, are my suspicions right? If that happens, I will jump out of the car and make noise, but can anyone hear me? I will be guilty of it myself.[4] "

The story shows that even if the girl gets out of the car and calls people for help, she realizes that she is to blame. The reality here is that women's rights are being violated in Indian society.

Let's analyze another example from the story.

एक विषैले सॉप का फन अपनी गर्दन पर महसूस करती हूँ। संपूर्ण शरीर उसके विषैले प्रभाव से नि:स्पंद हुआ जा रहा है। रेंगता-रेंगता वह सॉप मेरी कमर तक पहुंच गया है।

"It's like a poisonous snake skin on my neck. The whole body is suffering from its toxic effects. That snake crawled up to my waist. [5]"

The author likens the man to a venomous snake. His cruel touch to a girl's lust is what many women seen as a cheap doll, an item.

The images of all the women created by Mira Sikri attract attention with their closeness to life, their nationalism and

---

अकादमी, नई दिल्ली, 2015, पेज 171

[4] वही, पेज 172

[5] ममता कालिया, बीसवी सदी का हिंदी महिला साहित्य-लेखन, साहित्य अकादमी, नई दिल्ली, 2015, पेज 172

their easy identification.

In addition, in the literature of this period, along with the issue of women's freedom, domestic oppression, violence, it shows of the whole society as a low, dumb, languageless, lawless thing, a means of entertainment, its abuse, helplessness, insecurity. In general, it is necessary to acknowledge the services of this writer in raising the issue of gender with the utmost urgency.

Based on the events in the story, it can be said that in order for women to be able to bring up the younger generation in a scientific and healthy way, there is a hint that they need not only life experience and support from those around them, but also knowledge.The issue of early marriage and early marriage is also a problematic aspect of women's disenfranchisement. Currently, the number of girls married before the age of 18 in the world is 750 million. Only 52% of the world's women and girls marry voluntarily. Early marriages lead to sad and negative situations such as illiteracy, unpreparedness for motherhood, the possibility of an increase in the number of unhealthy and disabled children, unemployment, and dependency.

Fundamental documents such as the Rio de Janeiro Declaration on Environment and Development (Rio Declaration, 1992), the Cairo Conference on Population and Development (1994) and the Istanbul Conference on Human Settlements (1996) serve for this purpose. These include the Convention on the Elimination of All Forms of Discrimination against Women (CEDAW, 1979), the Beijing Conference on the Status of Women (1995), and others.[6]

Gender (English-seed) is a concept that expresses the socio-cultural aspect of the human gender. If we look at the socio-psychological image of humanity in the past, we see that

---

[6] https://www.un.org/sustainabledevelopment/gender-equality

in the landscape, their decisions are decisive on major, high and many issues, the influence of men on political, socio-economic life is high and their decisions are decisive on many issues. We also know from many historical sources that women were mainly involved in household chores and child rearing without interfering in these processes. There were even times when a woman was seen as a disgusting alien element. The notion that he was only a creature capable of satisfying a greedy need has long prevailed. That is why the Canadian Eskimos have a tradition of exterminating girls from infancy. The Arabs also had the practice of burying girls alive in the Arabian region before the advent of Islam. In India, there was a tradition of throwing a wife into a fire when her husband died. At the same time, similar actions were performed on boys. In Japan, for example, until the early twentieth century, there was a tradition of exterminating newborn boys as infants, making it difficult to sell them on the market and make a profit.[7] "

Thus, the plight of Indian women has long been a concern of many Indian writers, especially Rozia Sajad Zahir, Subhadra Kumar Chauhan, Rashida Jahan, Sodiqa Begam, Amrita Pritam, Mannu Bhandari. In their novels and stories, they talked about the role of Indian women in the family and society. These famous Indian writers defended women in every way with their creations, telling them in the content of their works what a woman should do and how to be a woman in order to have a place in society. The constant disenfranchised, discriminated status of Indian women in society was one of India's national problems. Throughout the centuries-old history of India, women have experienced all the hardships of life in a feudal society with a caste system and religious traditions. In the works of modern Indian writers, the

---

[7] ҚиёмиддинНазаров.Фалсафа қомусий луғати. "Шарқ".-Т: 2004. Б. 84.

subject of women, issues of family relations are among the Indian literary critics Hazari Prasad Dvivedi, Rashid Ahmad Siddiki and others, Indian orientalists S.K. Bannerji, N. Glebov and A.Sukhochev, V.Novikova, I.Serebryakov, I. Tovstyx, E.P. Chelyshev, Z.N. Petrunicheva, E.Ya. Kalinnikova and others, Uzbek orientalists O.S. Polinova, TA Khodjaeva and U.U. Muhibova are constantly reflected in the literature of Indian, Bengali, Urdu, Punjabi and other publics of India in prose, poetry, pamphlets and scientific articles.

References
1. Qiyomiddin Nazarov. Dictionary of philosophy. Sharq. – T: 2004. B.
2. Uzbek Oriental Studies: today and tomorrow. Scientific collection. T., 2010 Salimova F.S. Jenshchiny nezavisimoy Indii. Tashkent. 1979.
3. ममता कालिया। बीसवी सदी का हिंदी महिला-लेखन : खंड ,3-साहित्य अकादमी ,नई दिल्ली 2015
   https://www.un.org/sustainabledevelopment/gender-equality
4. Teacher of Hindi language at Uzbekistan State World Languages University, Researcher at Tashkent State University of Oriental studies, 90-096-37-31

Hindi Teacher,
Uzbekistan State World Language University,
Uzbekistan